The Holy Spirit of God

A biblical perspective

© Chad Sychtysz

To Mike Sams /
May God continue to
bless you with grace
and knowledge /

Published by
Spiritbuilding Publishing
15591 N. State Rd. 9
Summitville, IN 46070

Spiritual "equipment" for the contest of life.

Printed in the United States of America
ISBN:

Author's photo on back cover by **Todd Hobert**

Front cover photo by **Amar Ramesh**

Acknowledgements

I want to offer a general expression of thanks toward all those who have encouraged me to write this book. Works like this take a great deal of time and energy, as anyone knows who has done something similar, but they are made worthwhile by the support and appreciation of fellow Christians.

More specifically, I wish to thank Mary Wellington and Rod MacArthur for their generous loaning of books and materials from their private libraries. Many more thanks go to Sandi Williams and David Spaun for their time-consuming reading and critical reviews of early versions of my manuscript. Their helpful analyses and comments have made this work better and stronger than it was in the beginning. Special thanks to Carl "Mac" McMurray and his staff at Spiritbuilding Publishing for all the work they put into turning this manuscript into an actual book. And finally, I want to acknowledge my "family" in Anchorage (those who were there from 1994 to 2003) and my present "family" in Kent. These people have not only been patient and encouraging, but have endured my earlier, more primitive forays into the subject of this book.

Table of Contents

Introduction

Why study about the Holy Spirit? This seems an appropriate question to ask in the beginning of a book *on* the Holy Spirit. Some Christians may *never* engage in such a study. Others may only do so superficially, perhaps to answer a nagging question or two. But *you*, dear reader, are apparently ready to launch into an entire *book* on this oft-neglected subject. Why would you do such a thing?

Better yet, why did I *write* such a thing?

Of course, I cannot answer why you chose to read this book. The reason I chose to *write* this, however, is quite straightforward: I have a personal passion to introduce Christians of any level of spiritual maturity to the Holy Spirit of God in a manner I had not seen before. There are a number of very good books on the Spirit; I have read a number of them and will quote from some of them myself. Yet none of these approached the subject the way in which you will read it here. This book is not designed as merely a clinical study *of* the Holy Spirit; instead, it is designed as a tribute *to* Him. I feel strongly that Christians—even those seeking to *become* Christians—should not just know *about* the Holy Spirit, but that they should enjoy a rewarding fellowship *with* Him.

The researching and writing of this book has been tremendously rewarding for me personally. Beyond this, I cannot stress enough how important a study of the Holy Spirit is to anyone seeking to "draw near to God" (cf. James 4:8). It stands to reason that if you truly wish to draw near to God, then you would *strongly desire* to learn as much as you can about Him. It also makes sense that no one in the world should be as interested in God as those who wish to be saved by Him. Furthermore, if one truly desires to "walk by the Spirit" (Galatians 5:16), then he ought to know who this Spirit is that he is to follow.

The Holy Spirit is mentioned over 200 times in the New Testament, and yet He may be foreign to many of our spiritual conversations. In part, this is because some think there is little to *know* about Him. There is a considerable amount of information and insight concerning Jehovah God[1] of the Old Testament. Likewise, we have four gospels and a healthy amount of exposition—both theological and practical—concerning Jesus, who is both Messiah (Christ) *and* the Son of God (John 20:31).

But of the Spirit, we have comparatively little information. Even His name—"Holy Spirit"—is vague, even cryptic; it is more descriptive (of His essential nature) than it is personal. (This is evidenced by the fact that He is always called *the* Holy Spirit, and never just "Holy Spirit.") The King James Version (1611) has not helped matters: by referring to Him as the "Holy Ghost" gives the impression of a disembodied specter, a phantom, a paranormal oddity. This immediately characterizes the Spirit as a mysterious and unapproachable entity, which only further makes Him more alien to us. It is easy for us to disconnect ourselves from those things—or Persons—which are unfamiliar to us. Because of this, we tend to downplay or altogether ignore the Spirit's role in the church or the life of a Christian. We are much more comfortable and conversant in the redemptive work and mediatory role of Jesus Christ. Thus, we put our primary focus on Christ (which is what the gospel has taught us to do) but perhaps to the exclusion of the Spirit (which the gospel has *not* taught us to do).

We may also fail to learn more about the Spirit because it is a difficult thing to do (as you probably already know). A study like this takes time, dedicated concentration, prayer, and a healthy examination of the Bible—not just in *citations* of Scripture, but also in understanding the *context* of Scripture. Time is something a person is unlikely to devote to anything unless he anticipates a good return on his investment. Not every Christian is convinced that a better understanding of the Holy Spirit is even worth pursuing. A study of the Spirit does not seem to be as immediately rewarding or inspiring as, say, a study of the Beatitudes or the grandeur of heaven. Some feel that their present knowledge of the Word, or the direction of their walk with God, is already sufficient. They think (but may not put into words), "Since I already have a healthy relationship with the Lord *apart from* a deeper knowledge of the Holy Spirit, I really don't see the benefit of this."

Furthermore, many have been conditioned to think that God has provided the gospel for the "experts"—in this case, preachers and theologians. Yet God has provided the gospel for *every believer* to learn, not just the so-called "clergy." It is disturbing that one's knowledge of the Holy Spirit would be neglected only because we have deemed Him too difficult to understand—or too controversial to even try. God *expects* us to get beyond the "elementary teaching about the Christ" and "press on to maturity" in our faith (Hebrews 6:1).

The many references to the Holy Spirit in the New Testament are there for a reason: there are things God wants us to know about Him. It is one thing to know that God *does* work in our lives; it is quite another thing to know *how* He works—at least, according to what He has revealed to us in His Word. A deeper, more accurate understanding of how the Holy Spirit works in our lives leads to a deeper, more fulfilling relationship with God Himself. This also gives us a much greater appreciation for the Christ who *sent* the Spirit to us—and how He [Christ] is the Prime Mover behind all that the Spirit does for us. A better comprehension of our fellowship with God—the Father, Son, *and* Spirit—will give us an even greater understanding of our fellowship with one another.

Thankfully, there are those like you and me who are ready to jump into this study with both feet forward, unwilling to ignore it any longer. We are unconcerned with where this study will take us, as long as we are directed by God's truth. Since we can "bear fruit" *for* God only through the truth *of* God (Colossians 1:5-6), we want the truth—not some pre-scripted, "safe" doctrine that ties God's hands, holds the Holy Spirit hostage to human expectations, and doesn't really do anything for *us*. Our Bibles are open; our minds are filled with hope and looking forward to gaining knowledge; our hearts are filled with prayer imploring God's guidance in our study; we are poised and ready. The question as to whether or not we should learn about the Holy Spirit has already been answered: we cannot go any further *without* such learning.

So then, let's get started.

Chapter One
Who Is This "Holy Spirit"?

In the beginning God created the heavens and the earth. The earth was formless and void, and darkness was over the surface of the deep, and the Spirit of God was moving over the surface of the waters.
Genesis 1:1-2

If someone asked you to describe the Holy Spirit, how would you respond? Would you simply re-state the obvious ("The Bible says that He is God's Spirit")? Or would you defer to some personal conception of Him in your mind ("This is what He is to *me*")? Or would you appeal to the consensus of your own church or church leaders ("This is how *we* have come to describe Him" or "This is what *they* think He is")?

We can relate to the concept of a spiritual Father, since we all have fathers. Just as we can know, see, touch, and communicate with our earthly fathers, so we have at least a tangible form to associate with God the Father. So it is with God the Son: just as we are all children, and may have children of our own, so we can identify with that relationship. Just as Jesus "became flesh and dwelt among us" (John 1:14), so us parents can see the transformation of a dream or the anticipation of a child into a flesh-and-blood reality. Even angels in Scripture have manifested themselves in the form of glorified men, so at least we have some level by which to identify with them.

But to what or whom shall we liken the Holy Spirit?

The Unseen Spirit

Our perception of the Holy Spirit falls into the same category of other "spiritual" beings or concepts that we cannot quite wrap our minds around. Just as we struggle with eternity, God's omnipresence, and saving grace, so we struggle with the Holy Spirit. In reality, we struggle with the "spirit" part of the Holy Spirit, since we really have no fixed point of reference by which to understand what a "spirit" is in the first place. Intuitively, if by no other means, we *know* our own existence includes both a body *and* a spirit, but which of us has ever seen our own spirit? We know that the body *without* the spirit is dead, but which one of us has ever beheld one's spirit leave his body upon that person's death? We can observe a *living body* and know that it is animated by one's spirit; we can see a *dead body* and know that its spirit has departed. But that is where our earthly connection ends; the rest of what we know is by faith, not by sight.

This is why it is difficult for us to connect immediately with the Holy Spirit. Since He is *entirely* a Spirit, we are already at a loss as to what to do with Him. We have no earthly form or relationship by which to identify Him. Even those who have died once lived on earth and *had* a body. Even though they are now only a "spirit," they are still tethered to this life in earthly history or our past memories in a way that we can understand. The Holy Spirit, however, has never had a human-like body; He does not now have such a body. He is never represented in Scripture in any physical form except on one occasion: at the time of Jesus' baptism by John the Baptist. In that instance, "the Holy Spirit descended upon Him in bodily form like a dove" (Luke 3:22). This is the only tangible reference we have of the Holy Spirit: "like a dove." The connection still escapes us, simply because we cannot relate to the Holy Spirit as a bird any easier than we can relate to Him as an Eternal Spirit. At least we can say this much: the Holy Spirit *does exist*, because men have "seen" Him, even if He manifested Himself in a form no one ever expected.

Otherwise, the Holy Spirit remains what He is and has always been: God's *Spirit*. It stands to reason that God fashioned our body-and-spirit existence as a reflection of His own; indeed, this is at least part of what is meant by our having been made "in His image" (Genesis 1:27). Just as every person who has lived and who is now living *has* a spirit, so God has a Spirit. Just as our spirit is invisible to us while we are in this physical world, so God's Spirit is invisible to us here. Just as our spirit is what animates our physical bodies, so it is God's Spirit which *makes things happen* among God's physical creation; the Spirit "gives life" even in the spiritual world, though we see none of this (cf. John 6:63). Just as our spirit continues to exist beyond the death of our physical body, so God's Spirit continues to exist even after the death of the entire physical creation. [2]

While there are parallels between our spirit and God's Spirit, there are also critical differences. Our spirit had a "beginning" in time and existence: just as God breathed into Adam the "breath of life" (Genesis 2:7)[3] so God breathes life into every person in order to make him a *living being* (see Job 33:4; Ecclesiastes 12:7; and Isaiah 42:5; for example).[4] Yet we have nothing to do with bringing into existence or sustaining the Spirit of God; He exists independent of us. Not only this, but He has no beginning point, has no "birth," and is not bound by "time." No one has ever breathed life into the Holy Spirit, for He Himself is the "breath" of all life. Even in the spiritual context, no soul that has once sinned can be made "alive" to God—i.e., have fellowship with God—apart from the creative work of the Holy Spirit (to be discussed later).

Another critical difference between our spirit and the Holy Spirit lies in the realm of *ability*. Our spirit is limited to whatever context in which God has placed it; we cannot exceed the parameters imposed upon us by Him. Our spirit cannot be everywhere all at once; we are not even certain where our spirit *is* right now. We cannot peer into the hearts of other men; we struggle with coming to terms with what is in our *own* heart. Our spirit is bound by the decisions that we ourselves make while we are alive in the body; the results of these decisions are the only impact we make on the unseen spiritual world. We cannot direct the tide of history to accommodate the will of God; we have so little control even over our own life. We cannot impart spiritual life to a single soul of man; we cannot cause the death of any soul besides our own.

The Holy Spirit, on the other hand, can do all of these things. He can exceed all the limitations and restrictions that we attempt to impose upon Him. The Spirit is *not* bound by man-made decisions or circumstances. He *can* be everywhere all at once: just as God the Father is omnipresent (Ephesians 4:6), so is His Spirit. He *can* "judge the thoughts and intentions" of men's hearts (Hebrews 4:12).[5] He *does* have the ability to influence both heaven and earth. He *does* move human history to fulfill the will of God. He *does* bring souls to life, and He *does* convict men of their souls' condemnation (John 16:8-11).

A third critical difference lies in the realm of *holiness*. Once our soul has been corrupted with sin, our innocence is lost and we no longer enjoy fellowship with God. Our transgression of God's law severs our relationship with God, requiring that our relationship with Him is in need of reconciliation. [6] If we are never reconciled to God, then this separation will be made permanent: our spirit will "die." The holiness factor becomes, in essence, the ultimate distinction between who survives into eternity with God and who is destroyed: whoever is "holy and blameless" (Ephesians 1:3-6) is fit to dwell with God forever; whoever is "dead" in sin (Ephesians

2:1-3) is destined for destruction. Holiness is a state of being which only God can impart; our spirit is unable to confer holiness upon anything, even ourselves. Our spirit is made holy through the consecration of the "Spirit of holiness" (Romans 1:4). While it is *Christ's* sacrifice that makes our holiness possible, and it is He who mediates for us (1 Timothy 2:5), it is in reality the *Father* who anoints us with His Spirit (2 Corinthians 1:21). (We will discuss this in more detail later.)

The Holiness of the Spirit

As mentioned before, the name "Holy Spirit" seems more practical than personal. "Holy Spirit" is the name by which *we* know Him; it is hardly the name by which He is known in heaven. This name is adequate for us, however, given the inherent difficulties we have with His identity. He is indeed "Holy": He has not been *made* holy, as is the case of we who are "in Christ," but He is *intrinsically* holy. Just as the Father is holy, so His Spirit is holy; just as there was never a point in His existence when God was *not* holy—since this is impossible and inconceivable—so there was never a point when God's Spirit was not holy. "Holy," then, is not just a *characteristic* of the Spirit, but defines His essential *nature*. Since He is holy (or sacred), He possesses all the same qualities as any member of the Godhead. Thus, the Holy Spirit is:

❑ A **Living Being** (more discussion on this below).
❑ **Self-sufficient:** His existence or survival does not depend upon people or any external energy outside of Himself (as with God; Acts 17:24-25).
❑ **Sovereign:** He acts with supreme, unilateral authority (Isaiah 40:13).[7] (It is true that the Spirit carries out the will of the Father, but it is also true that no member of the Godhead consults with or answers to anyone else for decisions He renders.)
❑ **Spirit:** Just as "God is spirit" in nature (John 4:23-24), so the Holy Spirit is—by virtue of His name *and* divine essence—a "spirit." This means He cannot be defined, fully described, or contained in any earthly context, since He is already otherworldly and supernatural. His existence cannot be compared to our earthly existence, nor can His activity be limited to earthly activity. He is not of the Creation; He is *above* all that is created.
❑ **Omniscient:** Whatever God knows, the Spirit knows (1 Corinthians 2:11); since God knows all things, therefore the Spirit also knows all things. Just as nothing can be hidden from God, so nothing can

be hidden from His Spirit.

❏ **Omnipotent:** As God, the Spirit is more powerful than any other entity, authority, or spirit. While it is not the Spirit's *role* to exercise this power on His own, nonetheless it becomes evident through His Word that God's unlimited, unfathomable power is carried out through His unlimited, unfathomable Spirit.

❏ **Omnipresent:** As a divine being, the Holy Spirit is not limited to any one place at a time—"place" and "time" being earthly references which the Spirit inherently transcends. Just as God is everywhere all at once (Ephesians 4:6), so His Spirit is ever-present. [8]

❏ **Eternal:** Just as God did not have a beginning and cannot die, so the Spirit's existence is not bound by time or duration. The Spirit *is*, has always *been*, and will forever *be*; He is "the eternal Spirit" (Hebrews 9:14). On this point, R. C. Sproul writes: "Whatever God creates is by definition a creature. Whatever is created can be neither eternal nor self-sufficient. God could create an immortal creature, but not an eternal creature."[9]

❏ **Immutable:** Just as the divine nature of God the Father and God the Son are unchangeable (Hebrews 6:17-18; 13:8), so the divine nature of God the Spirit is unchangeable. He is already perfect in every way; therefore He cannot be anything more or less than what He is now. Again, Sproul writes: "Our [human] being is not *pure* being. Our being is mixed with becoming. We are both actual and potential. We are always changing. But God does not change. He has no [unrealized] potential. He is pure actuality. He is eternally what He is. As He said to Moses, 'I AM WHO I AM.'"[10]

❏ **Infinite:** Just as God is infinite—since He is *eternal* and *unlimited* in power, knowledge, and presence—so the Holy Spirit is infinite.

❏ **Indestructible:** This world is "passing away" (1 John 2:17), but God is not. He has the power to create and destroy all things (except Himself), but no one has the ability or authority to destroy Him. For God the Father to exist apart from God the Spirit—that is, to imagine the *Spirit* being destroyed, but not the *Father*—is impossible and inconceivable. Just as a living body cannot be separated from its living soul except upon death (cf. James 2:26), so the Living God cannot be separated from His Living Spirit.

❏ **Separated from sinful men:** Just as God cannot have communion with those who are outside of His fellowship (2 Corinthians 6:14-18), so His Spirit cannot indwell those who are not "in Christ"—that is, in Christ's body, His church (Colossians 1:18). The Spirit has performed miracles *upon* or *through* men, but the supernatural imposition of power *over* men (or the Creation) is not the same thing as having fellowship *with* men. God can perform a miracle anywhere or in any manner He chooses; but He cannot enter into agreement with sin, nor can He become "one" with the person who is not "joined" to Him through Christ (Isaiah 59:1-2; John 8:24; 14:6).

The Holy Spirit is not a human being, a ghost, or an angel. He is a Divine Personage who is only comparable to another Divine Personage (God the Father or God the Son). He is never portrayed as an abstract thought, a theological concept, or a nebulous and impersonal "presence." Instead, He is always described (directly or indirectly) as a very real Personage of the Godhead. [11] H. Leo Boles writes: "The fundamental meaning of 'Godhead' is the same as that of 'Godhood'; these terms express the state, dignity, condition, [and] quality of Jehovah."[12] Just as the Spirit searches the mind of God (1 Corinthians 2:11), so God searches the mind of the Spirit (Romans 8:27): in other words, the Spirit has a separate and distinct "mind" and personality of His own.

The Personhood of the Spirit

The Spirit is never referred to in Scripture as an "It," but always as a masculine Personage who is referenced by masculine pronouns ("He," "Him," "His").[13] This is a critical point: if we reduce the Spirit to a mere "It," then we reduce our *relationship* with Him to a mere abstraction; we will not see Him as anything but a mystical "energy" that somehow guides us to heaven. This reduces Him to a surreal "Force" that has no definition or explanation (as in, "May the Force be with you"); thus, our *spiritual life* will remain undefined and inexplicable. He will be a stranger to us, because we have estranged Him through our poor terminology and ignorance. To quote Boles again: "The Bible is not responsible for the vague mysticism which some ascribe to the Holy Spirit; the ignorance of the personality of the Holy Spirit belongs to religious teachers; they have not sought to present in a clear and definite way what God teaches on this subject."[14] God does not give us a foreign concept which cannot have an appreciable and life-altering effect on our thinking and behavior. Instead, He gives *His Spirit* who abides in those who obey Him (Luke 11:13; Acts 5:32; 1 John 4:13). Thus, we see the Spirit doing things that we would expect of a Personage, but that are impossible of a mere concept:

❑ He speaks to us (Revelation 2 – 3): "Hear what the Spirit says to the seven churches...."

❑ He testifies with us (Romans 8:16; 1 John 5:6).

❑ He leads us (Romans 8:14; Galatians 5:16).

❑ He teaches us (John 14:26).[15]

❑ He loves us (Romans 15:30).

❑ He can be lied to (Acts 5:3).

❑ He can be grieved (Ephesians 4:30).

❑ We have fellowship with Him (2 Corinthians 13:14; Hebrews 6:4).

These are things that a mere "concept" cannot do, but that a definable, personal Spirit most certainly *can* do.

The Spirit of Creative Activity

Beyond all these references and explanations, however, we are still at a loss with how exactly to regard the Holy Spirit. He is first mentioned in Scripture in the same way that God is first mentioned—as transcendent (of this Creation) and without introduction (Genesis 1:1-2): "In the beginning God created the heavens and the earth. ...And the Spirit of God was moving over the surface of the waters."[16] The Holy Spirit, by necessary implication, is identified with the "Us" of Genesis 1:26: "Let Us make man in Our image, according to Our likeness...." We know now, because of fuller revelation given to us by Christ and His apostles *through* the Spirit, that Christ Himself was the One in charge of the actual Creation (see John 1:1-3; 1 Corinthians 8:6; Colossians 1:15-17; and Hebrews 1:1-3). Nonetheless, this does not discount or nullify the role of the Spirit in either the creation of the world *or* a "new creation" in Christ (2 Corinthians 5:17; Titus 3:5).

God the Father is the cause of all good things (Romans 8:28; 11:36; James 1:17; et al) and "all things" exist by God the Son. It appears, however, that the Spirit is the One who actually carries out both the will of the Father and the Son (because the Son has been given "all authority," Matthew 28:18). We might say that the Father *upholds* all things, and Christ *makes* and *sustains* all things, but the Spirit makes things *happen*. This is how we see His role repeatedly in both the Old and New Testaments. The ancient prophets spoke from God but were moved by the Holy Spirit (2 Peter 1:20-21). Likewise, the apostles spoke by the authority of Christ (which was given to Him by His Father), but this authority was communicated through God's Spirit (John 16:13).

Perhaps we can consider the Spirit's role in this way: He is the "mind of God" *personified*, that is, as a distinctly separate entity from but inseparable in His communion with the Father. When God speaks, it is the Spirit who brings into reality what is in the mind of God. Similarly, when your conscious mind "speaks," it is simply bringing into reality what is generated within your otherworldly soul. If we were to view these two things—your conscious mind and your soul—as two distinctly separate "persons" yet inextricably linked in fellowship, this would become much clearer to us. Consider the following examples from the Old Testament of how the will of God is brought to reality through the work of the Spirit (all bracketed words are mine):

❑ "See, I [God] have called by name Bezalel [an Israelite appointed to work on the tabernacle]… I have filled him with the Spirit of God in wisdom, in understanding, in knowledge, and in all kinds of craftsmanship" (Exodus 31:2-3).

❑ "Then I [God] will come down and speak with you [Moses] there, and I will take of the Spirit who is upon you, and will put Him upon them [the seventy elders of Israel]; and they shall bear the burden of the people with you, so that you will not bear it all alone" (Numbers 11:17; see also verses 25 and 26).

❑ "'Woe to the rebellious children [Israel],' declares the LORD, 'Who execute a plan, but not Mine, And make an alliance, but not of My Spirit, In order to add sin to sin'" (Isaiah 30:1).

❑ "Behold, My Servant, whom I uphold; My chosen one in whom My soul delights. I have put My Spirit upon Him; He will bring forth justice to the nations" (Isaiah 42:1, in a prophecy of the Christ).

❑ "Then He [God] said to me, 'Son of man [Ezekiel], stand on your feet that I may speak with you!' As He spoke to me the Spirit entered me and set me on my feet; and I heard Him speaking to me" (Ezekiel 2:1-2). (There are numerous references to the "Spirit of the LORD" in Ezekiel.)

❑ "Then he [the angel] said to me [Zechariah], 'This is the word of the LORD to Zerubbabel saying, "Not by might nor by power, but by My Spirit," says the LORD of hosts'" (Zechariah 4:6).

This does not include the many references to those who carried out the will of God (by words or deeds) when "the Spirit of the LORD came upon" them (Judges 6:34; 11:29; 14:19; et al). In other words, we see an established pattern: God speaks, and the Holy Spirit brings into reality

God's spoken word (or revelation). Indeed, the oracles and prophecies of the Old Testament are in fact revelations of the Holy Spirit. For example, a lengthy quote from David (Psalms 95:7-11) is directly attributed to the Spirit (Hebrews 3:7-11). Likewise, the prophet Jeremiah's words are considered the testimony of the Holy Spirit (Hebrews 10:15-17). Peter is much more general in his comments, but reaches the same conclusion (1 Peter 1:10-12):

> As to this salvation, the prophets who prophesied of the grace that would come to you made careful searches and inquiries, seeking to know what person or time the Spirit of Christ within them was indicating as He predicted the sufferings of Christ and the glories to follow. It was revealed to them that they were not serving themselves, but you, in these things which now have been announced to you through those who preached the gospel to you by the Holy Spirit sent from heaven—things into which angels long to look. [17]

In light of all that has been written and preserved for us, we realize that the Spirit has been drawing men near to God throughout all of history in whatever way He saw fit to do so. In some cases, this was done directly (as when He "came upon" men or spoke through them); in other cases, this was done indirectly (as when He orchestrated certain events in order to carry out the will of God, as in Acts 8:26-40).

What the Spirit Says to the Churches

While many men—kings, prophets, priests, and others—have carried on conversations with God, we have no record of one's conversation with the Holy Spirit. It might be said that if one were talking to God, then certainly that person was also communicating with (or through) His Spirit. Even if we concede that point, the fact is that we know of no one *intentionally* speaking directly to the Holy Spirit.

Yet the Holy Spirit has certainly communicated with *us*. This has been done through both miraculous and non-miraculous means. While we will discuss this more thoroughly in a later chapter, suffice it for now to say that the Spirit has "spoken" to us through Moses, the ancient prophets, and more recently through Christ and His apostles (Hebrews 1:1-2). In this way, the Spirit both confirms what has already been declared (as in Ephesians 3:4-5) as well as prophesies of that which is yet to come (as in

1 Timothy 4:1 or Hebrews 9:8-10). The words of those who are genuinely "inspired"[18] are to be regarded as messengers of God. Thus Paul served as a "priest [of] the gospel of God" having been "set apart" by the Spirit (see Acts 13:2 and Romans 15:15-16). Thus, to reject those through whom the Holy Spirit has spoken is to reject God—and, by necessary implication, His Spirit (as in 1 Thessalonians 4:8).

This communication is perhaps nowhere as vividly clear in Scripture as in the book of Revelation. Despite the numerous interpretations ascribed to this book, we cannot deny the obvious: the Spirit is very much the guiding influence of the events described in it. Indeed, the revelation is from Jesus Christ, God the Father, and the "seven Spirits who are before His throne" (Revelation 1:4-5).[19] The entire book is the record of what John saw while "in the Spirit" (1:10; 4:2). It is a message of "what the Spirit says to the [seven] churches" (chapters 2 – 3), which includes a visionary behind-the-scenes account of the spiritual realm. John was "carried away in the Spirit" (17:3; 21:10) to see those things which would be of immediate benefit to the Christians of Asia [modern-day Western Turkey] who were facing enormous pressure to recant their faith. Certainly the message is beneficial to Christians of all time, in the same way that what the Spirit says to one Christian is beneficial for all. The Spirit Himself offered His brief but consoling encouragement: "And I heard a voice from heaven, saying, 'Write, "Blessed are the dead who die in the Lord from now on!"' 'Yes,' says the Spirit, 'so that they may rest from their labors, for their deeds follow with them.'" This is joined with Jesus' own encouragement: "Be faithful until death, and I will give you the crown of life" (2:10). This is the theme of Revelation, and it is the Spirit's proclamation to all who will accept it (22:17).

Summary Thoughts

The Bible opens with "the Spirit of God…moving over the surface of the waters" (Genesis 1:2), and closes with the Spirit of God "moving," in essence, over the "waters" of the world—its multitudes of people and nations (cf. Revelation 17:15). Just as the Spirit was intimately involved in the creation of the physical world, so He is the creative (yet hidden) activity of the spiritual world. From beginning to end, the Spirit is actively involved in everything that God does, and especially the work of Christ's church.

On the other hand, even though the Spirit was present at and involved in the creation of the visible world, we do not learn about Him by observing the visible world in the same way we can learn about God (cf. Romans 1:18-20). "…The study of the material universe does not reveal anything about the nature or work of the Holy Spirit in the redemption of man. The only source to which we can go to learn of the Holy Spirit is the Bible."[20] This means that regardless of what one *thinks* he knows about the Spirit, his conclusions must be supported by what the Spirit Himself has already *declared* through the inspired words of Scripture.

We have much more to say on the Spirit and His work, "and this we will do, if God permits" (Hebrews 6:3).

Fellowship with the Godhead

...His divine power has granted to us everything pertaining to life and godliness, through the true knowledge of Him who called us by His own glory and excellence. For by these He has granted to us His precious and magnificent promises, so that by them you may become partakers of the divine nature, having escaped the corruption that is in the world by lust.
2 Peter 1:3-4

God made us to be social creatures. Generally-speaking, we crave the company of other people, just as other people crave our own company. Just as it was "not good" for Adam to be alone (Genesis 2:18), so it is not good for people to be alone, completely removed from association with fellow human beings. This is what drives people to get married, have families, found churches, settle communities, and form nations. At the core of every society is an innate human need to *belong* to another person (or group of people), and thus to feel important and experience self-worth through that "belonging" experience.

This driving need is not limited to an earthly, human context. Man's longing for *otherworldly* company is what drives him to worship God (or "gods") in the first place. It is one thing to be acknowledged and accepted by an earthly equal; it is a far greater experience to enjoy communion with One who *exceeds* the greatness of earth and all humankind. While the craving for this experience has driven men to embrace numerous forms of transcendent religion—i.e., the worship of mythological gods, nature gods (paganism), demons, and even supposedly highly-advanced extraterrestrials—nonetheless the basic premise is an intelligent one. Man wants his existence to be validated by someone higher, more knowledgeable, and more powerful than himself. God designed us to think this way so that we might "grope for *Him*" rather than seek completion through gods of our own making (cf. Acts 17:24-28, emphasis mine).

We are not content merely to be acknowledged by a divine entity; we crave a *relationship* with this entity. We desire not only an established line of communication with the divine, but we seek *fellowship* with the divine. Men seek after God, for example, not only because they want to be saved from His wrath (although this provides powerful incentive to *begin* that relationship), but also because they desire a closeness with Him that is more satisfying and enduring than any relationship known in this world. Thus, the anticipation of an eternal union with an eternal God is more than interesting; for those who have a real expectation of this union, it is *enthralling* and deeply *inspiring*.

Once the relationship with God is established, we can then enjoy fellowship (or communion) with God. Once we are "reconciled" to God through Christ, we may then become "partakers of the divine nature"—in essence, *sharers* in the closeness that the Godhead itself already enjoys (John 17:20-22; 2 Peter 1:2-4). The very concept of "fellowship" includes a closeness (or intimacy) based upon what we have in common. People are able to have fellowship with each other because we all have, if nothing else, our *humanity* in common. The more we have in common, the deeper our fellowship is able to be. Likewise, as our relationship with God deepens and flourishes, then our fellowship with Him—and His fellowship with us—also deepens and becomes all the more enjoyable. Such fellowship is the epitome of what God has always wanted with us. It is *His* desire for *our* fellowship, based upon His inherent love for man, which compelled God to send His Son (1 John 4:9) and led that Son to the cross.

We long for a relationship with God, and we enjoy that relationship through our fellowship with His Son. Once we are made citizens of God's kingdom, we are brought into fellowship with all who belong to Him (1 John 1:1-3)—the "household of God" (1 Timothy 3:15), a community of believers. Thus, we pursue in Christ virtually the same objectives concerning fellowship that we do in the world, but on a level that far exceeds whatever we are able to accomplish among human beings alone.

The Relationship of the Godhead

What, then, are we to do with this Holy Spirit? We know the Father and His Son; we have communion with them; but does this communion extend to the Holy Spirit? Are we to also have a relationship with *Him*, one that is separately recognized from either the Father or the Son? Or is it sufficient that we have a relationship with "God," which includes the Father, Son, *and* Spirit? On that thought, consider what Paul wrote in 2 Corinthians 13:14: "The grace of the Lord Jesus Christ, and the love of God, and the fellowship of the Holy Spirit, be with you all."[21] If nothing else, this is a clear and unequivocal expression of the triune Godhead. Yet this also reveals the Holy Spirit to be a Divine Person with which we are *able* to have fellowship.

Naturally, we will struggle with fellowship with the Spirit simply because we cannot fully understand His *relationship* with the Father and Christ in the first place. When we come to the Holy Spirit, we may "relegate Him to the office of messenger boy" among the Godhead.[22] Prior to the incarnation—literally, the time when God was made "in the flesh" as Jesus Christ (John 1:14)—we see Israel's relationship with Jehovah, but we are not certain of Israel's relationship with the Holy Spirit. We do know that God's Spirit has been with Israel since at least the time of Moses (Isaiah 63:11-14), and we can safely conclude that His Spirit has always been with godly people, even though these have had to coexist with ungodly people (consider the reference in Genesis 6:3, for example).

Could an Israelite under the Law of Moses have had "fellowship" with the Godhead when he only knew of Jehovah and knew very little of His Spirit (and even less, if anything, of His Son)? This is more of a theoretical question than a practical one, since our lack of revealed knowledge prevents us from answering it conclusively. Suffice it to say that Israel was never required to have fellowship with God beyond what Israel *knew* of God. Intimate fellowship—which requires cooperative action, shared goals, and personal sacrifices toward achieving those goals—is not possible with an unknown party.

This is not comparable to our present situation, since we *do* know of God the Father, God the Son, and God the Spirit. Nonetheless, we should not be too quick to leave behind the Jehovah-Israel relationship, for our knowledge of the triune God in the New Testament builds upon what is known of Jehovah and His Spirit in the Old Testament. In fact, men knew of God's Spirit long before they knew of His Son; God *spoke* of His Spirit before He spoke of His Son. Regardless, Christ has always existed, even before He was mentioned (John 8:58), and thus the Godhead has always *been* what we know it to *be*, even though it is more difficult to explain prior to the incarnation of Christ than it is now. Prior to being identified to us as His "Son," we have little information concerning Christ's exact relationship with the Father. This "Father-Son" terminology, and the divine relationship to which it refers, is undoubtedly more for our understanding than a literal depiction of the triune Godhead. We have no doubt that Christ is God's "only begotten Son" (John 3:16); but until He came to us in the flesh, we would be hard-pressed to understand His position as

"Son," for there would have been nothing historical upon which to base that relationship. Even as it is, there is a great deal of sacred mystery surrounding the Godhead, for we essentially see a divine "Son" who is "begotten" of a divine Father in the absence of a divine mother.[23]

We do know that Christ was active in God's plan prior to His having been revealed to us in the flesh, however. We know that Christ's "ministry of reconciliation" is an "eternal purpose" which He brought about before His physical birth (cf. 2 Corinthians 5:18-21; Ephesians 3:11; 2 Timothy 1:9-10), and that fulfillment of this purpose necessarily involved God the Father *and* God the Spirit. We know that the Spirit of Christ *and* the Holy Spirit inspired the ancient prophets to speak of the gospel of God (1 Peter 1:10-12). Even in the beginning, we know that Christ (as God) created the world, but He did so according to the will of the Father *and* through the agency of the Spirit.

This cooperative, working relationship of the Godhead might be primitively illustrated in the context of a family-owned business—say, a manufacturing plant that "creates" things. In this illustration, the father is its owner and chief executive officer; he is the *authority* behind all that the business is and does, yet he does not literally engage in its daily operations. His son, however, is given full control of the business; he has every right to oversee the business by virtue of his intimate relationship with his father. His responsibility is to dictate *and* oversee everything that is done; he is the *creative force* behind all that the business is and does. The employees of the business, although they are not blood relatives of the father, are regarded as family. Their job is to fulfill the will of the father through the management of the son. These are the ones who perform according to what the father authorizes and the son dictates. The *will* and *inspiration* of the father is conveyed through his son to his employees. In essence, the *spirit* of the father permeates the entire workforce of his business.

Again, this is an oversimplified picture, and fails to fully define the Holy Spirit's role. At best, it may help put a very difficult and transcendent situation into an earthly context. Still, it does not satisfy all our questions that we have concerning the pre-incarnate Christ or the triune Godhead as it has existed from eternity. Christ's relationship with the Father was indeed directly affected by His incarnation. He had to "empty Himself" of His glory in order to "humble Himself" in obedience in the "form of a bond-servant," having been "made in the likeness of men" (Philippians 2:5-8). This is another insight into the cost of redemption: the Godhead itself had to be disrupted in order for God to bring salvation to men.

It is during Jesus' ministry, however, that we encounter the Holy Spirit like never before in Scripture. Instead of the Spirit being a vague or mysterious reference to God's work among men, He suddenly appears in a conspicuous and dynamic role in (first) Christ's ministry and (second) the church that Christ built. Thus, the Spirit was directly involved in Christ's conception (Matthew 1:20) as well as the birth of His herald, John the Baptist (Luke 1:15). Christ's earthly ministry was governed by the Spirit (the essential understanding of Matthew 3:16): it was the Spirit who led Him into the wilderness and elsewhere (Matthew 4:1; Luke 4:1), directed Him what to say (John 3:34), and performed miracles through Him (Matthew 12:28). From Christ's baptism to His death on the cross, it was the Spirit who "testified" of Christ's divinity and served as the source of His power (1 John 5:6-9).

After Christ's ascension to glory (Acts 1:9-11), we see a shift in emphasis: no longer is the Father directly sending His Spirit on such missions, but now it is *Christ* who sends the Spirit to carry out the will of the Father, since He has been given "all authority" (read, for example, John 7:37-39; Matthew 28:18-19; and Acts 2:33 in that order). The Spirit proceeds *from* the Father at the request of the Son; as Sproul observes, "In the work of redemption, as the Son is subordinate to the Father, so the Holy Spirit is subordinate to both the Father and the Son."[24] In other words, once Christ's authority *as* Redeemer was fully and historically established (Ephesians 1:19-23), the Spirit of God acts in the name of the Spirit of Christ.

The Unity of the Godhead

Even though we do not fully comprehend the Godhead, it is important that we appreciate the *unity* of the Godhead. "The plurality of persons in the Godhead does not negate the essential unity of God."[25] In Ephesians 4:1-6, Paul wrote:

> Therefore I, the prisoner of the Lord, implore you to walk in a manner worthy of the calling with which you have been called … being diligent to preserve the unity of the Spirit in the bond of peace. There is one body and one Spirit, just as also you were called in one hope of your calling; one Lord, one faith, one baptism, one God and Father of all who is over all and through all and in all.

"The LORD is our God, the LORD is one" (Deuteronomy 6:4), and yet God is plural ("Let Us make man in Our image," Genesis 1:26). There is *one* Father, *one* Son (Lord), and *one* Spirit, and yet "God" encompasses all three at once.[26] These three Persons function as *one God* with such harmonic cooperation and perfect efficiency, it is difficult for us to determine where the work of one ends and the work of the other begins. Thus, it is entirely appropriate that we find the triune Godhead mentioned separately but working in flawless, seamless fellowship (bracketed words and emphases are mine):

- ❑ "[The apostle Paul was] set apart for the gospel of **God**, which He promised beforehand through His prophets in the holy Scriptures, concerning His **Son**, ...who was declared the Son of God with power by the resurrection from the dead, according to the **Spirit of holiness**, Jesus Christ our Lord..." (Romans 1:1-4).
- ❑ "[Paul was set apart] to be a minister of **Christ Jesus** to the Gentiles, ministering as a priest the gospel of **God**, so that my offering of the Gentiles may become acceptable, sanctified by the **Holy Spirit**" (Romans 15:16).
- ❑ "Now I urge you, brethren, by our **Lord Jesus Christ** and by the love of the **Spirit**, to strive together with me in your prayers to **God** for me" (Romans 15:30).
- ❑ "Because you are sons, **God** has sent forth the **Spirit** of His **Son** into our hearts, crying, "Abba! Father!" (Galatians 4:6).[27]
- ❑ "[Peter wrote to those] who are chosen according to the foreknowledge of **God the Father**, by the sanctifying work of the **Spirit**, to obey **Jesus Christ** and be sprinkled with His blood..." (1 Peter 1:1-2).
- ❑ "[If animal blood served a sanctifying purpose,] how much more will the blood of **Christ**, who through the eternal **Spirit** offered Himself without blemish to God, cleanse your conscience from dead works to serve the living **God**?" (Hebrews 9:14).
- ❑ "The grace of the **Lord Jesus Christ**, and the love of **God**, and the fellowship of the **Holy Spirit**, be with you all" (2 Corinthians 13:14).

We do not see three rival gods vying for supremacy and control, but *one* God in three Persons, each one perfectly content to serve and glorify the others. As Basil of Cappadocia (late 4th century) noted, "For the sake of convenience we may speak of the Second and Third Persons of the Trinity, but there cannot be in fact any 'second' or 'third' in God.

The Unity lies in the common Godhead of the Three."[28] Thus, the Father glorifies the Son (John 8:54), the Son glorifies the Father (John 8:49, 17:1), and the Spirit glorifies the Father *through* the Son (John 16:14) and through the miracles which were performed in His name (Hebrews 2:4).

Notice, then, how the three Persons of God[29] work so closely together, yet retain individual identities (bracketed words are mine):

- ❑ "The angel answered and said to her [Mary], 'The Holy Spirit will come upon you, and the power of the Most High will overshadow you; and for that reason the holy Child shall be called the Son of God'" (Luke 1:35). What is remarkable in this passage—beyond the already unfathomable divine conception of a human child—is that this conception appears to have been conducted through the agency of the Holy Spirit, yet the Child is called the "Son of God." There is no contradiction here, only human incomprehension— and these are not to be confused with one another.

- ❑ "Go therefore and make disciples of all the nations, baptizing them in the name of the Father and the Son and the Holy Spirit" (Matthew 28:19). In order to become a disciple of Christ, one's conversion must be in agreement with *all three Persons* of the Godhead. Thus, no person can claim to be "of" one (i.e., the Father, Son, or Spirit) without being "of" the others (see John 13:20 and 1 Corinthians 12:3, for example). This forbids anyone claiming to act as "Christ's disciple" who knowingly contradicts the *revelation of the Spirit* (i.e., the gospel, Galatians 1:6-11). Likewise, no one can claim to honor the Father who dishonors the Son (John 8:42-49).

- ❑ "But the Helper, the Holy Spirit, whom the Father will send in My name, He will teach you all things, and bring to your remembrance all that I said to you" (John 14:26). The "Helper" (Holy Spirit) was sent *by* the Father *in the name [authority]* of Jesus Christ. The revealed gospel of redemption is predicated upon the full cooperation of all three Divine Personages.

- ❑ "But when the kindness of God our Savior and His love for mankind appeared, He saved us, not on the basis of deeds which we have done in righteousness, but according to His mercy, by the washing of regeneration and renewing by the Holy Spirit, whom He poured out upon us richly through Jesus Christ our Savior, so that being justified by His grace we would be made heirs according to the hope of eternal life" (Titus 3:4-7). While the process of one's salvation does not nullify the need for human faith (Romans 1:17), the ultimate *source* of salvation rests upon: the love and mercy of God, the [implied] sacrifice and grace of Christ, and the renewing power (consecration) of the Holy Spirit. God the Father cannot redeem the sinner without the blood of His Son; God the Son has no authority to save the sinner without having received His authority from His Father; and the Holy Spirit cannot save anyone on His own, yet no one is made holy apart from His consecratory work.

We must be careful not to blur the lines between these three Persons and their work. (Even though the lines may *seem* blurred to us already due to our finite perspective, we must avoid any *deliberate* distortions or misrepresentations of the Godhead.) For example, Jesus said, "I and the Father are one" (John 10:30), which might lead someone to conclude that Jesus *is* the Father. This is not true: the Son is not the Father, nor is the Father ever referred to as the Son. Perfect fellowship between two people does not nullify the individuality of each person;[30] perfect unity does not translate to literal oneness. Jesus is *not* the Father, but He is so *completely united* with the Father in desire, purpose, and love that He and the Father are viewed as *one God* (John 17:20-22). Likewise, the Spirit of God is so completely absorbed in the redemptive work of the Son, the two are expressed as one (2 Corinthians 3:17), even though the Spirit never *becomes* the Son or vice versa. Similarly, even though Christians are "one" with the Lord (1 Corinthians 6:17), we do not *become* the Lord; even though we "imitate" God (Ephesians 5:1), we certainly do not *become* God. However, we *can* (and are expected to) become "one" with Him in desire, purpose, and love. Thus, Augustine (AD 394) wrote, "Each Person of the Trinity is God, and all together are One God. Each is the full Essence, and all together are One Essence. The Father is neither the Son nor the Holy Spirit; the Son is neither the Father nor the Holy Spirit; the Holy Spirit is neither the Father nor the Son... The Three have the same eternity, immutability, majesty, power."[31]

What this "oneness" means is both profound and life-altering. The apostle Paul, for example, "died" to the world, which meant that his soul no longer served the desires of this world. Having done this, he confessed that "it is no longer I who live, but Christ lives in me" (Galatians 2:20). Shortly after this (5:18), he instructed that we should be "led by the Spirit." So which is it: Does Christ lead a believer, or does the Spirit? Does Christ indwell a believer, or does the Spirit? The answer to both questions is *yes*. Christ and the Spirit are on the same page, so to speak; they both have the same love, same objectives, and same earnest desire for our salvation. Their *functions* or *roles* are different, but their work in the life of the believer is so seamlessly interwoven that to have the one necessarily demands the presence of the other (as we see in Acts 16:6-7; Romans 8:9; 2 Corinthians 3:17; Philippians 1:19; et al). On this point, Gregory of Nyssa (4th century) observed that each Person of the Godhead has His own work, but does not work separately from the others; "…Every operation which extends from God to the Creation…has its origin from the Father, and proceeds through the Son, and is perfected in the Holy Spirit."[32]

Fellowship with the Holy Spirit

We have now laid the groundwork to answer the question posed earlier: How are we supposed to have fellowship with the Holy Spirit? Perhaps an appropriate response to this would be: Whatever fellowship we recognize and enjoy with Christ is also shared with the Holy Spirit. Since the relationship between Christ and the Spirit is inseparable, so is the relationship we have with the Spirit *through* Christ. Christ may be more familiar to us than the Spirit (if "familiar" is the right word here), but the Spirit is as essential to our fellowship with God the Father as Christ is: we cannot be saved apart from the help of either one.

It is not necessary, then, that we allocate our fellowship with the Godhead—as though we have to divide our fellowship into three parts. Since we have fellowship with the triune God, we have fellowship with the Father, Son, *and* Holy Spirit. The emphasis, then, should not be on trying to specifically detail our fellowship with the Spirit, but to recognize that in fact we *do* have fellowship with Him. He is not some abstract, ghostly "presence" with which we fail to ever connect; rather, He is a very real, distinctive, and personal member of the Godhead. He is our Comforter, our Intercessor, and Protector of all that has been entrusted to us (2 Timothy 1:14). As we will explore in later chapters, the Spirit indwells us in order to carry out these very objectives. We will also expound more specifically on how He works in the individual lives of believers as well in Christ's church overall.

This unity in the doctrine, work, and fellowship in *heaven* also ought to be expressed among believers in *churches* that claim to be "of Christ." As Paul wrote, "for God is not a God of confusion but of peace, as in all the churches of the saints" (1 Corinthians 14:33). It is to our shame when we make strenuous claims to exalt Christ in our assemblies while resisting the leadership of the Spirit in the same. We also misrepresent the Spirit entirely when we claim to be "led" by Him but fail to honor Christ appropriately. As one writer noted, "It is amazing how deaf the church is even when it is clearly written in Scripture" what we are to do and teach.[33] Likewise, we cannot give "acceptable service" to the Father if we fail to give "reverence and awe" to Christ and the Spirit of God (cf. Hebrews 12:28). (Furthermore, *God* dictates what is meant by "reverent" and "acceptable service," not us.) Divisions, schisms, sectarianism, and denominationalism are foreign concepts to the spiritual body (church) of Christ. "Has Christ been divided?" Paul asked rhetorically (1 Corinthians 1:13), and the answer is emphatically *no*. As impossible and ridiculous as it would be to divide the literal body of Christ and still have "one body," so it is impossible to sow seeds of division in Christ's churches and still practice the "unity of the Spirit in the bond of peace" (Ephesians 4:3).

However, if Christ is to live in us (cf. Galatians 2:20), then it is necessary that we be led by the Holy Spirit. The Spirit and Christ do not take us in two separate directions, but they both lead us straight to the Father. Jesus said, "I am the way, and the truth, and the life; no one comes to the Father but through Me" (John 14:6). But no one can be consecrated for service to God who has not been anointed with His Spirit. Suppose someone asked, "Who is most important for our salvation: Christ or the Holy Spirit?" The answer is *both*—in the context of what is required for our salvation. This does not make Christ and the Spirit's work or roles equal, but regards their work in the proper perspective. It is like asking, "Which is most important for our salvation: divine grace or human faith?" The answer again is *both*—in the context of what is *required* for salvation. Grace cannot be given in the absence of faith, and faith by itself saves no one apart from divine grace (Ephesians 2:8).

Hopefully our brief examination of the Spirit's relationship to the Godhead has helped us to gain a better perspective of our *own* relationship to God as Christians. While there are admittedly some challenging concepts to consider here, it is not as though we cannot understand them at all. In fact, as our understanding of the Spirit improves, our understanding of Christian fellowship ought to improve proportionately. Over time, we begin to realize that when we are led by God's Spirit, we grow together as those "of the same mind, maintaining the same love, united in spirit, intent on one purpose" (Philippians 2:2).

Chapter Three
Foreshadows of the Spirit

You shall make of these a holy anointing oil, a perfume mixture, the work of a perfumer; it shall be a holy anointing oil. ...You shall anoint Aaron and his sons, and consecrate them, that they may minister as priests to Me.
Exodus 30:25, 30

When God wants us to understand critical ideas on a spiritual level, He often begins with simple, physical illustrations. This is why Jesus described the powerful, universal, and eternal kingdom of God—a reality which challenges the most capable Bible student—with brief, story-like parables. By employing metaphors like seeds, soils, plants, leaven, pearls, coins, and sheep, for example, we are able to connect with the transcendent spiritual concepts that otherwise would remain vague or altogether foreign to us.

These illustrations of the kingdom of God actually begin in the Old Testament, particularly with regard to Jehovah worship. The physical forms which would later be translated into spiritual realities are known as "type" prophecies: they are, in essence, non-verbal snapshots of what is to come. A photograph cannot actually "be" what it represents, but is a reproduction of what "is." In anticipation of the greatest revelation of all—the divine incarnation—God used these physical types as well as the divine oracles spoken through His prophets. In this way, He purposely and progressively unveiled heavenly concepts to His people.

The Old Testament types or images may seem rather crude and primitive to us (in hindsight), but they were ideal for their time and are probably of more help to us than we realize. The slaying of animals, with the emphasis on the pouring out and smearing of blood, may seem distasteful to those who, say, have never dressed out a freshly-killed animal for consumption. Nonetheless, the pictures of this graphic, formulaic process are extremely valuable to our understanding of blood-based atonement. We would never really appreciate the idea of Jesus' perfect sacrifice, for example, if not for the less-than-ideal animal sacrifices described in the Law of Moses. The tabernacle with its furniture and rituals, the Levitical priesthood, and even the Law itself also serve as foreshadows of much better and greater things to come. Indeed, Christ is the summing up of all these things (Ephesians 1:9-10; see also Hebrews 10:5-10).

The Holy Spirit also is foreshadowed for us in the ancient system of Jehovah worship. Just as God prefaced the work of Christ with physical-based pictures that help us to grasp complex spiritual realities, so He prefaced the work of the Spirit with these same kinds of illustrations. While the foreshadowing *emphasis* is always on the work of the Redeemer, nonetheless the work of the Spirit is essential *to* redemption. This is exactly what these "type" prophecies concerning the Spirit reveal to us: Christ's work could never have been completed apart from the Spirit; but the Spirit could never have carried out this work apart from Christ. This means that our own salvation is impossible apart from the Spirit's direct involvement in the life of the believer just as it is impossible apart from Christ's atoning sacrifice. To illustrate this, we will now examine the type prophecies that foreshadow the Spirit's work.

The Olive Oil

In Exodus 25:31-40, God gave Moses the pattern for the lampstand that would be placed in the outer sanctuary of the tabernacle (see also 37:17-24). This golden lampstand or menorah was designed as a kind of tree with a single upright trunk (or "branch") with three "branches" on either side of it, all seven branches being on a single vertical plane. The lamps (and oil reservoirs) themselves were patterned after almond blossoms. The almond tree is the first to bloom in the year, signifying the first of many other blooms (of other trees) to come. The buds themselves signify a kind of resurrection, since the buds of a tree are a sign of life after the deadness of winter. We can also compare this with the "first fruits" concept of Christ's own resurrection (1 Corinthians 15:20-23): He was the first of His "brethren" to rise from the dead, indicating that many more would be raised as well.[34]

The only kind of fuel to be used for the seven-lamped menorah was pure olive oil obtained from beaten olives. This provided oil that burned clean and with minimal smoke—ideal for the indoor tabernacle setting. The priests were to keep this lampstand burning throughout the

27

night as an illustration of God's presence among Israel (Exodus 27:20-21; Leviticus 24:1-4). This was to be kept as a "perpetual statute," a prophetic expression that always anticipates a future spiritual fulfillment. Physical rituals in the Law are "a shadow of the good things to come and not the very form of things" (Hebrews 10:1), but these types are made permanent in the spiritual context of the church. The light of these lamps foreshadowed the brilliant light of Christ that would later come into a world darkened with sin and spiritual ignorance: "The Light shines in the darkness..." (John 1:5-9).

Light cannot be produced apart from a source of energy, however, and in the case of the menorah, the olive oil was that energy source. This oil also served as a type prophecy of that which was to be more fully revealed: the work of the Holy Spirit. The "power of the Holy Spirit" (Romans 15:13) is to be understood in this sense: He is the energy that gives life to those who carry out the will of the Lord (discussed below). The olive oil metaphor, then, is not only easy to see, it also makes perfect sense. Just as the oil fed the flame which lit the tabernacle, so the Spirit feeds the fire of those who serve in God's "house" (Christ's church). He is, in essence, the "zeal of the Lord" which accomplishes the will of the Father (Isaiah 37:32).

In connection with this—and to make the idea more clear to us— we should consider the vision given to the prophet Zechariah (4:1-14). This vision revealed God's endorsement of Zerubbabel (as governor) and Joshua (as high priest) in post-exile Judea.[35] The reason for this vision was to inspire these men to oversee the completion of the temple in Jerusalem, which remained unfinished due to procrastination and seemingly insurmountable obstacles. The prophet was shown a seven-branched lampstand, very similar to the one which Moses had made, with an olive tree standing on either side of the lampstand. The olive branches provided the oil for the lamps, but the original source of this oil was the Spirit Himself. (Remember, it is a vision: it does not have to conform to natural expectations.) God told Zechariah, "Not by [human] might nor by [human] power, but by My Spirit" this temple would be completed (4:6, bracketed words mine). The Spirit would be the *power* behind what Israel needed to accomplish for the Lord. Indeed, this is the process by which God has always worked: God the Father gives the directive; God the Son oversees the work to be done; but God the Spirit is the power or energy behind the work itself.[36]

As mentioned earlier, the *emphasis* of such type prophecies is always on Christ, but even the ministry of Christ was not possible apart from the direct involvement of the Spirit. While the light of the menorah signified God's presence among His people, Christ was the true Light which signified God's presence in the world. In the same way that the olive oil fueled the presence of God in the tabernacle, so the Spirit "fueled" the ministry of Christ. As we saw in the previous chapter, the Holy Spirit was the driving force of Jesus' earthly ministry from His baptism to His ascension; He was given the Spirit "without measure" (John 3:34) for this purpose. Jesus exemplified perfectly what He expects us only to imitate: being "led by the Spirit" is the key to one's successful ministry to God. "It is the Spirit who gives life; the flesh profits nothing," Jesus said; "the words that I have spoken to you are spirit and are life" (John 6:63).

It is then no coincidence that Jesus was identified as the Branch of David or Olive Tree of Israel (Isaiah 4:2; 11:1; Jeremiah 23:5; Romans 11:17-18;[37] and Revelation 5:5, "the Root of David"). The nation of Israel, generally-speaking, was a disappointment to God as a fruit-bearing plant, having failed to produce what He expected of it (Isaiah 5:1-7). We could easily say that Israel did not surrender itself to the *power of God's Spirit* so as to serve properly as God's people. For this reason, God's prophets spoke of the Branch who would bring light into a darkened world (Isaiah 9:2; see also Matthew 4:15-16). Christ's light would characterize the nature of the kingdom of God—a kingdom filled with light, knowledge, goodness, safety, and glory. The "zeal of the Lord" would usher this kingdom presence into reality for the people of God (Isaiah 9:7). The Spirit is the actual personification of this "zeal."

It is evident that Christ is the spiritual Menorah who brings light not only to the "temple" (His church, which is "a dwelling of God in the Spirit," Ephesians 2:21-22), but has also enlightened the entire world. As He said, "I have come as Light into the world, so that everyone who believes in Me will not remain in darkness" (John 12:46). The *reason for* or *power behind* Jesus' brilliant light is the *Spirit* with whom He was filled.

This helps us to understand what Jesus meant by, "You are the light of the world" (Matthew 5:16). One cannot be a "light" if he has nothing with which to produce that light; likewise, one cannot bear "fruit" if he has no power to generate the life of that fruit. To be the "light of the world," then, means two simultaneous things: first, one must be "in Christ," which means that one must belong to Him; and second, one must be anointed with the Spirit of God, which means that one must be filled with His presence in one's essential being. No one can be "in Christ" who does not have the Spirit, and no one can have the Spirit who is not "in Christ"; these are mutually dependent states of being.

This also helps us to understand the "lampstand" symbolism associated with the seven churches of Asia in Revelation 2 – 3. The message is clear: Jesus is the One who establishes the lampstands in the first place, but the Spirit is the *life* of the congregation (Revelation 1:12-20; see also 1 Corinthians 3:16, which refers to the entire church at Corinth). This is why the letters are written by the authority of Christ, but "spoken" to the group by the Spirit (2:7, et al, "let him hear what the Spirit says to the churches"). The Spirit, like the olive oil of the menorah, is the energy behind the health and growth of any of Christ's churches. This also anticipates the glory to come, as William Brown has observed:

> As the first apartment in the tabernacle was illuminated by the sevenfold light of the candlestick, and as the church composed of all genuine believers on earth in every age, is enlightened by the Holy Spirit, so will the church triumphant in heaven, that great temple, not made with hands, be a place of glorious light; and the light will never go out, it will burn always; so that there will be no night there; nor sun, nor moon, nor stars will shine in that happy place—"For the glory of God did lighten it, and the lamp thereof is the Lamb" (Rev. 21:23, RV).[38]

If a church will not repent of its sins, however, then the Spirit departs and the lampstand is removed: that group has no more "light" because it has no more *life*.

The Holy Anointing Oil

Let us now consider another Old Testament symbol that foreshadows the Spirit and His work. In Exodus 30:22-33, God instructed Moses to make a special compound of oils, spices, and perfumes known as the "holy anointing oil." All the people, furniture, and utensils used in the ministry of the tabernacle were to be anointed with this oil. It was forbidden to be used for any other purpose, or to have it compounded in these same proportions by any other (common) person.

We must remember that holiness is a status conferred upon

something or someone by God, not men. "Holy" refers to the nature of God Himself; whatever (or whoever) is used in conjunction with God's holiness must itself (or himself) be made holy. While certainly a person *participates* in this process of becoming holy, and must consent to perform the service for which he is being *made* holy, nonetheless it is God who pronounces one as holy.

This "holy anointing oil," then, was a physical, visible means of designating those who were ordained by God. (This process is called consecration; see Exodus 29 and Leviticus 8 for the highly symbolic detail of Aaron and his sons' consecration for the priesthood.) After being anointed, Aaron was known thereafter as "the anointed priest" (Leviticus 4:3, 5, 16, et al), which indicated he was set apart in a special way for the ministry to the Lord. This already anticipates a much greater application: "The fragrant graces of the Holy Spirit seem to be typified by this holy perfume."[39] While serving in the capacity of an anointed priest, a man could not participate in any secular functions, and especially could have nothing to do with mourning or death (Leviticus 10:6-7; 21:10-12).

Thereafter, the anointing *process*—not the "holy anointing oil" itself—was used for consecration in other ministries, most notably in the appointment of kings (1 Samuel 10:1; 16:13; 1 Kings 1:39; et al). It is here, in fact, that a direct connection between the Holy Spirit and anointment begins. For example, when Saul refused to follow the Lord's commandments, God's Spirit "departed from Him" and (as a result) he was tormented by an evil spirit (1 Samuel 16:14; 28:16). Even though Saul had been anointed as a holy instrument of God's, he did not conduct himself accordingly; God's Spirit will have nothing to do with willful rebellion (cf. 1 Samuel 15:23).[40] David, however, continued to honor Saul as "God's anointed" with respect to the *office* it signified, not the man who occupied it (1 Samuel 26:9-10, 16).

This anointing process can also be understood figuratively, as in the case of Cyrus, the first Emperor of Persia (538 BC). In Isaiah 45:1, God called Cyrus "My anointed," even though there is no record that Cyrus was ever literally anointed or formally consecrated by a prophet of God. The *work* that he would perform for the Lord, however, set him apart in a special way, so that God employed the same symbolism as used for those who were anointed. Likewise, David used this metaphorically in Psalm 23:5, for example, when speaking of himself as a servant of God (and not as a literal king). Thus, to be "anointed" meant, in a figurative sense, to be set apart by God, consecrated for service, and specially employed by God for a particular work or ministry.

This idea took on a transcendent, universal perspective among the Jews of the post-exilic period.[41] Those who returned from Babylonian captivity to Judea lamented the pathetic state of Israel. They began looking forward expectantly to a Redeemer who would restore the glory and fortunes of ancient Israel (under David and Solomon) and remove the shame of their subjugation to a foreign power. This Redeemer figure became known simply as "Messiah," which is a transliteration of the Hebrew word for "anointed."[42] ("Christ" is the Greek form of this same word.) Thus, Messiah became the name given not to one who was merely anointed, but to the One who is *the* Anointed: He would not be *a* redeemer (like the judges of Israel's pre-kingly days), but *the* Redeemer.

Indeed, Jesus Christ *was* anointed of God in a unique and special way. He was not anointed with a horn of olive oil or daubed with the holy anointing oil, nor was He anointed only in a metaphorical sense. Having identified Christ as "the Lamb of God who takes away the sin of the world" and "the Son of God"—not one identity or the other, but both[43]—John the Baptist baptized Jesus in water, and at the same time God anointed Him with His Spirit (Matthew 3:13-17; John 1:29-34). Upon His baptism, the Holy Spirit descended upon Him in the form of a dove, which served as a visible sign of the fact of this anointing. The Father also confirmed this anointing with an audible voice from heaven: "This is My beloved Son, in whom I am well-pleased." This anointing, then, took the function of the holy anointing oil to an ideal and spiritual level. What was prophesied *of* the Spirit through the type prophecy of the anointing oil was fulfilled *by* the Spirit when He was poured out (so to speak) upon Jesus' head.

Being anointed with God's Spirit served as the beginning point of Jesus' earthly ministry. This is not to suggest that the Holy Spirit was absent from the picture until this time. Such a conclusion is no more logical than to say that the Spirit was not involved in the lives of God's people until Pentecost of Acts 2. However, it is true that Christ's ministry was *incomplete* apart from the direct involvement of the Spirit. The Spirit provided the power (for miracles), guidance, and supernatural inspiration for Christ's ministry. Jesus, then, did not operate alone: He was filled with the Spirit of God, which is to say that He was in constant and intimate communion with the Father. "You know of Jesus of Nazareth," Peter later told Cornelius, "how God anointed Him with the Holy Spirit and with power, and how He went about doing good and healing all who were oppressed by the devil, for God was with Him" (Acts 10:38). This "God was with Him" phrase is loaded with profound implications: God was not just monitoring His progress, or merely in agreement with what Jesus was doing, but was *with* Him through the Spirit that was given to Him "without measure" (John 3:34). Indeed, Jesus' prophetic name was "Immanuel" (Isaiah 7:14; Matthew 1:23), which means "God with us": God was with Israel through Jesus the Messiah. More specifically, God was with Israel because God's Spirit was with Jesus *and* because Jesus was Israel's Spirit-anointed King (see also Luke 1:30-33).

Not only was Jesus anointed with the Spirit, but so are those who are "in Christ." We are sealed "in Christ" by the anointing of God's Spirit, and thus are "established" by the Father Himself (2 Corinthians 1:21-22). We are not anointed in the same way, for exactly the same purpose, or to produce the same exact visible results (i.e., miracles), but our anointing with the Spirit is real and necessary all the same. While the Levitical priests had the holy anointing oil poured upon their heads, we have the Spirit "poured out" upon our *souls*.

An important point that is often overlooked is this: we must *come into contact* with the substance of our salvation, for it cannot remain a mere concept or teaching. It is not enough, for example, that the blood of Christ *exists*; if we are not *sprinkled* with that blood, it cannot make atonement for *our* sins.[44] (This "sprinkling" is not with the *literal* blood of Christ, but it is with *reference* to the physical blood of Christ and the historical reality of its having been shed; Romans 3:25; 5:9; et al). In this same way, it is not enough that the Spirit *exists*; if we are not *anointed* with Him, then we are not consecrated for service for God—and we cannot have communion with the Father. (We will explore these concepts in more detail in later chapters.) Knowing *about* the Spirit and being anointed *with* the Spirit does not necessarily describe the same thing or produce the same result. Yet with the sprinkling of Christ's blood *and* the anointing of God's Spirit—both processes defined metaphorically but being *real* and *necessary* all the same—we are "born again" to a new life with a new and "living hope" (1 Peter 1:1-3).

The Liquid Metaphor

There is also something remarkable in how the Holy Spirit is nearly always defined with an indefinite shape.[45] Just as a liquid does not have any particular shape of its own, so the Spirit cannot be described in a physical form. Just as a liquid is able to adapt to the shape of whatever vessel into which it is put, so the Spirit is able to adapt to any person of any age, size, status, color, ethnicity, or nationality. Just as a liquid can be applied (or daubed upon) any person, so the Spirit can be universally "applied" to any person. The Spirit's fluid, pliable, and completely versatile "application" to the human soul is perfectly conducive for His sanctifying work. In a similar thought, a person's physical or social circumstances are of no difficulty for the Spirit, and He has already proved His mastery over the human context (as illustrated in Acts 2:4-11 with regard to language, for example). In other words, no human or earthly obstacles can prevent the Spirit from carrying out the will of God in those who belong to Him— except for one: human *unbelief.* The Spirit simply cannot perform in the best interest of one who will not trust Christ's authority or follow the Spirit's direction.

This "liquid" description of the Spirit is carried out in a figurative sense as well. Just as the anointing oil was poured upon Aaron's head to anoint him (Exodus 29:7) and olive oil was poured upon every grain offering (Leviticus 2:1), so there are several passages that use a "pouring" metaphor to indicate the indwelling of the Spirit (all bracketed words are mine):

- ❑ "…The palace has been abandoned [because of judgment]…Until the Spirit is poured out upon us from on high…" (Isaiah 32:14-15).
- ❑ "Thus says the LORD, '…I will pour out water on the thirsty land and streams on the dry ground; I will pour out My Spirit on your offspring and My blessing on your descendants…'" (Isaiah 44:2-3).
- ❑ "'I will not hide My face from them any longer, for I will have poured out My Spirit on the house of Israel,' declares the LORD God" (Ezekiel 39:29).
- ❑ "'It will come about after this That I will pour out My Spirit on all mankind; And your sons and daughters will prophesy, Your old men will dream dreams, Your young men will see visions. Even on the male and female servants I will pour out My Spirit in those days'" (Joel 2:28-29; see also Acts 2:14-21).
- ❑ "Therefore having been exalted to the right hand of God, and having received from the Father the promise of the Holy Spirit, He [Christ] has poured forth this which you both see and hear"

(Acts 2:33).

❑ "All the circumcised believers who came with Peter were amazed, because the gift of the Holy Spirit had been poured out on the Gentiles also" (Acts 10:45).

❑ "and hope does not disappoint, because the love of God has been poured out within our hearts through the Holy Spirit who was given to us" (Romans 5:5).

❑ "[God] saved us, not on the basis of deeds which we have done in righteousness, but according to His mercy, by the washing of regeneration and renewing by the Holy Spirit, whom He poured out upon us richly through Jesus Christ our Savior" (Titus 3:5-6).

The anointing (pouring) imagery is used consistently in both the Old and New Testaments: the first set of revelations (the Old Testament) discloses what is to come; the second set (the gospel of Christ) discloses what has already happened or is happening now. We need both perspectives in order to understand the role and power of the Spirit in the life of the believer.

Summary Thoughts

The Spirit's work in the life of the believer and in the body (church) of Christ is analogous to the anointing process described in the Old Testament. These actions—the pouring out of olive oil or the holy anointing oil upon those who were commissioned to serve the Lord—help to illustrate *how* and *why* the Spirit is given to us. Once again, those who are "in Christ" are most certainly "anointed" with the Spirit of God— not visibly, and not for the same exact purposes as were others, but our anointing is *real, necessary*, and *productive* all the same.

Just as the holy oil dripped down from Aaron's beard to his body (cf. Psalms 133:1-2; Hebrews 1:9), so the Spirit is poured upon the Head of God's Church (Christ) and drips down, so to speak, to the body of the saints.[46] When we are filled with God's Spirit, we radiate with the light of God and bear the "fruit of the Spirit," which is all in preparation for our entrance into the eternal kingdom (cf. 2 Corinthians 5:5; 2 Peter 1:10-11).

Chapter Four
Holy Spirit Baptism

As for me, I baptize you with water for repentance, but He who is coming after me is mightier than I, and I am not fit to remove His sandals; He will baptize you with the Holy Spirit and fire.
Matthew 3:11

In the last chapter, we discussed how the Holy Spirit has fulfilled Old Testament "type" prophecies concerning how God consecrates His people. This was once a purely physical process, rich with symbolism. Now it is a spiritual process that is invisible to us but is very real nonetheless. Just as the olive oil or holy anointing oil was poured upon the head of the one being consecrated (or ordained, in the case of priests), so the Spirit has been "poured out" upon the spiritual body of Christ, consecrating (ordaining) all who belong to Him. Thus, the Holy Spirit—and His work—should be of great interest to Christians.

Peter declared that Joel's prophecy concerning the "pouring out" of the Spirit ("I will pour forth My Spirit upon all mankind") did indeed commence upon the day of Pentecost when he [Peter] delivered his first discourse to the Jews (Acts 2:17). This "pouring out" is generally referred to among Christians as the "baptism of the Holy Spirit." This "baptism" is supposed to elicit rejoicing and celebration, since it underscores Christ's triumph over death and His subsequent reign at the right hand of God (Acts 2:33). It is unfortunate, then, that this subject has also become a sticking point of controversy among so many believers. In our present study, we will do our best to be as objective as possible regarding this and will accept whatever conclusions the New Testament Scriptures draw for us.

The Source of the Baptism

To begin with, what is popularly called the "baptism of the Holy Spirit" is really a misnomer. Nowhere in the New Testament is this exact phrase used. John the Baptist spoke of One who would come after him who would baptize *with* the Spirit (Mark 1:8) or *in* the Spirit (John 1:33), but he never spoke of a baptism *of* the Spirit. Jesus later underscored John the Baptist's words as being authentic and accurate, since He repeated John's words verbatim (Acts 1:5).

This is not a mere quibble over the use of prepositions. Rather, it emphasizes the *source of authority* that governs the activity of the Spirit. To speak of the baptism "of" the Spirit indicates that the Spirit is the One who, by His own volition and independent decision, "baptizes" people as He sees fit. This is not the case: the Spirit does not act unilaterally, but acts in response to what He is told to do. This does not mean He is a mindless robot who cannot make decisions; it means His decisions are not made apart from the One who "sends" Him: the Father, in the name of His Son. Whatever this "baptism" is, it is Christ who authorizes it, commands it to be done, and oversees its procedure. This is John's point: "He who is coming after me is mightier than I...; He will baptize you with the Holy Spirit" (Matthew 3:11). It is Christ who baptizes *with* or *in* the Spirit, not the Spirit who baptizes on His own.

This is consistent with what we see elsewhere of the present relationship between Christ and the Spirit. While Christ was "in the flesh," He had to be guided by the Spirit since He [Christ] had divested Himself of His heavenly glory and privileges (Philippians 2:6-8). Once Jesus died, resurrected, and ascended into heaven to the right hand of the Father, He was given full authority over all things in heaven and on earth (Ephesians 1:20-23). The Spirit then submitted Himself to the authority of Christ, and thus serves the interests of the kingdom over which Christ rules. The Spirit did not decide on His own to "baptize" men with Himself, but Jesus *sent* Him for this reason (as discussed below).

When one is baptized in water, it is not the water that baptizes him, but someone else. That person is baptized *in* (or *with*) water, but the responsibility or authority *for* that baptism lies outside of the water itself. Likewise, when Christ's church[47] is "baptized" in the Spirit, it is not the Spirit that baptizes it, but Someone else. The church is baptized *in* (or *with*) the Spirit, but the authority *for* that baptism lies outside of the Spirit Himself. Does this diminish the role of the Spirit in the salvation of believers? Absolutely not: no one can be sanctified or consecrated to God apart from His Spirit (1 Corinthians 6:11). We need the Spirit in order to be saved; this is the means God has chosen to identify to Himself those who belong to Him (Ephesians 1:13-14). It is for this reason that Jesus clearly stated what was soon to come: "Truly, truly, I say to you, unless one is born of water and the Spirit he cannot enter into the kingdom of God" (John 3:5). So it is: one cannot enter the kingdom of God—an expression that necessarily implies salvation—without having been "born again" of water *and* the Spirit of God.

A Comparison to John's Baptism

There are relatively few verses that speak of the Spirit in connection with baptism. Below is the entirety of those verses, except for those which deal with Jesus' own literal baptism in water (bracketed words are mine):

❑ Matthew 3:11, "As for me [John the Baptist], I baptize you with water for repentance, but He who is coming after me is mightier than I, and I am not fit to remove His sandals; He will baptize you with the Holy Spirit and fire." (This passage, and the duplicate ones found in Mark, Luke, and John, will be discussed below.)

❑ Matthew 28:19, "Go therefore and make disciples of all the nations, baptizing them in the name of the Father and the Son and the Holy Spirit." (This passage deals with *water* baptism, not a purely spiritual baptism, and therefore goes beyond our present discussion. However, water baptism is commanded by all Persons of the Godhead.)

❑ Mark 1:8, "I [John the Baptist] baptized you with water; but He [who is coming] will baptize you with the Holy Spirit."

❑ Luke 3:16, "John answered and said to them all, 'As for me, I baptize you with water; but One is coming who is mightier than I, and I am not fit to untie the thong of His sandals; He will baptize you with the Holy Spirit and fire.'"

❑ John 1:33, "I [John the Baptist] did not recognize Him, but He who sent me to baptize in water said to me, 'He upon whom you see the Spirit descending and remaining upon Him, this is the One who baptizes in the Holy Spirit.'"

❑ Acts 1:4-5, "Gathering them together, He [Jesus] commanded them [the apostles] not to leave Jerusalem, but to wait for what the Father had promised, 'Which,' He said, 'you heard of from Me; for John baptized with water, but you will be baptized with the Holy Spirit not many days from now.'"

❑ Acts 2:38, "Peter said to them, 'Repent, and each of you be baptized in the name of Jesus Christ for the forgiveness of your sins; and you will receive the gift of the Holy Spirit.'" (This baptism refers to *water* baptism; see Acts 2:41. The "gift of the Holy Spirit" expression will be discussed in a later chapter.)

❑ Acts 10:44, 47, "While Peter was still speaking these words, the Holy Spirit fell upon all those who were listening to the message. ...[Then Peter said,] 'Surely no one can refuse the water for these to be baptized who have received the Holy Spirit just as we did, can he?'" (The occasion here is Peter's visit to Cornelius, the first Gentile to have been given the miraculous manifestation of the Spirit like what had been seen in Acts 2 with the apostles.)[48]

❑ Acts 11:16, "And I [Peter] remembered the word of the Lord, how He used to say, 'John baptized with water, but you will be baptized with the Holy Spirit.'" (This is Peter recounting the incident with Cornelius to the Jewish Christians in Jerusalem.)

❑ 1 Corinthians 12:13, "For by one Spirit[49] we were all baptized into one body, whether Jews or Greeks, whether slaves or free, and we were all made to drink of one Spirit." (The emphasis here is not Jesus' baptism with the Spirit, but the *oneness* of all believers *in* the Spirit; see verse 12.[50] The reference to "drinking" of the Spirit alludes to what Jesus Himself had said in His ministry concerning the Spirit; John 4:13-14; 6:63; and 7:37-39.)

All of the passages dealing with Jesus baptizing anyone in (or with) the Spirit share the same thing: they are all used as *comparisons* to the baptism of John the Baptist. What is really being emphasized is threefold: first, the *authority* behind each baptism; second, the *nature* of each baptism; and third, the *purpose* for each baptism. We will briefly examine each of these aspects separately.

Authority: John the Baptist began his ministry in fulfillment of divine prophecy (Isaiah 40:3-5; Malachi 3:1; Luke 3:2-6). He was not a rogue prophet, a radical nationalist (like many Zealots),[51] or a lunatic. Instead, he was the "messenger" sent to pave the way for the coming of the Messiah[52]; aside from Christ Himself, John was the only prophet whose own birth was specifically prophesied in Scripture. He was the symbolic "Elijah" who was to "restore the hearts of the fathers to their children and the hearts of the children to their fathers" (Malachi 4:5-6). The importance of his ministry, while brief (about six months), is not to be understated. Jesus declared that John spoke with heavenly authority, and that he was the greatest prophet to have preceded the establishment of the kingdom of God under Christ (Luke 7:24-28).

John's *baptism*, then, was not a mere ritual or self-determined feature of his ministry, as though only a means to attract attention. John called people out to the wilderness—away from the comforts of home and the conveniences of the cities—in order to snap their attention back to their covenant relationship with God. Israel had been languishing in darkness and doubt; the priests had imposed unrealistic expectations and self-serving teachings upon the people. John's mission was to touch the people's hearts with a powerful message: Messiah is coming! *Prepare your hearts to receive Him!* The *way* in which the people were to prepare their hearts was through repentance; the *visible demonstration* of this repentance was immersion in water.[53] John spoke with authority, prophesied with authority, and baptized with authority.

All this notwithstanding, John's authority paled in comparison to that of the One whom he said was to come. Christ's authority was infinitely greater than John's, and John knew as much (John 1:19-27). While John baptized in water with heavenly authority, the Messiah would baptize "with the Holy Spirit and fire" with *supreme* heavenly authority. Thus, in each passage that speaks of His baptizing with the Spirit, Jesus' authority is being compared to John's and is found to be far superior to his or any other prophet's.

Nature: John baptized in water; this is indisputable. John's ministry took place in the wilderness areas around the Jordan River, and he baptized people in that river—including Jesus (Matthew 3:13-17; John 1:28-33). Baptism in water was not mandated by the Law of Moses for those who were not priests. John did not add to the Law by baptizing people in water, but was employing baptism as a sacred ritual to turn people *back* to the Law (discussed below). Furthermore, baptism was not used exclusively by John to signify ritual cleansing and inward purity. The Pharisees and Essenes, at least, practiced baptism for these same reasons.[54] While John's baptism was similar in nature to the practices of others, it was not meant to duplicate them. It had a specific and unique purpose: to prepare one for the coming of Israel's King.

Jesus' baptism with the Holy Spirit, however, was completely different in nature. While John employed a physical, earthly substance (water) to indicate one's renewed identity to God, Jesus used a Living Spirit; while John's baptism was limited to this world, Jesus' baptism involved the spiritual realm of God. Jesus could have duplicated what John did—in fact, His disciples *did* baptize at the same time as John, though Jesus Himself did not baptize anyone (John 4:1-2)—but John could *never* have done what Jesus did. Jesus' baptism with the Spirit is something only

He could do; no one else could perform it; He does not expect anyone else to perform it.

Purpose: John's baptism was not to replace one's sincere repentance, but to serve as an indication that such repentance was *real* and thus did *exist*. John refused to baptize those who did not repent, as graphically demonstrated by his rebuke of the hypocritical Pharisees and Sadducees who came to him (Matthew 3:7-12). Of course, repentance or baptism by itself cannot save anyone. The repentance John expected—and thus the baptism he performed—was in *preparation* for being saved by the Messiah. This was not in conflict with the Law of Moses, but simply anticipated what the Law itself prophesied would come (see Acts 26:22-23).[55] Israel had not been keeping the Law, which violated her covenant with God; the repentance John sought was to rectify this transgression. Repentance must have a point of reference, something to which a person must return, just as there must be something from which he must turn away. In this case, the Law is that to which the people were to return even as they turned away from their sins. In this process, neither John nor Jesus meant to amend the Law in any way (Matthew 5:17-19).

John's baptism was not a different means of salvation than through the Law of Moses or Christ's gospel. In fact, when the apostle Paul later encountered men who had been baptized with John's baptism, he instructed them to be baptized into Christ (Acts 19:1-5). It was obvious to Paul that these men had not yet done what Christ required of them, given what had transpired since John; otherwise he would have taken no action with them. (We can safely assume, too, that some of the 3,000 who were baptized into Christ on the day of Pentecost [Acts 2:38-41] may have also previously been baptized by John.) John was a Jew who preached to Jews about Jewish law and God's covenant with the Jews—and the anticipation of (what was at that time) a very Jewish concept of the "kingdom of God." John could not baptize people into Christ, for no one could do this until Jesus had ascended to His rightful place in heaven.

Jesus' baptism with the Spirit *did* indicate a different means of salvation than what one pursued through the Law of Moses. Thus, while John's baptism with water only prepared people *for* the fulfillment of God's covenant with Israel, Jesus' baptism with the Spirit proved that the change had indeed been made. By immersing His church in the Spirit of God, Jesus showed that sanctification—the process by which one is made holy—required not only a "once for all" *physical* sacrifice (Hebrews

10:8-10), but also the divine *spiritual* consecration of God's Spirit (1 Corinthians 6:11; 2 Thessalonians 2:13; 1 Peter 1:2). It is Christ who ties all these things together, for He *was* the physical sacrifice and He *sent* the Spirit of God to His church. Through His blood a "new covenant" is made between God and men that could not be made by anyone else (Luke 22:20).

A Comparison with Water Baptism

While baptism with the Spirit inaugurated a new means of salvation—i.e., a new covenant system, since God's covenant with Israel had been fulfilled (cf. Jeremiah 31:31-34; Hebrews 8:6-13)—this still remained a special action, and not a perpetual one. Just as a man is only baptized in water once to demonstrate his allegiance to Christ (Romans 6:3-7),[56] so Christ only had to "baptize" once in order to demonstrate the reality of His ascension to power. The immersion of the church in the Spirit is proof positive that Christ truly *has* ascended to the right hand of God, since He could not have sent the Spirit otherwise (John 14:15-16; 16:7; Acts 2:33). The *miracles* that were performed by the early Christians are proof that the Spirit really *has* been "poured out" upon the church, in fulfillment of Joel's prophecy (Acts 2:14-21). *This* baptism is the result of a promise; it is not a command or expectation of believers. "Promises may be enjoyed, but cannot be obeyed. Commands are to be obeyed in order that the promises connected therewith, if any, may be enjoyed."[57]

When we say that Jesus only had to baptize with the Spirit *once*, we need to recognize that there were two groups that needed to be baptized by Him: Jews and Gentiles. *Each group* had to be baptized *once* with the Spirit; there had to be sufficient proof that this had occurred with each group. Jesus brought the two groups together into "one new man," but He did so "through the cross" *and* "in the Spirit" (Ephesians 2:13-18):

> But now in Christ Jesus you who formerly were far off have been brought near by the blood of Christ. For He Himself is our peace, who made both groups into one and broke down the barrier of the dividing wall, by abolishing in His flesh the enmity, which is the Law of commandments contained in ordinances, so that in Himself He might make the two into one new man, thus establishing peace, and might reconcile them both in one body to God through the cross, by it having put to death the enmity. And He came and preached peace to you who were far away, and peace

to those who were near; for through Him we both have our access in one Spirit to the Father.

The Jews—the first group—were the first to be baptized with the Spirit, since the gospel was offered to them first (Romans 1:16). The miraculous event that marked this occurred in Jerusalem on the day of Pentecost, when the apostles spoke in tongues as "tongues as of fire" rested upon their heads and the sound of a mighty wind invited men to see this great sign (Acts 2:4-11). John promised that the *Jews* would be baptized with the Spirit; this was the audience to which he spoke in Matthew 3:11. However, Jesus promised *power* only to the apostles: "You shall receive power when the Holy Spirit has come upon you" (see Acts 1:4-8). Not all Jews were promised this "power," but only the apostles. However, the Jewish people (as a group) were promised baptism with the Spirit. Power was given to the apostles; but the Spirit was given to *all* who called upon the name of the Lord (Acts 2:21). What happened with the apostles on Pentecost indicates the *visible, historical event* of this outpouring or baptism; but Joel's prophecy is clear that the effects of this baptism could not be *limited* to that event.

It seems some of us have spoken in error on this point in the past. We have said, "The baptism with the Spirit was limited to the apostles," because we understood that only the apostles were recipients of the *power* that Jesus promised them. We have thus married together two separate (but related) things: *power* given exclusively to Christ's apostles and *promise* given generally to the church of those who call upon the name of the Lord. Power (or apostolic authority) was necessary in order for God to fulfill His promise; but the promise (of the Spirit's presence in Christ's church) cannot be defined only by apostolic power. *Both* groups—the apostles and all those who are not apostles—were baptized with the Spirit; but while *authority* was given to the apostles, *signs* were given to the church.[58]

The Gentiles—the second group—also were baptized with the Spirit. The miraculous event that indicated this occurred in Caesarea, when Cornelius (and company) also spoke in tongues (Acts 10:24-48).[59] God used this occasion to open the door of salvation through Christ to the Gentiles, as indicated by the Spirit's manifestation upon him (them). What happened with Cornelius is the *historical event* of this outpouring upon the Gentiles; but Joel's prophecy once again is clear that the *implications* of this baptism went far beyond Cornelius.

The historical *reality* of the baptism itself—upon the apostles, then upon Cornelius—serves as an invitation for both groups (Jews and Gentiles) to become fellow members of Christ's church (Ephesians 3:6). If both groups (through their representatives, the apostles and Cornelius) are shown to be *with* the Spirit, then both groups are united *by* Him. Whatever barrier stood between the two groups was removed so that they might be reconciled to God as *one new man*—"in Christ" and "in the Spirit." As Christ sees the body of believers, we are all "one" in Him (Galatians 3:28).[60]

The resulting *effects* of this baptism were the miracles performed by the early Christians—first among the Jews, then the Gentiles (as each group was "baptized" in the Spirit). Joel's prophecy foretold that God's Spirit would be poured out upon "all flesh"—literally, this means believers from all peoples or nations, not upon every individual believer—and that the *evidence* of this outpouring would be signs and wonders (Acts 2:16-21). The hyperbolic language of Joel's prophecy ("blood, fire, and vapor of smoke"; "the sun will be turned into darkness"; etc.) also indicates a *great upheaval* to the present system. To the Jews, the covenant they had known for 1,500 years was superseded by a "better covenant, which has been enacted on better promises" (Hebrews 8:6). To the Gentiles, all the pagan and philosophic attempts at achieving ideal human potential were trumped by Christ's own perfect life and His invitation to the Gentiles to join Him in His success. In both cases, the Jews and Gentiles' worlds were turned upside-down; it was the end of one world just as it was the commencement of another. Never before in the history of mankind had God ever dwelt among men as He does through those in the body of Christ; never before had He baptized *any* group of men in His Spirit. Thus, the "one new man" (Jews and Gentiles) of Christ's church has been immersed in the Holy Spirit, and has since benefited from the Spirit's gifts and activity.

Spirit Baptism versus Water Baptism

This baptism with the Spirit did not nullify the need for *water* baptism, however. What Christ does through the Spirit of God is His business; it is an act of His authority, not an action required of those who call upon Him. In Acts 2, even though the twelve tribes of Israel (as represented by the twelve apostles) were baptized with the Spirit, they still had to demonstrate their faith in Christ *personally* and *visibly*. This was accomplished through their being immersed in water (Acts 2:38-41). Likewise, even though Cornelius and company were immersed in the

Spirit, they still had to be immersed in water (Acts 10:47-48). In other words, the one kind of baptism did not replace or remove the need for the other. Both are needed: each "man" (Jews and Gentiles as groups) had to be baptized by Christ in God's Spirit; likewise, every *individual member* of each "man" must be baptized in water according to the gospel's commands.

Jesus' baptism with the Spirit cannot be confused or made interchangeable with our baptism in water. These two baptisms do not mean the same thing, are not done for the same reason, and do not accomplish the same result. One is from heaven, the other is from earth; one is performed *by* God, the other is performed by men in the *name* (authority) of God (Matthew 28:18-19). Water baptism is what we do for Christ; baptism with the Spirit is what Christ has done for us. Water baptism is directly linked to one's salvation (1 Peter 3:21); baptism with the Spirit indicates the power *of* (or *supporting*) that salvation. Water baptism is our response *to* the gospel; baptism with the Spirit is the power *of* the gospel—it is proof that this gospel can truly help those who "call upon the name of the Lord" (Acts 2:21; Romans 10:11-13). If anyone today claims that he does not need to be baptized in water because he has already been baptized by the Spirit, that person reveals a misunderstanding of these crucial facts.

What these baptisms—in the Spirit *and* in water—have in common is this: they both serve to establish an *identity* with the Godhead. The baptism of the Spirit associates us with God, regardless of nationality or any previously insuperable barrier; our baptism in water associates us with Christ through our having died *to* the world and *with* Christ, in order that we might "walk in newness of life" with Him (Romans 6:3-7; 2 Timothy 2:11). More specifically, our baptism with the Spirit identifies us with the Father, while our baptism in water identifies us with Christ. We have access to the Father in the Spirit (Ephesians 2:18), and we have our access to Christ (who *gives* us the Spirit) in the church. By being baptized in the name (authority) of the Father, Son, and Holy Spirit, we become the possession of God: we are bought with the Son's blood, filled with God's Spirit, and given access to the Father Himself. Through *both* of these baptisms—one having already been performed *by* Christ, the other performed upon each sinner's conversion *to* Christ—we are able to be "partakers of the divine nature" (2 Peter 1:4).

The Implications for the Believer Today

One might still ask the question: "In becoming a Christian, have I been baptized with the Spirit?" Certainly Christ's *church* is immersed in the Spirit, while "the whole [unregenerate] world lies in the power of [in a sense: is immersed in] the evil one" (1 John 5:19, bracketed words mine). When we are brought into Christ through our obedience to His gospel, we are transferred from the domain of Satan to the kingdom of Christ: our identity with Satan is severed, while our identity with Christ is established (Galatians 3:25-27; Colossians 1:12-14).

Each person who becomes a Christian is added to the Spirit-filled body of believers. Since the body (church) itself has been baptized in the Holy Spirit, each person who is added to the body (by the Lord, Acts 2:47) becomes a partaker of the Godhead, which includes fellowship with the Spirit. Each Christian is not *himself* baptized with the Spirit, for his entrance into the body of Christ bestows upon him all the rights and privileges of the entire *body* having been immersed in the Spirit. There is only "one baptism" with which we need to be concerned now (Ephesians 4:5), and that is the one Christ requires of *all* who come to Him: water baptism. This is the visible means by which we "[call] upon His name" (Acts 22:16).

In contrast, there is no New Testament passage that directly or indirectly requires each believer to be baptized with the Holy Spirit. (We are, however, to receive the *gift* of the Holy Spirit; He is to *indwell* the believer; and He is our *access* to God. These are some of the "rights and privileges" mentioned above, and will be discussed in later chapters.) Christ does not need to baptize each individual person with the Holy Spirit; this is redundant and unnecessary. He has already proved that *all men* are invited into His church by having representatively baptized *both groups* (Jews and Gentiles) with the Spirit. He has also proved that His church is a Spirit-filled church, as evidenced by the many miracles that were once performed within it (1 Corinthians 12:4-7; Hebrews 2:4). Once a fact is established, it does not have to be endlessly repeated. In a court of law, once a verdict is reached, the case is closed; we do not reconvene the court, reenact the entire trial, and repeat the jury's deliberation every time someone wants to review the case. Once it is a matter of court record, it can simply be read and understood. Likewise, the fact of Christ's having baptized the redeemed among both Jews and Gentiles—which is to say, the redeemed of *all mankind*—with the Spirit of God has been forever documented in the gospel record.

The church has been and will always be immersed in the Spirit. There is no need for miracles to continue in order to substantiate this fact. This does not mean that the absence of miracles necessitates the absence of the Holy Spirit; it only means that genuine miracles are possible only through the Spirit and not by any other power. Miracles are a "sign," not the substance; they point *to* the object of our attention, but they are not the object itself; they visibly manifest (in this case) the power *of* salvation, but we do not need to see or perform them *for* salvation. We have no record of anyone in the New Testament who was saved by a miracle alone; instead, we are saved by faith *inspired* by miracles performed by the Holy Spirit (cf. Romans 1:17; Hebrews 2:3-4).

Furthermore on this point, it is necessary to view "the part" as it relates to "the whole." In the Law of Moses, the "first fruits" of the harvest, which was only a symbolic part of the crop, was offered in order to consecrate the entire harvest (Leviticus 23:9-11; see also Romans 11:16). Jesus Himself was raised from the dead, which is sufficient to prove that all who are "in Christ" will be raised from the dead; He is the "first fruits" of all who will be raised (1 Corinthians 15:20-22), the "firstborn among many brethren" (Romans 8:29). In this same way, when the representatives for Jews and Gentiles—the twelve apostles and Cornelius (and company), respectively—were baptized with the Spirit, they were baptized for all Jews and all Gentiles. Because of what happened to them *specially*, we can be confident of what has happened *generally*. They serve as fitting representatives of all men; they represent the "first fruits" of the entire "harvest," which is the body of those who are "in Christ."[61]

There are some who argue the "baptism of the Spirit" from personal experiences and not biblical precedent. "For many humans the occasion of receiving the baptism in the Holy Spirit is a memorable dynamic, stirring, deeply emotional event. To be seized by the Spirit, to enjoy the abundance of God's filling, and to experience the Spirit's assumption of His control, may press the human physical and emotional natures to their limit."[62] This baptism is allegedly necessary in order to achieve "experiential sanctification," that is, to experience sanctification in a life of holiness, as evidenced through miraculous gifts.[63] While one's relationship with God is indeed a deeply *personal* experience (as Paul indicated in Galatians 2:20), we must guard against reducing that relationship to a *subjective* or *emotional* experience.

Summary Thoughts

From the standpoint of the Spirit's work in the early church, we might regard Acts as having the two following objectives. The first is to define which people *collectively* (i.e., as a group) are invited into God's kingdom for salvation. This invitation may be offered through the mediation of men (i.e., the apostles), but it comes directly from heaven. The second objective is to identify *individually* those who rightly respond to that offer. These are two separate but related objectives; we cannot make them into one. The first describes a once-for-all action, inasmuch as God has invited *all* men—both Jews *and* all non-Jews—into His kingdom. The second describes a perpetual action: people are responding to God's invitation all the time.

Christ does not ask us to be baptized with the Holy Spirit. Christ *never* asks us to do something that only He can do or that is impossible for us to perform. Likewise, Christ does not need to baptize you *personally* with the Spirit, since this action has already been accomplished once and does not need to be continually repeated. It would not only be redundant to do this, it would challenge what already *has* been done: in essence, it would call into question what was done in the beginning. (The same can be said if Christ had to continually offer Himself as a sacrifice for sin: if His *first* offering was not sufficient, then how can we know that any *subsequent* offerings will be any better?) The fact is: Christ has been offered once, and His church has been immersed in the Spirit once. In each case, the first and only time was sufficient for *all* time.

On the other hand, if you have not been baptized in water for the forgiveness of your sins (Acts 2:38; 22:16) *and* to unite with Christ in the likeness of His own death (Romans 6:3-7), then the fact that Christ's church has been immersed in the Spirit does not help you. The means by which we gain entrance into Christ's church is through the demonstration of our faith in Christ Himself. While we are not saved by our works of faith, we are not saved apart from them, either. If we want the salvation that is found in Christ, then we must do what the Spirit has asked us to do: we must be obedient to the commands of the gospel (cf. 1 John 5:1-4).

Chapter Five
The Gift of the Holy Spirit

Peter said to them, "Repent, and each of you be baptized in the name of Jesus Christ for the forgiveness of your sins; and you will receive the gift of the Holy Spirit."   Acts 2:38

Certainly one of the more controversial subjects in the New Testament concerns what is meant by the phrase "the gift of the Holy Spirit." The question, of course, has never been whether or not God gives gifts, for God has always bestowed gifts upon those who turn to Him for salvation. God even gives gifts to the unconverted in hopes that they will respond favorably to His kindness and call upon Him (Luke 6:35; Romans 2:4).

But what of this "gift of the Holy Spirit," which is at the center of so much religious debate? Some believe that this "gift" refers to the ability to perform miracles. Some agree with this, but since they also believe miracles have ceased, this "gift" is no longer relevant for Christians today. Still others believe that it refers to eternal life and nothing more: the Holy Spirit has no interactive function with the saints other than to acknowledge our salvation—similar to the function of a customs clerk who stamps passports.

The intention of this study is not to dissect all the different views on the "gift of the Holy Spirit." Instead, we would do well to examine the New Testament Scriptures themselves to see if we can come to an objective and accurate understanding of what this phrase means. It does not appear that God has given us something too difficult to understand here, but He does expect us to be diligent and methodical in our study of His Word.

What is Required in Order to Receive the Gift

Perhaps we should just dive into the one passage that, more than any other, is cited with regard to this subject (Acts 2:37-39, bracketed words mine):

Now when they [the Jews who gathered on the day of Pentecost to hear Peter's message] heard this, they were pierced to the heart, and said to Peter and the rest of the apostles, "Brethren, what shall we do?" Peter said to them, "Repent, and each of you be baptized in the name of Jesus Christ for the forgiveness of your sins; and you will receive the gift of the Holy Spirit. For the promise is for you and your children and for all who are far off, as many as the Lord our God will call to Himself."

There are some immediate conclusions we can draw concerning this "gift." First, whatever it is, one must *repent* and *be baptized* in order to receive it. Repentance is a change of attitude *and* action, as demonstrated by "fruits" (i.e., visible demonstrations, Matthew 3:8; Acts 26:19-20; 2 Corinthians 7:10). Baptism is (in this context) immersion in water, which symbolizes one's death to sin and spiritual re-birth in Christ (Romans 6:3-7). It is grammatically and contextually impossible to separate "baptism" from "repentance" here. If one is necessary, the other is equally so; both are required in order to receive whatever is promised; it cannot be otherwise. In fact, neither forgiveness *nor* "the gift of the Holy Spirit" is possible apart from these actions.

Second, whatever this "gift" is, it is conditional and not automatic. Since repentance and baptism are *at least* required[64] in order to receive this gift, then it stands to reason (and is supported by Scripture) that if one does not fulfill such conditions, neither will he receive what is being offered (Matthew 7:21-23; 1 John 2:4-5; et al). Some want God to save people (including themselves) simply because He is a good and merciful God. It is absolutely true that God is good, but He still requires commandments to be obeyed (Matthew 19:16-17; John 3:36); and it is absolutely true that God is merciful, but He extends mercy (or kindness) in order that people would respond rightly to it (Romans 11:22; 2 Peter 3:9; et al). In other words, God only saves those who are willing to put their full confidence in Him *and* demonstrate moral responsibility for their own souls. This is the kind of faith God seeks among men (Romans 1:17). Without this faith, one forfeits all of God's priceless gifts, including the "gift of the Holy Spirit."

Third, this gift cannot be merely "forgiveness." This would make Peter's invitation pointlessly redundant; Acts 2:38 would read, in essence: "Repent, and each of you be baptized in the name of Jesus Christ for the forgiveness of your sins; and you will receive forgiveness as a gift." Besides this, forgiveness is what is extended to the believer *so that* he may receive the "gift of the Holy Spirit." Repentance and baptism are preparatory for forgiveness, and forgiveness is preparatory for the reception of the Spirit's gift. God does not cleanse people of their sins just so that they can be cleansed; He always does so in order that *something else* may be done—really, so that we are *made fit* to do serve Him.

These clarifications make the "gift" more easily definable, but do not entirely remove all difficulties associated with this subject. They do, however, help us to focus on the essential facts without trying to support a predetermined agenda. It is already evident that when God offers gifts, He has the right to dictate the conditions for their reception. We should not confuse payment for gifts (which contradicts the very concept of gift-giving) with preparation to receive gifts (which is legitimate and expected). God's conditions for receiving the "gift of the Holy Spirit" on *our* part include repentance and baptism; on *His* part, the forgiveness of our sins.

Furthermore, to receive the "gift of the Holy Spirit" (as with all gifts of God) requires the acceptance of whatever responsibilities come with it. This may be likened to parents giving their teenager a car to drive: the car may indeed be a free gift, but it necessarily demands responsible behavior in order to drive it, including obeying the rules of the road. God gives His children gifts, but He also expects us to behave responsibly, to "walk in a manner worthy of the Lord" (Colossians 1:10). Such gifts, then, are not for mere show, nor are they given without *purpose*. By giving the "gift of the Holy Spirit," God gives His children something productive to *do*.

Different Contexts of "Gifts"

The New Testament speaks of three different uses of "gifts" in relation to the Holy Spirit. While we will only briefly examine each usage, the meaning of Peter's words will likely become even clearer to us as a result of this.

❑ **"the gift of the Holy Spirit" (Acts 2:38):** Some believe that this phrase has to do with the impartation of miraculous abilities: those who are given this "gift" are thus able to perform miracles. But this is not what we see happening as a result of Peter's words. In fact, it is only the apostles who are thereafter performing miracles (Acts 2:43), until a *separate* action is done, namely, the apostles lay their hands upon certain people in order for *them* to perform miracles (as in 8:14-19). While "all" believers received the Spirit (5:32), not all were given the ability to perform miracles *by* the Holy Spirit.

❑ **"the gift of the Holy Spirit" (Acts 10:44-48):** The speaking in tongues by Cornelius and company (i.e., Gentiles) was the same *kind* of miracle demonstrated by the apostles in Acts 2:4-11 (see also Acts 11:15-17 for a parallel account). This does not mean that it was for the exact same *purpose*, however (see below). Furthermore, this miracle was performed on Cornelius *before* he was baptized. This is important to note because it is the opposite order of what Peter said in Acts 2:38: "Repent and... be baptized...for the forgiveness of your sins, and you shall receive the gift...." But here, Cornelius is given "the gift" before having demonstrated that which was required of the Jews earlier. Thus, the same phrase is being used differently (for two separate purposes) in both accounts.

❑ **"gifts" of the Spirit, or "spiritual gifts" (1 Corinthians 12:4-7, 11):** The Corinthians, *having already been baptized* into Christ, were then given the ability—by necessary implication, through the laying on of Paul's hands—to perform miracles *of* the Spirit. These miracles (as explained in 1 Corinthians 12 and 14) were for the purpose of: edification (in lieu of the full revelation of the gospel, as we have today); a "sign for unbelievers" (14:22), so that the unconverted would be convinced of God's power; and, in the case of an apostle, to authenticate the source of one's authority (2 Corinthians 12:12).

Each usage or endowment of such gifts must be kept in its rightful context:

❑ The **context of Acts 2:38** is *not* for edification, a "sign" for unbelievers, or to confirm the genuineness of an apostle. Rather, the context here deals directly with personal salvation. In 2:39, Peter says that "the promise is for you...and for all who are far off"—the "promise" being the direct intervention of the Holy Spirit by the authority of Christ (2:33). The miracles that had been demonstrated through the apostles (2:4-11) were visible proofs that the invisible Spirit of God was in Christ's church. The "promise," then, was not primarily to perform miracles, but to be sanctified by God's Spirit (1 Peter 1:2), which itself is only possible through the redemption of Christ.

❑ The **context of Acts 10:44-48** is *not* for salvation, but to demonstrate God's acceptance of Gentiles into the kingdom of God. Cornelius did not become a Christian until he was immersed in water as an act of faithful obedience; he could not even be forgiven of his sins until he repented and was baptized (2:38). Peter did not give the Jews and Cornelius two different methods by which to call upon the Lord. No one has ever been saved by a miracle alone; likewise, no one has ever been saved simply because God involved that person *in* a miracle. Even the anointing of the Holy Spirit is not for the purpose of removing sins, for only the blood of Christ is able to do this. The anointing can only be done *after* forgiveness is accomplished, not before. Cornelius was a representative of all Gentiles, as we have already established; the part sanctifies the whole. It was not necessary to repeat the process for every Gentile that which has already been established in the case of a fitting representative. The Holy Spirit, by His *own* determination (not by any action or imploring of Peter) opened the door for the Gentiles (see Acts 15:7-9). In *this particular case alone*, the baptism *with* the Spirit is set equal to the gift *of* the Spirit.

❑ The **context of 1 Corinthians 12** is *not* the salvation of souls *or* designation of a certain group of people as being acceptable for salvation. Rather, it is the regulation of spiritual gifts (*charisma*) that had been endowed upon certain Christians in Corinth. (Even though all had been baptized into Christ and thus received the "gift of the Holy Spirit," not every Christian there was a "worker of miracles," 1 Corinthians 12:29.) The purpose, as stated above, was for edification, as a "sign" for unbelievers, and to substantiate authority. Just because one had the ability to exercise a "gift" did not automatically mean that he had the spiritual maturity to do so rightly. First Corinthians 12 – 14 serves as a guide for those who were given such gifts, so that they might use them as they were intended.

What these "gift" contexts do have in common is this: they were all given by the will of the Father, through the authority of Jesus Christ, and with direct intervention of the Holy Spirit. No one can receive the "gift of the Holy Spirit" through manipulation or usurpation. God cannot be coerced, deceived, or extorted; it is impossible to obtain gifts from Him through illegitimate means. No one will receive such gifts if he is not first seeking God, does not have his heart prepared to receive them, and has not demonstrated his preparedness through legitimate acts of faith. Finally, if there is any confusion about what the "gift of the Holy Spirit" is, it lies with us: God is not confused about His gifts, nor is His Holy Spirit.

However, it should be clear that these "gift" contexts are not interchangeable. We ought not to expect that the Holy Spirit will impart to us the ability to perform miracles, as the Corinthians enjoyed. We ought not to expect that He will specially designate us as being acceptable for salvation, as He did for Cornelius and friends. We ought not to point to what happened to Cornelius' situation and compare it point-for-point to what Peter said to the Jews in Jerusalem on Pentecost. It *is* true that all of these contexts employ similar or comparable language or terms; it is *not* true we can ignore the context (or environment) in which these terms are used simply because of such similarities. "...The same word in *different contexts* may refer to different things."[65]

Another important point is this: all these "gifts" are spiritual in nature and have their source in heaven and not here on earth. This means that men (or churches) are not the origin of God's gifts, and neither can men arbitrarily define them. We cannot go *outside* of Scripture—say, to an ancient church tradition, a Bible commentary, or some preacher of distinction—to determine what God alone has already defined *by* Scripture.

The Gift Defined

Now that we've examined the different contexts used in the New Testament concerning any "gift" (or "gifts") of the Spirit, we are drawn back to Acts 2:38 to determine the *ideal* usage of this subject. The reasons for this are: 1) this is the first time this phrase (or concept) is used; 2) all other uses are subordinate to this one—e.g., if Acts 2:38 is taken out of the picture, Acts 10:44-48 makes no sense; and 3) this applies in principle to *all* those whom the Lords calls to Himself and who *at the same time* call upon the Lord.[66]

The "gift of the Holy Spirit" is that which is given to *all* persons who "call upon the Lord" by repenting of their sins *and* being baptized into Christ (compare Acts 2:21 with 22:16). This "gift" is *not* the ability to perform miracles, for this goes beyond the context of Acts 2:38.[67] It cannot be limited to "eternal life," for this would conflict with other New Testament passages which speak of the Spirit's work in the church in the here and now. On the other hand, this "gift" *must*: originate with God;

be given by the authority of Jesus Christ; and have something to do with consecration and fellowship.

This latter point is the key to understanding the "gift of the Holy Spirit." According to the Law of Moses, no Levitical priest could approach God (via the tabernacle or the solemn assemblies) without atonement first having been made for him through the blood offerings prescribed by God. Once atonement was made for his sins, then he could be consecrated for service: literally, he was anointed with the holy oil, as we have discussed in an earlier chapter. (Also read Leviticus 8, which describes the literal ordination of priests.) This formulaic process serves as a distinct pattern that God has *always* used in regard to the salvation of men:

❑ **First,** sin must be dealt with, and this atonement is impossible without (ultimately) a blood sacrifice—an offering of life in place of the life of the sinner (Leviticus 4 – 6). Thus, in every case, sin offerings are *offered* first in sequence, even though burnt offerings are often *mentioned* first (because of their higher objective).

❑ **Second,** consecration is what God desires, since this prepares us for service. God's objective is not only that we would be forgiven, but that we would enter into His service, to do "good works" in His honor (Matthew 5:16; Ephesians 2:10; Colossians 1:9-10; et al). Under the Law, this consecration involved burnt offerings (Leviticus 1) and the anointing of the one being set apart for such service.[68] In principle, one cannot serve the Lord who is not prepared (or fit) for service (note the language in, say, Luke 9:62).

❑ **Third,** the believer's expected response to having been brought into God's service is gratitude or thankfulness. Thus, the third group of offerings prescribed by Law was called "freewill," "peace," or "thank" offerings—which all refer to one's voluntary desire to give visible praise to God through sacrifice (Leviticus 3).

Thus, for each Israelite, the Law prescribed *in this order* atonement, consecration, and fellowship offerings. God's covenant with Israel stipulated that this is how one was able to draw near to Him despite the fallible human condition. As Gordon has observed (bracketed words mine),

[The Old Testament types] fix the sequence of events in redemption as rigidly as the order of sunrise and sunset is fixed in the heavens. Nowhere in tabernacle or in temple shall we ever find the laver placed before the altar. The altar is Calvary and the laver is Pentecost. One stands for the sacrificial blood; the other, for the sanctifying Spirit. ...It was impossible that Pentecost could have preceded Calvary, or that the outpouring of the Spirit should have anticipated the shedding of the blood.[69]

Since the Law served as a shadow of the things to come (Hebrews 10:1), we can cite the process by which one drew near to God under the Law and apply the principles to the present time. Just as God required the Israelite to be cleansed of sin and consecrated for service (and expected his gratitude in return), so we must be cleansed of sin and consecrated for service (and our gratitude is expected in return). Christ is our blood offering, since animal blood is insufficient for the cleansing of human sin (Hebrews 10:4). The Holy Spirit is our consecration, since by Him we are anointed and set apart for service to God as priests (1 Peter 2:9). The Father then expects our gratitude as part of our "acceptable service" (Hebrews 12:28).

The Jews in Peter's day would be familiar with the terms and conditions of covenant, so he could speak to them with allusions to the patterns in the Law without having to describe them in detail. What Peter told the Jews on Pentecost (Acts 2:22-38), then, was essentially this: "A new and superior covenant has been inaugurated which fulfills the first covenant. In order for you to enter into this new covenant, your sins must be atoned by the body and blood of Jesus, and no longer by the offerings of animals; only in this way can you now be forgiven. Also, just as Christ died in order to be resurrected, so *you* must 'die' to all former allegiances and give your allegiance to Him, this being signified through your burial in water. Only when these actions are completed can you be consecrated to service for God, in which you are anointed with His own Spirit."

Just as God promised a relationship with ancient Israel (Exodus 6:7), so He promised a *new* relationship with the Jews (Jeremiah 31:31-34) and even with those who are "far off" (John 10:16; Acts 2:39). This covenant would no longer be defined by "type" sacrifices, nor would it merely lead to yet another covenant relationship. This new covenant relationship would be defined by each participant's *individual consecration* by the Holy Spirit; it would no longer be limited to one nation or ethnic group. This "gift"—for it certainly could not be earned, nor could it be purchased—served as the culmination of centuries of preparation and anticipation. By bestowing His Spirit upon each believer, God would create a completely new and unprecedented body of people, one "predestined" for justification and glory (Romans 8:28-30; Ephesians 1:3-14). By the authority and providence of "one Spirit," all believers would become the "many members" of the "one body" of Christ (1 Corinthians 12:13).

All of these things have been fulfilled through Christ and have been realized in His church. Furthermore, these facts define the "gift of the Holy Spirit" in its rightful context. This "gift" is one's *access to the Father* through the *agency of the Spirit* because of the *redemptive work of the Son.* This "access" (cf. Ephesians 2:18) is defined through the Spirit's activity in the life of the believer—which is the essential definition of *grace* as used in the New Testament.[70] The Spirit provides what we need (that we cannot provide for ourselves) with regard to salvation:

- ❏ Intercession for prayers (Romans 8:26-27).
- ❏ Guidance for our walk with God (Galatians 5:16-17).
- ❏ All spiritual blessings, which are found "in Christ" (Ephesians 1:3) for those who are "sealed" by the Holy Spirit (1:13; 4:30).
- ❏ Divine activity in the heart of the believer (Philippians 2:13, "…it is God who is at work in you").
- ❏ Assurance of all future blessings and promises (2 Corinthians 1:21-22).

Once again, no one can come to the Father who has not been anointed with the Spirit, and no one will be anointed with the Spirit who does not surrender himself to the authority of the Son. Our fellowship with God—the fundamental implication of "access"—is not something we are able to assume into existence or impose upon God. It is the real and functional state of being that exists between the believer and his God based upon a covenant relationship having been established between the two parties. The terms and conditions of this covenant are spelled out in Christ's gospel; one enters into this covenant through the life-giving blood of Christ *and* the believer's faithful obedience to its terms and conditions. As a *result* of this relationship having been established, God seals the spiritual transaction with His Spirit, conferring all the privileges and blessings—all the gifts—that He [the Spirit] provides for the believer (Galatians 3:14). Just as the believer gives his spirit to God, in a sense, so God gives His Spirit to the believer.

A passage that parallels Acts 2:38 doctrinally is 1 Corinthians 6:11 (bracketed words are mine): "Such [unregenerate people, see verses 9-10] were some of you; but you were washed [i.e., baptized, 1 Peter 3:21], but you were sanctified [i.e., set apart, made holy], but you were justified [i.e., declared legally innocent, without condemnation] in the name [or by the authority] of the Lord Jesus Christ and in the Spirit of our God." Or we could paraphrase this passage accordingly: "You all were once guilty people; but having died with Christ in baptism, you have been atoned of your sins, you were consecrated for service, and you thus gained access to the Father as innocent people. All of this was accomplished by the redemption of Christ *and* the anointing of the Holy Spirit." Both Peter and Paul reached the same conclusions by the same reasoning process, since they were both inspired by the same Spirit. All who are "in Christ" are given access to the Father by the grace of God; this is the "gift of God" (Romans 3:23-24; Ephesians 2:8-9), which is also the "gift of the Holy Spirit." Everything God does for us is a "gift": the Father's gifts, the Son's gifts, and the Spirit's gifts are all aspects of saving grace. In a finely-wrapped package filled with many other gifts, fellowship with the Father is indeed "the gift." It is the greatest gift any human being could hope to receive.

Some have said, "The 'gift of the Holy Spirit' is simply His presence in the life of the Christian." This makes sense, to a point: certainly the gift *of* the Spirit includes our communion *with* the Spirit. But as we will see in later chapters, the Spirit *does* things for us as well; He *gives* us things that we cannot have otherwise. To say that the "gift" is *only* the presence of the Spirit regards Him as a mere companion to the soul and not the dynamic, soul-transforming, and life-giving Deity that He is. We must be very careful to avoid insulting the "Spirit of grace" by not believing in His power to *draw* us near to God and *lead* us heavenward (cf. Hebrews 10:29). The Spirit ought never to be reduced to a mere static "presence" in or "disposition" toward the life of a believer.

Receiving the Holy Spirit (Acts 8)

Some have gone to great lengths to "prove" that the "gift of the Holy Spirit" is interchangeable with the ability to perform miracles. In Acts 8:20, for example, this power is referred to as the "gift of God." To "receive the Holy Spirit" (Acts 8:15), then, appears directly linked to receiving miraculous gifts of God. Therefore, some have concluded that the "gift of the Holy Spirit" in Acts 2:38 must be the ability to perform miracles.

This reasoning assumes that "gift of God" is being used in the *same context* in Acts 8 as it is in Acts 2. It also implies that to "receive the Holy Spirit" has no function except to perform miracles. (You can see where this leads: if no one is performing miracles today, then neither is anyone receiving the Holy Spirit.) Third, it assumes that what has *already happened* prior to this situation (in Acts 8:14-20) has no bearing on the situation itself, when in fact it does. Fourth, it assumes (by implication) that Peter's words in Acts 2:38 do not really mean that upon one's submission to the gospel (as evidenced by his repentance and immersion in water) a person really does *receive the gift of the Holy Spirit.*

In response to the Acts 8 scenario: First, the same terms or phrases in Scripture can have different meanings or uses, based upon different contexts.[71] The context of Acts 2:38 concerns the spiritual salvation of the individual believer; the context of Acts 8:14ff concerns something *different* than this. We know this because the Samaritans had already *rightly responded* to the same gospel Peter preached in Jerusalem (8:12-13). These Samaritans believed; they repented of their sins [necessarily implied]; and they submitted to water baptism. As a result of this, they were forgiven of their sins. Therefore, they received what all receive who believe, repent, are baptized, and (thus) forgiven: the gift of the Holy Spirit. Whatever "receiving the Holy Spirit" means *after* this cannot in any way be imposed upon all candidates for salvation for all time, for these people had already done what is required of all other people. They had become Christians through this process; there can be no disputing this.

Second, Peter and John were dispatched from Jerusalem to Samaria *not* to give these people "the" gift of the Holy Spirit—i.e., the gift that *all* believers receive (Acts 5:32). It was not within their power to do this; mere men cannot grant or refuse salvation based upon their own decisions or actions. The matter of salvation of the Samaritans was between them [the Samaritan believers] and God. Nonetheless, it was still necessary—to the Jews, the Samaritans, and all Christians everywhere—that God put His seal of approval upon the Samaritans' reception of the gospel. This was not because it was in question in the mind of God, but in order to remove all doubt in the minds of men. If mixed-blooded Samaritans can perform the same miracles that pure-blooded Jews can perform (by the same Spirit that the Jews had received), then they are no less citizens of the kingdom than these Jews themselves. To communicate this endorsement, however, Christ sent His hand-picked apostles, Peter and John, to lay their hands upon these people and provide them the proof of common citizenship that they and others required. (We will save the discussion of "laying on of hands" for chapter 10.)

Third, to "receive the Holy Spirit"—in the context of Acts 8:14-17—means to be endowed with miraculous power *from* the Spirit in order to witness the presence *of* the Spirit in one's life. Once the context is established, the individual pieces of the passage fall properly into place. Peter, by inspiration of the Holy Spirit, said what he said and meant what he meant in Acts 2:38: If you rightly respond to the gospel of Christ, then you will receive the gift of the Holy Spirit. There can be no question of this; that was not a "limited time offer"; this is still as valid today as it was 2,000 years ago. However, what Peter and John did for the Samaritans *was* limited, since the purpose for which they did it has already been fulfilled. We cannot mix these two contexts together. As one Bible scholar put it, "To confuse the power given by the Spirit and the Spirit Himself is to miss the whole point."[72]

To "receive the [gift of the] Holy Spirit" with regard to (in the context of) *salvation* is absolutely necessary. This is what Jesus promised (John 7:39); to maintain otherwise nullifies one's spiritual fellowship with God (Romans 8:9). To "receive the Holy Spirit" in the context of spiritual (miraculous) gifts, however, is another matter altogether: the manner in which this power is given, the purpose for which it is done, and how it is manifested are all different than the previous usage. If I am a Christian, it is imperative that I receive the Spirit *and* His gift(s); I cannot draw near to God otherwise. However, I have no reason to receive or expect the ability to perform miracles, since that function is no longer necessary for Christ's church. (This will be further discussed in chapter 10). That which is recorded in Scripture is sufficient for convincing me and anyone else of God's truth (cf. John 20:31).

Summary Thoughts

Identifying the "gift of the Holy Spirit" does not require superior intelligence or scholarly debate. But we should not oversimplify the subject, either. This "gift"—access to the Father, and all that is involved in this—is certainly not small: it is incomprehensible in scope, power, and effect. Neither should we minimize the role of Christ in order to accentuate the Spirit's gift. Without the gift of Christ's own body and blood to redeem us, the Spirit would have no gift to offer us; none of us could have access to the Father. It is only because of the gift of Christ's death, resurrection, and ascension to the right hand of God that we have any other divine gifts at all. "It [the Spirit] is as much a gift of a person to the church, as Christ was the gift of a person to the world [cf. John 3:16]."[73]

All that has been said here leads to one's personal examination. First, do *you* have the gift of the Holy Spirit? You cannot obtain this gift if you have not done *at least* what Peter instructed the Jews to do: repent and be baptized into Christ by His authority. If you have done these things, and continue to "walk by the Spirit," then you are blessed with the grace of God and have access to the "throne of grace" (Hebrews 4:16) by this same Spirit.

Second, what are you *doing* with this gift of the Holy Spirit? Often, the response is something like, "I didn't know I was supposed to 'do' anything." But of course you are! The Spirit's involvement is not limited to a singular occurrence at the point of one's conversion. Furthermore, God never gives gifts just to be generous, but to *engage* us in ever-deepening fellowship with Him. Those who rightly respond to God's gifts draw nearer to the Father through the intercession of His Son and the ministry of His Spirit.

Hopefully, drawing near to God is exactly what you are striving to do.

Chapter Six
The Indwelling of the Spirit

However, you are not in the flesh but in the Spirit, if indeed the Spirit of God dwells in you. But if anyone does not have the Spirit of Christ, he does not belong to Him. Romans 8:9

Sometimes Christians treat the subject of the Holy Spirit like they do, say, black holes in space or the discovery of a new planet: it's a fascinating read, but it really doesn't change things. After having read a few articles in the paper on the subject, and maybe having watched a slickly-produced segment on Discovery Channel, life simply resumes where it left off when they had their interest piqued. The same old thinking, same old habits, and same old reactions resurface and take their comfortable place in those people's lives.

This may sound unfair (at first), but I have seen this response far too many times among Christians for it to be an anomaly. It is unlikely that Christians will take time to engage in a study of this Holy Spirit at all, much less allow the conclusions of that study to affect how they think, love, function, and praise God *as* Christians. After the study is over, many will simply move onto a different subject, but they themselves are not much different than when they began. I'm not suggesting that these people are deliberately trying to *remain* unchanged, but that they simply do not see the importance or benefit of walking by the Spirit. Indeed, some may even equate churchgoing by itself to be a sufficient "walk" with God, and that anything beyond this is unnecessary, even excessive.

Thankfully, when others begin learning about the Spirit and His work in the life of the believer, they become *changed people* because of such education. These people become pillars of strength and sources of great faith in the church. They no longer merely learn *about* the Spirit but have learned to surrender their heart *to* the Spirit, allowing Him to dictate the course of their life rather than serve as a mere doctrinal concept in their belief system. They actually welcome the Spirit's oversight, knowing that His divine guidance will better prepare them for service to God—and the eternity to come.

After many years of trying (wrongly) to bring myself to perfection *apart* from the Spirit, I too have become a changed person. I no longer rely on my own spiritual strength, but seek strength, endurance, and intimacy through the Spirit. I no longer resist the Spirit's work in me, but gladly *anticipate* His work in my walk on this earth. Through the priestly intercession of the Son of God *and* the guidance of the Spirit of God, I am able to overcome the limitations and inadequacy of my own human condition. As the Scripture says, "By the grace of God I am what I am" (1 Corinthians 15:10), and while I cannot hold a candle to the apostle Paul, I can appreciate how he credited all of his success to God's grace. The One who makes grace possible is Jesus Christ; the manifestation of His grace is seen through the work of the Holy Spirit. So it was with Paul, and so it is with me, and so it will be with *you*, if you continue to believe God's Word. God can only help those who are willing to accept His help. He does not drag anyone kicking and screaming into a deeper relationship with Him—or into His heaven. At the same time, He is not unconcerned with our needs and always seeks our best interests.

The better we understand *how* the Spirit works (to the extent that we are able), the better we will be able to submit ourselves to His influence. This is not to imply that the Spirit gives us teachings beyond or even regardless of what is written in the New Testament. At the same time, one might misunderstand what the Scripture *does* teach concerning the work of the Spirit in the life of the believer. This may especially be true concerning the "indwelling of the Spirit" (taken from Romans 8:9, et al). Some appear to take this phrase too far; others may not take it far enough. This is a difficult subject to begin with; it is made even more difficult when we must first unlearn some of what we have already thought was true, if indeed the Bible does not support our views.

Laying the Groundwork

Whatever this "indwelling" ultimately means, we can confidently make a few observations. First, we never read in the New Testament of the Spirit completely overwhelming a person's body and senses. We *do* see demons taking over people's bodies and causing those people to do things against their own will. In Mark 5:1-5, for example, we read of a man in whom dwelt "many" demons (collectively known as "Legion"). This man was out of control: he was driven mad by the presence of such evil; he could not be restrained, even with chains; he ran naked through a graveyard, screaming in his mental torment. In another incident, a demon threw a young man to the ground or into the fire or water to destroy him (Mark 9:17-22). This is what demons do to people, if left to themselves.[74] Such uncontrolled, unrestrained, and undignified activity is not a manifestation of God's Spirit, but a different kind of spirit altogether.

Second, even if one believes that the "indwelling of the Spirit" referred to the use of miraculous gifts, we would not see a person acting out of control as a result of this. In fact, Paul actually admonished the Corinthians *not* to act in such a manner. Those who had the gifts of tongue-speaking or prophesying, for example, were instructed to exercise those gifts in a respectful, organized, and reverent manner. They were to speak in turn, giving no cause for reproach, and had to remain silent in the absence of an interpreter (1 Corinthians 14:22-33). "The spirits of prophets are subject to prophets," (verse 32), which means that those who were given the ability to perform miraculous gifts also had the responsibility to exercise them appropriately. "For God is not a God of confusion but of peace, as in all the churches of the saints" (verse 33). These people were not "possessed" by the Spirit (like a person was possessed by a demon), but were given special gifts *of* the Spirit. There is a vast difference between these two ideas.

Third, if the Spirit's presence is *only* manifested through the working of visible miracles, then we are left with the following assumptions:

❑ The only reason *for* the indwelling of the Spirit must be to perform visible miracles, which assumes that the Spirit has no other real purpose or function within Christ's church. (On the contrary, the Bible teaches that the Spirit is given to *all* those who obey God, regardless of miraculous activity, Acts 5:32).
❑ Given the point above, everyone who has the Spirit must be able to perform miracles. (But we do not see this in the New Testament record, and especially in the book of Acts, where this ought to be most evident.)
❑ Everyone who *cannot* perform a miracle obviously does not have the Spirit—and thus he cannot be sanctified *by* the Spirit (1 Corinthians 6:11, et al) and has no access to God *through* the Spirit (Ephesians 2:18).

In light of these, and of the evidence offered below, this "indwelling" must be for something other than the sole purpose of performing miracles.

Fourth, the Spirit's "indwelling" must be something more than the mere internalization of Bible verses and the study of biblical concepts. The written Word was given to us *by* the Spirit for our instruction; but this was not meant to limit His work. The Holy Spirit did not reveal the gospel to us for *His* sake—to instruct *Him* as to what He can or cannot do—but for our sakes. The Bible as a *book* cannot produce fellowship anymore than a book on love can produce love or a book on marriage can replace an actual marriage. The Bible defines the doctrinal basis for our relationship with God—the Father, Son, *and* Holy Spirit (see 2 Corinthians 13:14); it cannot be equated with or a replacement for such fellowship. Since the fellowship experience that every believer has with God is spiritual in nature, it cannot be reduced to mere words on a page or verses in a book. The relationship itself transcends the instruction upon which it is based. As Boles states plainly,

> Some have made the gross error in concluding that the indwelling of the Holy Spirit is nothing more than the presence of the word of God in the mind or memory of the Christian. It may be that we cannot tell the difference so that others may see or understand it; however, there is a difference between our words and our spirits. In like manner there is a difference in the Holy Spirit and the words of the Holy Spirit.[75]

The written New Testament is the instrument the Holy Spirit uses to reveal God's truth and to convict the sinner's heart; however, "We should not mistake the *instrument* for the *agent*."[76] The "sword of the Spirit" (Ephesians 6:17) is not one and the same as the Spirit who wields or has given this "sword."

On this point, consider the passage in Ephesians 3:14-21, a prayer of Paul's on behalf of the saints in Ephesus. There is no way to limit these words to those who have miraculous "gifts"; what he says in this prayer simply cannot be reduced to mere Bible-reading as a means of fellowship with God:

❑ "[I pray] that He would grant you...to be strengthened with power through His Spirit in the inner man" (3:16, bracket words mine): This speaks of an active, dynamic process of spiritual transformation. The *source* of this transformation is not only the discovery of more Bible verses, but necessarily involves the very real and mysterious work of the Spirit "in the inner man," that is, in one's heart (or soul).

❑ "so that Christ may dwell in your hearts through faith..." (3:17): While it is Scripture that teaches us of Christ and His will for us, we cannot reduce Christ's indwelling of the believer's heart to mere words and memorization of Bible verses. Christ *lives* in the heart of the believer (cf. Galatians 2:20); He is not merely "recorded" there as an intellectual concept.

❑ "...[that you may be able] to know the love of Christ which surpasses knowledge..." (3:19, bracketed words mine): In essence, Paul is contrasting what is learned through mere human knowledge with the incalculable knowledge of God (i.e., earthly knowledge versus heavenly knowledge). Exactly *what* this knowledge is, we are not told, though we are certain that it cannot contradict whatever the Spirit has already revealed (Galatians 1:8).[77] No one can be "filled up to all the fullness of God" only by reading the Bible; this verse necessarily implies that there is a *divine activity* occurring in the heart of the believer *as a result of* his devotion to the Word of God.

❑ "Now to Him who is able to do far more abundantly beyond all that we ask or think..." (3:20): We might be inclined to think of this as referring to God's power generally (since, after all, He is omnipotent). But the context in which this is said involves what God does *within the heart of the believer*, which is more than the believer is able to accomplish on his own. Reading the Bible teaches us about the Spirit who works in us and (to a limited extent) what the Spirit does, but it cannot describe or define everything that is "beyond all that we ask or think."

❑ "...according to the power that works within us" (3:20): It is worth noting that the Holy Spirit is commonly associated with "power" (e.g., Luke 4:14; 24:49; Acts 1:7-8; 10:38; and Romans 15:13). It stands to reason that any reference to "power" within the context of the work of God necessarily involves the Spirit of God. This includes the power to perform miracles (1 Corinthians 2:4-5) as well as the power to achieve spiritual maturity (Colossians 1:28-29).[78] If nothing else, it is evident that there is a *supernatural power* that performs within us which supersedes whatever we are able to perform on our own. It is also evident that without this power, we are unable to be perfected (cf. 2 Corinthians 12:9; Philippians 1:6; and 1 Peter 5:10).

What we *cannot* say is, "Forget about reading your Bible—just let the Spirit lead you!" This is what many devout Christians want to guard against, and rightly so. This also contradicts the message of the Spirit, which emphasizes devotion to the study of the Scriptures (2 Timothy 3:16-17). One who ignores "sound doctrine" cannot worship God "in spirit and truth" (John 4:24), since he has rejected the very basis for his fellowship in God.

What it Means to "Indwell"

We have taken a roundabout path to talking about the indwelling of the Spirit, but we have also laid some very important groundwork for this discussion. Next, we need to define terms. The original Greek New Testament uses several different (but very similar) words that are often translated "dwell":

- ❑ *enoikeo* (Strong's #1774): to inhabit, as in Colossians 3:16.
- ❑ *episkenoo* (Strong's #1981): to tent (tabernacle) upon; to abide with; to rest upon, used only in 2 Corinthians 12:9.
- ❑ *kathemai* (Strong's #2521): to sit down (beside); to remain or reside, as in Luke 21:35.
- ❑ *katoikeo* (Strong's #2730): to house permanently; to reside, as in Ephesians 3:17.

While the above citations use "dwell" in a positive sense, it can also be used in a negative one. For example, Paul spoke of sin "dwelling" in him when he lives in violation of the law of God (Romans 7:17-20). Jesus called Pergamum a place "where Satan dwells" (Revelation 2:13). In John 13:27, we read of how Satan entered into the heart of Judas—in essence, he [Satan] was given a place to "dwell" in Judas. None of these expressions are meant to be taken literally: sin does not occupy a physical space within a person, nor does Satan assume a physical form in order to dwell in one's heart or within a city. These do speak of both influence *and* activity, however: Satan was given *control* in each of these examples.

The same conclusions can be drawn concerning the indwelling of the Spirit. The Spirit of God does not assume a physical presence within a person's body.[79] If you were literally to cut a Christian open, you would not find the Spirit dwelling in one of his organs, or any evidence of a spiritual "presence." However the Spirit indwells a person, He does not do so in a physical or visible manner.[80] He is a *spirit* after all, and therefore His indwelling must be a *spiritual* indwelling, even though this indwelling has a direct influence upon one's physical body.

With these thoughts in mind, let us turn our attention now to Romans 8:3-11, which helps to explain the context of the indwelling of the Spirit:

> For what the Law could not do, weak as it was through the flesh, God did: sending His own Son in the likeness of sinful flesh and as an offering for sin, He condemned sin in the flesh, so that the requirement of the Law might be fulfilled in us, who do not walk according to the flesh but according to the Spirit. For those who are according to the flesh set their minds on the things of the flesh, but those who are according to the Spirit, the things of the Spirit. For the mind set on the flesh is death, but the mind set on the Spirit is life and peace, because the mind set on the flesh is hostile toward God; for it does not subject itself to the law of God, for it is not even able to do so, and those who are in the flesh cannot please God. However, you are not in the flesh but in the Spirit, if indeed the Spirit of God dwells in you. But if anyone does not have the Spirit of Christ, he does not belong to Him. If Christ is in you, though the body is dead because of sin, yet the spirit is alive because of righteousness. But if the Spirit of Him who raised Jesus from the dead dwells in you, He who raised Christ Jesus from the dead will also give life to your mortal bodies through His Spirit who dwells in you.

Now we will briefly expound upon this passage: We who are saved through the offering of Christ's physical body and blood are no longer to conform to "the flesh," that is, the worldly, self-serving, satanic realm of human existence here on earth (Ephesians 2:1-3; 1 John 2:15-17; 5:19). We continue to live here, but must separate ourselves from the wickedness that is all around us (see 2 Corinthians 6:14 – 7:1). Our mind is not set on the flesh (the attitudes and desires of this world), but on Christ and the things above (Colossians 3:1-4). Such godly *thinking* naturally produces godly *behavior*, which is evidenced through our conduct. The mind that *is* set on the "flesh" leads to spiritual ruin ("death"), whereas the heart governed by the Spirit of God enjoys spiritual "life and peace." That person's "walk" (conduct and lifestyle) and "mind" (heart) are no longer governed by the world, but by the Spirit of God. These two "walks" cannot peacefully coexist, but are entirely incompatible (Galatians 5:16-17). Likewise, the "mind" set upon the world is hostile to the mind that conforms to the Holy Spirit.

Having the "Spirit of Christ" is the same as having the "Spirit of God"—we do not have two outside "spirits" indwelling us, but *one* Spirit being directed by *one* Savior. In essence, we have one Spirit accomplishing many things according to the will of the King who reigns over God's kingdom. Regardless of one's spiritual allegiance, the physical body will die because of the curse placed upon the "family" of man (cf. Genesis 3:19; Romans 5:12-21). Yet whomever the Spirit indwells continues to live to God in righteousness, and anticipates a glorious resurrection from the dead (1 Corinthians 15:20-24; Philippians 3:20-21; 1 Peter 1:3-5; et al).

This indwelling is not a physical one, as we have already concluded. Instead, it is spiritual in nature—but very *real* all the same. ("Spiritual" does not mean "pretend" or "illusionary," but refers to that which truly exists beyond our physical vision.) The Holy Spirit "dwells as an abiding gift—not as a doer of miracles, not as a wonder-worker except through natural and ordinary channels—in the mind, heart, and conscience of every obedient believer."[81] Robertson Whiteside is more to the point: "He [Holy Spirit] dwells in the Christian; that is plainly affirmed [in Romans 8:6-9]. And I dare not deny what Paul here affirms."[82]

James Needham agrees, but with conditions: "There is no denying the *fact* of the Spirit's indwelling, but it is imperative that we understand that there is a vast difference between the *fact* of the indwelling and the *method* of it. These are two different questions."[83] These *are* two different questions, but they are mutually-dependent: how you answer the one bears directly upon the other. Needham cannot deny the obvious—the Spirit *does* indwell the believer—but claims that this must be an entirely natural process, not a supernatural one.[84] This view does not make sense. He also writes, "There is no passage that states that the Spirit directly and personally indwells the Christian separate and apart from the written word."[85] If he means that the Spirit's indwelling cannot *contradict* the written word, this makes sense. But if he means that the Spirit's indwelling is nothing more than an internalization of Bible-based knowledge, there is sufficient evidence in Scripture to prove the contrary. The implication that "Only the words of the Bible indwell you" is nothing like Paul's inspired claim that "the Spirit of God dwells in you"; these two statements say different things. The people to whom Paul wrote these words did not even *have* the full revelation of Scripture; yet there is no doubt that the Spirit indwelled them.

Ideally, the will and desire of the Christian's spirit is directly influenced and controlled by the will and desire of God's Spirit who indwells us—not at the expense of Scripture, but in perfect harmony with it. Just as a man's body is dead when separated from his spirit (James 2:26), so also is a man's soul dead to God when it is separated from His Spirit. But just as the Spirit *gives* life (John 6:63), so also one lives to God in whom His Spirit dwells. Thus we are able to say like Paul, "I have been crucified with Christ; and it is no longer I who live, but Christ lives in me; and the life which I now live in the flesh I live by faith in the Son of God, who loved me and gave Himself up for me" (Galatians 2:20). Did Paul's own spirit disappear upon his conversion? Of course not— otherwise, he would be physically *dead*. Then what was "crucified with Christ"? It was Paul's *allegiance to the world*—his sin-controlled, self-serving, self-righteous conformity to "the flesh" (cf. Romans 6:3-7; 7:4-6). Paul himself most certainly continued to live, but he lived to *Christ* and no longer to himself. Thereafter, he was led by the Spirit of God, and no longer by the spirit of the world.

Fellowship with God

The presence of the Holy Spirit in one's heart necessarily implies *fellowship* with God. No one can have the Spirit who lives outside of God's fellowship; that person is considered (spiritually) "dead" to God (Ephesians 2:1). When a person "dies" to the world, as symbolized by his "burial" in water (baptism), he is raised to walk in "newness of life" (Romans 6:4). This newness of life necessarily involves entering into covenant with God—a covenant of life which was ratified by the offering of Christ (Matthew 26:27-28; Hebrews 9:11-16). Through Christ's blood, one is cleansed of his sins; through the Spirit's sanctification, he is given gifts of grace and access to the throne of God. The indwelling of the Spirit, then, refers to the fact of one's fellowship or communion with God. If one does not have the Spirit *of* God, it is impossible for him to have fellowship *with* God (and vice versa).

Let's examine some parallel passages (arranged topically) that also speak of an "indwelling" of God as an expression of fellowship with God:

❑ "The one who keeps His commandments abides in Him, and He in him. We know by this that He abides in us, by the Spirit whom He has given us" (1 John 3:24). God "abiding" in us is used interchangeably with the Spirit being given to (and thus abiding within) us. Does God abide within you? If so, then the Spirit indwells you. Wherever God is, the Spirit is; this is John's essential point.

❑ "Let the word of Christ richly dwell within you, with all wisdom teaching and admonishing one another with psalms and hymns and spiritual songs, singing with thankfulness in your hearts to God" (Colossians 3:16). The meaning of "word of Christ" here is metaphorical and spiritual all at once. Metaphorically, it refers to the full message of the gospel—not just its *words*, but also its meaning and the lifestyle it produces. Spiritually, it refers to Christ Himself: inasmuch as His *gospel* is in you, so *Christ* is in you. We can cite this verse as an example of how the Holy Spirit dwells within us, for that also is metaphorical and spiritual all at once. Metaphorically, our body has become a temple for the Spirit, and this indwelling ought to produce a behavior commensurate with that indwelling. Spiritually, inasmuch as the Spirit is in us, *God* is in us.

❑ "Guard, through the Holy Spirit who dwells in us, the treasure which has been entrusted to you" (2 Timothy 1:14). The "treasure" here likely is the "word of Christ"—not the mere recollection of Bible verses, but the message, effect, and promises of the living gospel (Colossians 1:23; 1 Peter 1:23). This message is not something limited to Paul and Timothy, but is given to all Christians ("us"), just as the Holy Spirit is given to all who obey God (Acts 5:32).

❑ "But the one who joins himself to the Lord is one spirit with Him" (1 Corinthians 6:17). This speaks of communion (as in John 10:30), not involuntary "possession" (like what we see with demons in the gospel accounts). The believer's spirit is in fellowship with God's Spirit. It is true, however, that we do *belong* to God; we are His possession (Titus 2:14; 1 Peter 2:9), having been purchased from the state of our condemnation with the blood of Christ (Revelation 5:9). But God's Spirit does not overwhelm our own; this is not a leveraged "takeover." Instead, we are "one spirit" with God because we have elected to *give* Him control continually. He is, then, the real, active, and dynamic influence upon our hearts that leads us to salvation. Indeed, we cannot be saved otherwise. This makes sense of what Paul says shortly after informing us that we are "one spirit" with God once we are "joined" (or "cleaved," like in Ephesians 5:31) to Him.

❑ "Or do you not know that your body is a temple of the Holy Spirit who is in you, whom you have from God, and that you are not your own? For you have been bought with a price: therefore glorify God in your body" (1 Corinthians 6:19-20). One's body serves as a kind of sanctuary for the Holy Spirit; He does not indwell a believer in a purely theoretical or conceptual sense, but in a manner that involves that actual person. God is "in your body" in the sense that He *uses* your body (with *your* consent) to carry out His righteousness. (We will discuss the *result* of this indwelling in a later chapter.)

❑ "Do you not know that you are a temple of God and that the Spirit of God dwells in you?" (1 Corinthians 3:16). This is similar language to 1 Corinthians 6:19 (discussed above), but in a different context. Paul is not talking of the individual believer here, but the entire church at Corinth: the Spirit of God "indwells" each church of God's people, just as God dwells in the entire body of believers (2 Corinthians 6:16). This concurs with what we see in the seven letters to the seven churches of Asia (Revelation 2 – 3). Jesus walks among the lampstands (which symbolize the churches' fellowship with God), but this necessarily involves the Spirit's presence *within* those churches (an association implied in 4:5, and by the expression, "Hear what the Spirit says to the churches…").

❑ "…but you are fellow citizens with the saints, and are of God's household…in the Lord, in whom you also are being built together into a dwelling of God in the Spirit" (Ephesians 2:19, 22). This is yet a different context: Paul is not speaking of the individual believer or a single congregation, but references the spiritual body of Christ—which includes *all* who have been "clothed" with Christ (Galatians 3:26-27). Everywhere there are faithful Christians, the Spirit is present—it cannot be otherwise, for then we would not *be* Christians. Thus, the Spirit indwells: 1) the individual believer, 2) each congregation of believers, and 3) the entire body of all believers.

Summary Thoughts

The indwelling of the Spirit does not render the written Word of God useless. On the contrary, the Word is absolutely essential in instructing us as to what commandments are required of Christ's disciples *and* defining the "fruit" that identifies us with God (to be discussed in the next chapter). The written gospel serves as a kind of legal document for us, spelling out our covenant relationship with God. It has all the elements of a formal covenant agreement:

- ❑ Introduction of the parties: mortal man, God the Father, and God the Son (Intercessor).
- ❑ Purpose and objective of the covenant: man lives in a fallen state and thus faces an awful condemnation, and only God ("because of His great love with which He loved us," Ephesians 2:4) is both willing and able to save him from this.
- ❑ Stipulations of the covenant: its terms and conditions; what is required from man (faith and obedience to Christ); what is required of God (mercy and grace); and recourse for man's sin while he is under covenant.
- ❑ Expectations of behavior: habitual expressions of Christ-like love; keeping God's commandments; clinging to what is good; abstaining from every form of evil (cf. 1 Thessalonians 5:21-22); and things corresponding to these.
- ❑ Guarantee for those who honor the covenant: eternal life with God.
- ❑ Consequence for disregarding the covenant: eternal separation from God.

In other words, this is very similar in form to that which is spelled out in the Law of Moses. (The Law itself was not *the* covenant, but described the expected behavior of those *under* covenant.) Just as the Israelite required the Law of Moses to define his covenant relationship with God, so we need the gospel of Christ to dictate *our* covenant relationship with God. The Spirit's indwelling does not replace or nullify this, but perfectly *complements* it. The gospel's instruction and the Spirit's presence in our lives are mutually dependent—neither one can exist without the other.

In a loose analogy, the Holy Spirit is like the executor of an estate. He did not write the testament of the One who owns the inheritance; it is the Father who did this. He did not die to ratify this testament; it is Christ who did this. The Spirit does, however, carry out the Father's will as instructed by the Heir of all things, the resurrected Son of God. He is, then, the divine *influence* and *activity* in the lives of God's children, who are "fellow heirs with Christ" (Romans 8:17). We are not heirs only because the Bible says so, but because we are given God's Spirit as a pledge of what is yet to come (2 Corinthians 5:5).

Someone says, "Yes, but what exactly does the Spirit *do?*" We will discuss this shortly, even though the fact remains that we simply cannot know everything the Spirit does in us, through us, and for us. His work is largely a mystery to us, just as God Himself is largely a mystery to us. He is an infinite Being; it is impossible that a single book (the Bible) can fully explain who He is and what He does[86]—nor was that ever His intention. We do not need to know exactly *how* the Spirit works within us; we only need to know that He *does indeed* work within us. This is similar to our understanding of saving grace: we do not need to know everything there is to know *about* grace (which is humanly impossible); we need only to believe in the *reality* of grace—and in the One who makes it possible.

"For the word of God is living and active..." (Hebrews 4:12). Words on a page cannot be "living and active"; legal terms and conditions of covenant cannot be this; but a *living Spirit* most certainly can be this. The Holy Spirit—the "living and abiding word of God"—dwells in us, animates our spiritual lives, and identifies us with Christ. This indwelling does not give us the ability to perform miracles, but there is certainly something miraculous about having fellowship with a Divine Being. How He performs in us is not necessary to answer; how we *benefit* from how He performs in us is the appropriate question.

Accordingly, this is exactly where we are going next in our study of the Spirit.

Chapter Seven
The Fruit of the Spirit

But the fruit of the Spirit is love, joy, peace, patience, kindness, goodness, faithfulness, gentleness, self-control; against such things there is no law.
                                                            Galatians 5:22-23

In my front yard is a large, mature cherry tree. I know it's a cherry tree because of its shape, bark, leaves, and blossoms, but not by its fruit. This is because mine is a "self-unfruitful" tree: it produces no cherries. Apparently, a cherry tree requires pollination from another cherry tree close enough for bees and other insects to carry pollen from the one to the other. Since we have no such tree near us, our tree cannot bear fruit.

A cherry-less cherry tree is fine by me; I do not expect it to be anything but ornamental. If it were a different kind of fruit tree, however, it should have borne fruit on its own. This is why Jesus cursed the fig tree that bore no figs (Mark 11:13-14, 20-21). First, it had the *appearance* of being fruit-producing (because normally the leaves and figs appear at the same time), but had nothing of substance to offer. Second, it was apparently *capable* of producing fruit but did not. Third, it simply *failed* to produce fruit (most fig tree varieties are "self-fruitful," which means they need no outside pollination), even though it was created to be a fruit-producing tree.

These three characteristics—appearance without substance, capability without productivity, and (thus) failure to perform as expected—serve as the basis for what Jesus did. (As a necessary inference, Jesus would not have cursed a tree—or anything else—from which the impossible was expected.) God created fig trees to produce figs; likewise, He created cherry trees to produce cherries (when the trees are properly pollinated); and so on. When a tree fails to produce that for which it was created, it defies its Maker and is destined for destruction (Luke 13:6-9).

An Expectation to Bear Fruit

What Jesus did to the fig tree served as a sign for Israel: either bear fruit or be destroyed. This principle certainly applies to all those who claim to believe in God but fail to show proper evidence for this.[87] A Christian who bears no "fruit" is (according to spiritual expectations) unnatural and therefore unacceptable. God does not extend saving grace only to forgive sins but nothing more. He is looking for a good return on His investment; He desires produce from His people. In light of this, consider the following passages:

- ❑ "And the one on whom seed was sown on the good soil, this is the man who hears the word and understands it; who indeed bears fruit and brings forth, some a hundredfold, some sixty, and some thirty" (Matthew 13:23).
- ❑ "Therefore, my brethren, you also were made to die to the Law through the body of Christ, so that you might be joined to another, to Him who was raised from the dead, in order that we might bear fruit for God" (Romans 7:4).
- ❑ "…[The gospel] is constantly bearing fruit and increasing, even as it has been doing in you also since the day you heard of it and understood the grace of God in truth" (Colossians 1:6).
- ❑ "For this reason also, since the day we heard of it, we have not ceased to pray for you and to ask that you may be filled with the knowledge of His will in all spiritual wisdom and understanding, so that you will walk in a manner worthy of the Lord, to please Him in all respects, bearing fruit in every good work and increasing in the knowledge of God" (Colossians 1:9-10).

A non-fruit-bearing disciple is essentially a freeloader. He soaks up all the benefits and opportunities given to him without producing anything for which those blessings were intended. Such a person is like a field that receives good rain but produces nothing beneficial. On the other hand, one who "brings forth vegetation useful to those for whose sake it is also tilled" finds favor with God, and is blessed accordingly (cf. Hebrews 6:7-8).

This is graphically illustrated in John 15:1-8 in the parable of the vine and branches. God the Father is the "vinedresser," which refers to a farmer (or husbandman) who owns the vine and the field in which it grows. Jesus is the "vine," which refers to the essential fruit-bearing plant itself that is rooted in the vinedresser's field. He is distinctly defined as the "true vine," which means He is the only One upon whom the Father has set His approval (John 3:35; 14:6). "You are the branches," He told His disciples (15:5), which refers to the actual fruit-bearing extensions of the vine itself.[88] The purpose of the branch is not just to exist as a branch; in fact, if a branch is not producing fruit, then it is going to be "taken away," where it will "dry up" and be "cast…into the fire."

The meaning here is unmistakably clear: the Christian's purpose is to produce "fruit," and not merely be called a Christian. Unfortunately, some are content with being "members of the church" without realizing their intended purpose as *fruit-bearing branches* of Christ. Those who are producing fruit will be "pruned" in order to bear more fruit, for God is always preparing His faithful servants to "excel still more" (cf. 1 Thessalonians 4:1). Those who refuse to do what branches are expected to do will ultimately be removed and cast away; by not remaining true to the Vine (Christ), they forfeit the life supplied by Him. This is not to suggest that Jesus has no patience or compassion for such people, for we are told elsewhere of the patience and kindness of God which is intended for repentance (Romans 2:4; 2 Peter 3:9; et al). But Jesus' words here are factual—this *is* what will happen if changes are not made—and are intended to inspire us to act.

Maximizing the Growth Potential

We should say something about the "pruning" process here for those fruit-producing branches. The reason fruit growers prune trees or vines is to promote greater health in the plant and (thus) productivity. Pruning cuts away the unnecessary twigs and shoots that distract from the branch's full potential. By removing these extemporaneous growths, the branch can then put its entire effort into its ideal activity: producing fruit. The energy of the vine (or trunk) can then achieve maximum growth, and a high-yielding crop is inevitable. But while vine branches do not feel the "pain" of pruning, Christians most certainly do; it is an uncomfortable and sometimes excruciating[89] experience. Peter uses a different analogy—the flame of a crucible—for the same effect (1 Peter 1:6-7). Neither pruning nor purifying fires are easily endured, but they serve the best interest of the one who undergoes them. As each sinful practice, bad habit, improper attitude, distraction, and interference is removed from the disciple's life— painful as that removal may be—it allows him to focus completely on the business *of* discipleship: bearing fruit. The removal of such "stumbling blocks" may be likened to the pain of cutting off one's hand or gouging out one's eye (cf. Matthew 5:29-30); nonetheless the objective is far too important to compromise. Those who do not bear fruit for the Lord are simply not going to be *with* the Lord; they will be cast into the fire (see also Matthew 25:46).[90]

"Abide in Me, and I in you. As the branch cannot bear fruit of itself unless it abides in the vine, so neither can you unless you abide in Me" (John 15:4). When Jesus asks His disciples to "abide" in Him, He means to *have the same mind* as Him (as in Philippians 2:5), to remain with Him as a believer. This necessarily includes keeping His commandments, for one cannot "abide" with Christ by refusing to do what He asks (Luke 6:46; 1 John 2:4-6; 3:24). Discipleship is not reduced to mere commandment-keeping, however. The sense of this passage (John 15:1-8) implies a mutually-beneficial fellowship between the Vine (Christ) and the branches (disciples). This fellowship is built upon a common goal: producing fruit, which leads to the preservation (salvation) of the branch. Jesus does not want merely nominal disciples; He desires fruit-bearing disciples. In order to become fruit-bearing, we must first "abide" in Him, for apart from Him we are unable to bear any fruit for God (15:5).

When we abide in Christ, we not only produce much fruit, but He listens to our prayers and makes them effective (15:7). Whatever we ask of the Father—as long as it is in agreement with His Father's will (1 John 5:14-15)—Christ will make it happen. Certainly a disciple of Christ will not deliberately pray for something that contradicts the Father's will. At the same time, we do not always know what His will is, and thus we allow Christ to answer our prayers as He deems appropriate. The point here is: by abiding in Christ, we are blessed with His high-priestly intercession regarding our needs and requests, and He is happy to help us.

Furthermore, as productive, fruit-bearing branches, we bring glory to the Father (John 15:8). This is because we have sought His will ahead of our own, even to our own hurt and loss. What we are saying is, in so many words, "I *choose* to be a disciple of Christ in order to exalt my Father." In this same way, Christ chose to exalt His Father, the God of His life, even to the point of death on a cross; this obedience was the "joy set before Him" (Hebrews 12:2). Such is also the admonition of Paul (1 Corinthians 6:20): "For you have been bought with a price: therefore glorify God in your body." We did not make the "vine"; individual Christians are not natural branches, either, but have been "grafted" in (cf. Romans 11:17-18); even the fruit we produce is not our own, but is generated by a power beyond our human effort. We are *purchased* of God, if indeed we are "in Christ"; in humility and obedience, then, we should ever seek to glorify God through the earthly vessels He has given us for this very purpose (cf. Romans 9:22-24; 2 Corinthians 4:7; 2 Timothy 2:21).

But what exactly is the *source of power* that generates this "fruit" in each "branch"? What *is* this "fruit"? To answer these questions, we now need to return to our discussion of the Holy Spirit. It is impossible to answer these questions otherwise.

The Source of Fruit-bearing Power

God the Father did not give "all authority" to Jesus Christ just to honor His Son (Matthew 28:18; Philippians 2:9). It is true that Christ proved Himself *worthy* of heaven and earth's honor, but this "proving" was necessary for a higher objective: the salvation of human souls. If Christ was not worthy to be our Savior, then we could not be saved by Him. God made Christ the King over His kingdom in order to secure the redemption of men's souls. Christ's physical life was given on the cross so that we might have spiritual life with Him; His blood serves as atonement for our sins so that we can be made holy to the Father.

We could easily continue to speak of the great work of Christ and His worthiness. Yet the point here is this: Christ was made our King and High Priest for a specific *purpose*. Likewise, everything God does is done with foresight and purpose; He never acts recklessly or unintentionally. So it is with His having "anointed" and "sealed" us with His Spirit: these actions have been done with a specific objective in mind. We who are "in Christ" are not given the Spirit to indwell us just so that we can claim such status.

Instead, the Spirit is given to believers so that they may "bear fruit." In other words, the *presence* of the Spirit in our lives is the dynamic *energy* that makes fruit-bearing possible. Take away the Spirit, and we have no power by which to produce fruit for God. If we did have such power, then we never would have needed the Spirit in the first place. This would imply that Christ sent the Holy Spirit into His church unnecessarily. This, of course, contradicts all the teachings of the gospel, which teaches that we are all inadequate to produce "good fruit" on our own since we all "fall short of the glory of God" (Romans 3:23).

Jesus is the Vine, Christians are the branches, and the Spirit is the *spiritual energy* that gives life to the fruit generated through the branches. This in no way reduces Christ's role in the life of the believer, for He continues to serve as our King and High Priest. Indeed, the Spirit does not work apart from Christ, but in complete cooperation with Him; such is the nature of the Godhead. Christ works in us daily *through the agency of the Spirit, and not apart from Him*. Consider the following comparisons, which show the integral work of Christ and the Holy Spirit:

❑ Christ performs "circumcision" on the heart of the believer (Colossians 2:9-12); we are circumcised "by the Spirit" (Romans 2:29).
❑ Christ intercedes for us (1 Timothy 2:5); the Spirit intercedes for us (Romans 8:26-27).
❑ Christ lives in us (Galatians 2:20); the Spirit lives (or dwells) in us (Romans 8:9).
❑ Christ gives us liberty (Galatians 5:1); we have liberty in the Spirit (2 Corinthians 3:17).
❑ Christ is our strength to do "all things" (Philippians 4:13); we are strengthened with power through the Holy Spirit (Ephesians 3:16).
❑ We are to set our minds on Christ (Colossians 3:1-2); we are to set our minds on the Spirit (Romans 8:6).
❑ We walk as Christ walks (1 John 2:6); we walk as the Spirit guides us (Galatians 5:16).
❑ We are sons of God by faith in Christ (Galatians 3:26-27); we are sons of God who are led by the Spirit (Romans 8:14).
❑ We are sanctified in Christ (1 Corinthians 1:2); we are sanctified by the Spirit (2 Thessalonians 2:13).
❑ We have fellowship with Christ (1 Corinthians 1:9); we have fellowship with the Spirit (2 Corinthians 13:14).
❑ We have access to God through Christ (John 14:6); we have access to God through the Spirit (Ephesians 2:18).
❑ Christ is the truth (John 14:6); the Spirit is the truth (1 John 5:16).

Such passages ought to confirm the ever-present energy of the Spirit in the life of the believer. We therefore cannot reduce the Spirit's role to that of a mere chaperone that stands by and watches us labor in God's kingdom. Nor can we assume that the Spirit's only role was to enable us to perform miracles, for then we are admitting that His presence has no practical value in the everyday walk of the believer even though the verses above teach otherwise.

As we have said before, the Spirit is the "power" within Christ's church. God the Father *authorized* the church to be built; God the Son *built* the church; and God the Spirit *makes things happen* in the church. Just as the human soul animates the physical body, so the Spirit of God animates the physical church. Christ is the "head" of His church (Colossians 1:18), and the Spirit is the nervous system that directly connects every member of the body to the head and by which the will of the head is carried out in the body.

Vine, Branches, and Fruit

We may now re-emphasize the plant analogy we cited earlier: The Father is the Vinedresser; the Son is the Vine; we are the branches; and the Spirit is the energy by which the fruit is grown. No branch can survive if it is removed from the vine, because in doing so the energy that the vine supplies is severed. No branch can bear fruit all by itself, for it is simply incapable of producing (or duplicating) the energy that is required for this. But if the branch is one with the vine, and the power that flows through the vine now fills the branch, then most certainly that branch will produce good fruit.

To illustrate this yet another way: In John 4:13-14, Jesus spoke of a "well of water springing up to eternal life" within the soul of one who believes in Him. Later in John 7:37-39, He spoke of "rivers of living water" in one's "innermost being," which John specifically identified as the Spirit. Thus, the "waters" of the world—both the liquid substance itself and its metaphorical use, the multitudes of humanity—offer no satisfaction for the soul, but the Spirit provides an everlasting spring of life-giving nourishment. No wonder, then, that virtually the last words spoken in the Bible are offered as an invitation by the Spirit: "The Spirit and the bride say, 'Come.' And let the one who hears say, 'Come.' And let the one who is thirsty come; let the one who wishes take the water of life without cost" (Revelation 22:17).[91]

The world is *filled* with water, cannot *exist* without water, and is benefited by the manifold *uses* of water. Likewise, the soul was meant to be filled with the Spirit of God, cannot live without Him, and is benefited by the manifold blessings that He provides. "It is the Spirit who gives life; the flesh [i.e., human effort by itself] profits nothing," Jesus said. "The words that I have spoken to you are spirit and are life" (John 6:63, bracketed words are mine). John Chrysostom (5th century) wrote: "The Spirit is called 'living water' because He is ever at work; no fountain gushes forth more freely, never ceasing, never running dry or stopping in its course. The Lord [John 7:37-39] speaks of 'rivers,' not of 'a river,' to shew [*sic*] the unspeakable variety of the Spirits' operations."[92] Without water, we will die. Without God's Spirit, we are already dead (cf. Ephesians 2:1)—but we can be re-born through the life-giving blood of Jesus Christ *and* the sanctifying work of the Spirit (1 Peter 1:2-3). Just as apart from Christ we can do nothing (John 15:5), so then apart from the Spirit we can do nothing.

The same needs a vine (or fruit tree) has in order to produce a bountiful crop are likened to those required for the growth of spiritual fruit. This is not surprising, since the spiritual life of man is richly illustrated by the natural world (in both positive and negative ways). Consider, for example, the following comparison of a fruit tree with the soul:

Fruit Tree	The Lord's Disciple
Begins as a seed planted in good soil.	Begins when a "seed" is planted in fertile "soil" of his heart (cf. Matthew 13:18ff; 1 Peter 1:23).
The seed dies and is reborn in an inexplicable conversion.	The "seed" planted within him "dies" as a mere seed and a disciple is "born" in an inexplicable conversion (cf. John 12:24; Romans 6:3-7).
The new plant must be rooted and grounded to ensure its success.	The new disciple must be rooted and grounded in Christ in order to ensure his success (Colossians 2:6-7).
The plant extracts energy from the sun in a complex chemical process called photosynthesis.	The disciple extracts energy from Christ, who is the Source of his spiritual growth. This process is also complex and invisible to the human eye, but is just as real and is even more efficient than that which occurs in living plants.[93]
The plant requires water, for without water it will die.	The disciple requires the "water" of the Spirit, without which he will most certainly die (John 4:13-14).

The plant requires a safe, healthy environment in which to flourish.	The disciple finds an ideal growing environment within Christ's church—the local congregation *and* the spiritual body of Christ (Ephesians 4:11-16).
The plant must be protected from destructive elements— parasites, disease, calamity, etc.—in order to survive.	The disciple is protected from the forces of the ungodly world by the "full armor of God," which includes the "sword of the Spirit" (Ephesians 6:10-17). Despite his individual strength, he simply cannot survive without this protection.
The mature plant, when provided with these ideal conditions, will bear fruit to its fullest potential.	When a mature disciple is provided with all of these ideal conditions, he will also bear fruit to his fullest potential.[94]

The fruit of a tree or vine will not be different than the kind of plant from which it came. This is what God has ordained from the beginning (Genesis 1:11-12); it is naturally impossible otherwise. Likewise, it is impossible for one to be a Christian whose fruit looks much different than the "true vine" from which he is supposed to have originated. "Can a fig tree, my brethren, produce olives, or a vine produce figs?" (James 3:12). No, a fig tree produces only figs, an apple tree produces only apples, and an orange tree produces only oranges. In other words, if any so-called "Christian" produces "fruit" (i.e., doctrines, thinking, or behaviors) that does not look like Christ (cf. 1 John 2:6), then he does not belong to the "true vine." He belongs to a different plant, one which will be uprooted in due time (Matthew 15:13).

We can evaluate fruit not only by its type (or kind), but also its quality. There is good fruit and there is bad fruit; disciples of the Lord are supposed to learn the difference between the two. This difference really is dictated by what kind of *spirit* is giving life to either one. The "spirit of the world" (1 Corinthians 2:12) inevitably generates bad fruit; the Spirit of God only produces good fruit. Jesus lays the responsibility for the kind of fruit one produces upon the individual himself: "Either make the tree good and its fruit good, or make the tree bad and its fruit bad; for the tree is known by its fruit" (Matthew 12:33). While the Spirit only produces good fruit, He does not force anyone to listen to Him, either.

Admittedly, "false prophets" (i.e., false teachers) have arisen and will continue to arise within the brotherhood, even among its own leaders (Acts 20:28-30). Jesus warned us of such people, and taught that these can be identified by the type of fruit they produce (Matthew 7:15-20). The Spirit of God cannot be the source of teachings that contradict what He has revealed through Christ and His apostles. The self-serving spirit of ambitious men (and women), on the other hand, will most certainly contradict and "malign" the teachings of God (cf. 2 Peter 2:1-2).

The Evidence of the Spirit's Indwelling

One of the difficulties a Christian faces is the absence of visible shrines or icons by which to tether him to a historical religion. For example, we believe in the cross of Christ, but we cannot go visit that literal cross to validate that belief. We know that Jesus' tomb was empty on the first day of the week after His death, but no one is certain today which tomb was His—or if it even still exists. We know that the early churches existed—in Jerusalem, Ephesus, Corinth, Philippi, etc.—but there are no church buildings or ancient rosters of those first congregations (nor do we need them). In other words, we have nothing *material* except for the written Word itself by which to identify with this transcendent religion known as Christianity. Even though Christians anticipate their own future resurrection, for now "we walk by faith, not by sight" (2 Corinthians 5:7). It would seem, then, that the Christian belief system has little to support it outside of the Bible, the people who believe in the Bible, and the transient memorial of the Lord's Supper.[95]

So it would seem. While we have no visible, tangible evidence which connects us with God, our "connection" (really, our *fellowship*) is manifested instead through something far superior to earthly memorials: "the fruit of the Spirit." What the Spirit produces *within* the believer is far greater than what men produce for themselves, or even the physical remnants of historical events. This "fruit" is manifested by Christ-like attitudes and virtues, which themselves are translated into visible behaviors and even tangible benevolence (cf. 1 John 3:17-18). Some of the specific descriptions of this "fruit of the Spirit" include (Galatians 5:22-23):

- ❏ **Love:** Jesus said that "by this all men will know that you are My disciples, if you have love for one another" (John 13:35). But no one can even acknowledge the Lord—much less *love* Him—apart from the evidence which the Spirit has provided (1 Corinthians 12:3). The Spirit cannot endorse one who claims to love God yet refuses to keep His commandments (1 John 2:3-6) or who refuses to love the brethren (1 John 4:20-21).

- ❏ **Joy:** Worldly people rejoice over superficial, temporary, or pointless victories (cf. Romans 1:32; Revelation 11:7-10; et al). Their joy is limited to this life; they have "no hope" in the life to come. But the Spirit inspires the believer with hope and confidence of a future life with God, so that he is able to rejoice in all that he does (Philippians 4:4), knowing that he has an inheritance reserved for him (Ephesians 1:13-14).

- ❏ **Peace:** "World peace" is a fictitious, utopian idea that provides an illusion of hope and at best unites people only temporarily. World peace is impossible because the *spirit* of the world is inherently selfish, uncooperative, and unstable. But the believer can enjoy spiritual peace regardless of the state of the world, for the *Source* of his peace lies with Christ who has "overcome the world" (John 16:33). This peace is realized through the work of the Holy Spirit whose energy radiates throughout the body of Christ (cf. Romans 8:6; 14:17; 15:13; et al).

- ❏ **Patience:** The *purpose* of patience (or "longsuffering") is a belief that something good will come of one's endurance of a particular difficulty or situation. Of course, if one's hope is fixed only upon this world, whatever patience he demonstrates is ultimately pointless, since he *and* this world are "passing away" (1 John 2:16-17). But the Holy Spirit inspires patience among those who follow Him, since "we through the Spirit, by faith, are waiting for the hope of righteousness" (Galatians 5:5). The righteousness that is *practiced* by us serves to enhance the *hope* that we have in God, so that we may with confidence endure the difficulties, injustices, and even persecutions of this life.

- ❏ **Kindness:** The "kindness of God" appeared in the form of Jesus Christ, but has been extended to us also through the "renewing by the Holy Spirit" (Titus 3:4-5). This invisible "renewal" has been made real through the historical, flesh-and-blood presence of Christ; since the one, so the other. Just as God has been kind to us by inviting us into fellowship with Him, so we are expected to show kindness to others (Matthew 5:43-47).

❑ **Goodness:** "The fruit of the Light consists in all goodness and righteousness and truth" (Ephesians 5:9), and the *energy source* of this "Light" is the Spirit of God, as we have discussed in an earlier chapter. Those who are in Christ are to "let your light shine before men in such a way that they may see your good works, and glorify your Father who is in heaven" (Matthew 5:16; see also Ephesians 2:10).

❑ **Faithfulness:** Christ redeemed us *so that* we would have "the promise of the Spirit through faith"; and "through the Spirit, by faith" this redemption will one day be visibly realized (Galatians 3:14; 5:5). It is impossible to manifest the "fruit of the Spirit" apart from being faithful to the Son of God who has *given* us this Spirit by the authority of the Father. "Without faith it is impossible to please Him" (Hebrews 11:6), but *by* our faith we are justified by God, and *because* of our faith we are sanctified by His Spirit. It is also clear—because faithfulness is a *result* of His activity in our lives—that the Spirit also *helps* us to remain faithful in times of fear or weakness (cf. Mark 9:24; Ephesians 6:16; 1 John 3:19-22; et al.)

❑ **Gentleness:** Like kindness and humility, this is something that God expects us to *demonstrate*, not just talk about. Gentleness is the quiet spirit of consideration for others which allows them to retain their human dignity *and* reflects the divine patience that God has shown to each one of us. The gentle attitude and its corresponding behavior are essential in pursuing "the unity of the Spirit" (Ephesians 4:1-3), forgiveness (Colossians 3:12-13), and re-directing those who are in error (Galatians 6:1-2; 2 Timothy 2:24-25).

❑ **Self-control:** Paradoxically, we *gain* control of our lives by *relinquishing* all control to the Spirit's oversight. This does not mean we cease to be responsible for our actions; on the contrary, we are trained by the Spirit how to be *ideally* responsible for them. One who is controlled by the Spirit is thus in control of himself; one who is controlled by some other spirit—in particular, the careless spirit of the world—is actually spiraling *out of control*, even though he may be oblivious to this. Worldly people are naturally self-centered instead of Christ-centered, since they are under the spell of a worldly spirit. God's Spirit does not bewitch people, but teaches us to be "peaceable, gentle, reasonable, full of mercy and good fruits, unwavering, without hypocrisy" (see James 3:13-18).

"Against such things there is no law" (Galatians 5:23). In the context, this means that there are no *limits* as to the practice of such "fruit": one can produce as much love, joy, peace, patience, kindness, etc. as he desires! There is "no law" (or boundary) to restrain him; just as the Spirit's energy is boundless and limitless, so the believer's life can generate an incalculable amount of fruit. This, of course, defies natural expectations, but is made possible because of the supernatural work of the Spirit within the life of the believer. Fruit trees can only produce one, maybe two crops a year; the disciple of the Lord can produce many kinds of fruit all of the time. (Perhaps this gives more meaning to the symbolic picture portrayed in Revelation 22:2.) All of these fruits will be considered "fruit of the Spirit" if indeed they are inspired and generated by the Spirit's work in the believer's heart.

Summary Thoughts

The *reality* of the Spirit's indwelling (or "abiding") is manifested through our keeping of God's commandments (1 John 3:24) *and* the "fruit of the Spirit." While we may initially understand these in an abstract or conceptual way, they are of no benefit to us until they are actually *put into practice*. Thus, while God's laws and the Spirit's "fruit" are spiritual in nature, they must be carried out "in the flesh," so to speak. Just as Jesus' obedience may have been in His heart all along, He still had to *manifest* that obedience in His life here on earth. It was only in this way that He was "made perfect" to God *and* to us (cf. Hebrews 5:8-9).

In other words, Christians can talk about "bearing fruit" all day long, but we have nothing to show for it until something literal, visible, and definable is actually *accomplished*. The "members of your body" are no longer to accommodate sinful practices, but the will of God (see Romans 6:11-13). Fruit trees that produce no fruit may be attractive and ornamental, but they are of no advantage to the farmer who looks to profit from his investment. Non-producing fruit trees may provide some aesthetic value to the homeowner, but that was not their original purpose; they do not *produce* anything. God made fruit trees to produce *fruit*, for within the fruit are the seeds of even more fruit trees and thus countless other crops.

Likewise, God makes men and women Christians *not* to sit ornamentally upon a church pew or provide some aesthetic value to a congregation, but to *produce fruit*. Christians who refuse to produce fruit are suppressing the work of the Spirit in their lives (a problem we will address in a later chapter). Yet he who welcomes the Spirit's guidance and prays for God to bless him *through* His Spirit is among those "who indeed bears fruit and brings forth, some a hundredfold, some sixty, and some thirty" (Matthew 13:23).

Given the faithful heart of a willing believer, the Holy Spirit is able to bring about an abundant crop of "fruit" for God in even the most unfavorable, unsuitable earthly conditions. The believer is not dependent upon ideal physical conditions, the absence of adversity, the cooperation of others, or even his own personal abilities; the Spirit is able to perform remarkably in him regardless of all of these things. In the natural world, this is impossible, but with God—and the Holy Spirit most certainly *is* God—"all things are possible" (Matthew 19:26).

Chapter Eight
The Work of the Spirit in the Christian's Life

In Him [Christ], you also, after listening to the message of truth, the gospel of your salvation—having also believed, you were sealed in Him with the Holy Spirit of promise, who is given as a pledge of our inheritance, with a view to the redemption of God's own possession, to the praise of His glory. Ephesians 1:13-14

Certainly there are some who resist the "indwelling of the Spirit" for what it is—not because the concept is too difficult, but because it challenges long-held beliefs. This is similar to what Jesus encountered in Capernaum when He spoke figuratively of eating His flesh and drinking His blood. "Therefore many of His disciples, when they heard this said, 'This is a difficult statement; who can listen to it?'" (John 6:60). It wasn't that His words were too difficult to understand. Rather, they flew in the face of their expectations of Messiah and forced the people to recalibrate their view of Him (which many refused to do).

In many cases even today, people want the Holy Spirit to conform to their own perceptions of Him. This is not a reference to those who are genuinely trying to learn about the Spirit but are still unfamiliar with what the Bible teaches concerning Him. Instead, this refers to those who have had sufficient time and opportunity to know better, but still have not come to a more mature understanding about God. The deliberate resistance of biblical knowledge distorts people's view of Christ's gospel, His church, and the work of the Holy Spirit in the lives of believers. The Spirit's work is not disconnected from the work of Christ, but is inextricably bound to it. One cannot, therefore, purposely remain uninformed about the Spirit and still end up with a correct view of the Christian's relationship with God. Take the Spirit out of the picture—or assign to Him an improper role *in* the picture—and the picture is corrupted altogether.

Yet even among knowledgeable Christians are those who are hesitant to accept that the Spirit *does* play an active role in the lives of believers. Some will concede that He does, but are overly guarded in explaining *how* He does this. Others enthusiastically embrace the Spirit's work, but their approach may be more emotional than practical. Rather than trying to defend one position or another, Christians need to know:

Does the Bible teach that the Spirit actively works in the life of a believer today or not? If so, what is that work—and how is it manifested? We will now turn our attention to this subject, for it is a most important one.

The Christian's Source of Energy

We have already discussed some of the fundamental principles of the Spirit's involvement with the believer. This involvement begins, of course, upon that person's reception of the gospel message. No one comes to God without having first been invited *by* God. "While there is no conversion without the Holy Spirit, there is no operation of the Holy Spirit in conversion independent of God's word."[96] The Spirit calls the sinner through His gospel (Acts 2:39; 2 Thessalonians 2:13-14), and the sinner must respond to that call with his *own* appeal to God (cf. Acts 2:21; 22:16; Romans 10:13). We cannot make the Spirit responsible for one's conversion; the sinner must *do what is required* in order to call upon the Lord.[97] In Acts 2, 3,000 Jews received the Holy Spirit; in Acts 7, the Jewish Council rejected the Holy Spirit and killed His spokesman (Stephen). So it is today: men either receive the Spirit or they reject Him; it is left to each individual how he or she will respond to His Word.

Simply reading or knowing the gospel does not by itself initiate any supernatural involvement; in fact, one can know the gospel thoroughly and still not respond to it in faith (Hebrews 4:2). However, when one demonstrates his obedience to God in whatever manner the gospel has instructed him, then something *supernatural* occurs—not upon the believer's physical body, nor within the believer's scope of vision, but upon his *heart*, within his *soul*. God calls into being a "new creature" (2 Corinthians 5:17; Ephesians 2:10)—in the sense that a new *relationship* (sonship) is established—upon the union of human faith and divine grace. Sins are forgiven (Hebrews 8:12), life is imparted (Ephesians 2:4-5), access to the Father is granted (Ephesians 2:18), and salvation is promised (Romans 10:9-10). No *one* of these things is accomplished through an earthly, human, or natural process (John 1:12-13); such things *demand* supernatural activity.

We have seen that the Holy Spirit most certainly indwells the heart of the believer. This indwelling is not physical anymore than is sin's indwelling (cf. Romans 7:17). The Spirit's indwelling (or presence) is real, necessary, and productive all the same. We have also discussed the "fruit of the Spirit" and how the dynamic presence of the Spirit is required in order to generate this "fruit." The soul that has not yet been sprinkled with the blood of Christ can neither be consecrated by the "eternal Spirit"; such a person can only produce "dead works" (Hebrews 9:13-14). "Good works" are those which the Father expects from His disciples because of the "power" that is within them—"power" that is *beyond* them otherwise (Romans 15:13; Ephesians 3:16, 20).

Let's back up and take in a big picture perspective. The entire physical universe is filled with various forms of energy (or "light"). The seven different forms of this energy[98] radiate throughout our solar system and the cosmos. Likewise, all physical matter can be expressed as a static form of energy.[99] Not only is the universe filled with energy, but it cannot function or exist *without* it. All the natural laws that govern the universe—laws of light properties, thermodynamics, physics, momentum, etc.—dictate how energy is expressed, used, and transformed. These laws also govern the effects of energy (as heat, radiation, gravity, motion, etc.). In other words, the universe operates within a pre-determined, organized, and purposeful system. Take away these laws, and energy cannot function or perform: it cannot be stabilized, and thus no work or objective can be accomplished. The entire universe would plunge into unending chaos. Take away energy itself, and the physical universe vanishes altogether, since energy is the fundamental substance of its existence.

The natural context of the physical universe serves as an ideal illustration of the unseen spiritual world. The Christian is also filled with energy—not just physical energy (which relates only to a physical context), but also *spiritual* energy. This is what the indwelling of the Holy Spirit provides: an inexhaustible, supernatural form of *power* that is able to accomplish what the Christian himself cannot. The Spirit operates according to immutable "laws"—not the Bible, for that is His law to *us*, but according to the divine nature of the Father Himself. This cannot mean that the Spirit operates regardless of what is written *in* Scripture, for He is the source of and authority *for* Scripture. "This does not mean that the Holy Spirit has a will for us which is not revealed in the Word, but it does mean that in this He does a work on our behalf which He does not do through the written Word."[100] Because He is God, the Holy Spirit is absolutely reliable: there are things that He will *always do* (that conform to God's divine nature), and there are things that He will *never* do (that violate God's nature).

Take away these divine laws and God ceases to exist, for God's laws and His existence are mutually dependent. Likewise, when a Christian continues to "willfully" violate these laws, then the Spirit cannot exist within him; such a person has "insulted the Spirit of grace" (cf. Hebrews 10:26-31) and forfeited his fellowship with God. The Holy Spirit is the energy and essence of one's spiritual life; just as the universe is completely dependent upon the energy within it, so the Christian's fellowship with God is completely dependent upon the presence of the Spirit. Just as the universe would die if its energy were removed, so the Christian's fellowship with God would die if the Holy Spirit were to be taken from him. (If a person physically dies in this state of separation, then his soul dies as well.[101]) The Spirit is the energy and power that gives *life* to the Christian, just as God gave life to this world through the energy He extended to it. "The life-giving and origin of life is in the Christ, but he gives life through the Holy Spirit."[102]

Trying to explain the Christian life apart from the Spirit's active involvement is like trying to explain the universe—or human, animal, or vegetative life—apart from the energy that makes everything happen: it is impossible to do. Likewise, it is impossible to biblically and accurately explain the work of a *Christian* without referring (either directly or by necessary implication) to the work of the *Spirit*. Just as the universe cannot function without God-given energy, so the Christian cannot function *as* a Christian without God's Spirit. Instead, that person's spiritual life would plunge into darkness and chaos; his heart would no longer be filled with light; he would no longer have access to power. He would simply succumb to a slow and pointless spiritual death—which is exactly what *all* people face who refuse to receive Christ and (thus) God's Spirit.

The one in whom the Spirit indwells has access to supernatural power and spiritual intercession. This power does not enable us to perform actual miracles, but it is a miraculous power all the same. Whatever we cannot accomplish on our own, but that *needs* to be accomplished in order to save our souls, God does for us—in Christ, through the power of His Spirit. This is the essence of *saving grace*: God doing the impossible for us so that we can be saved from our own ruin. Whatever that is, whatever that involves, and however often it needs to be done, this is the work of divine grace.

God's Activity in the Life of the Believer

God has not given us of His Spirit simply as a matter of protocol, or as a token insignia of divine approval. Rather, the Spirit is given to us to *perform His work* in us, since we are unable to perform without Him, and whatever work we *do* perform is insufficient by itself. We can only do what God has told us to do (cf. Luke 17:10), but the Spirit is not bound by our limitations. With this in mind, we will now consider the various works of the Holy Spirit in the Christian. (Some of this will be review from previous chapters, but it is helpful to see all the information together.)

Anointed for consecration: "Now He who establishes us with you in Christ and anointed us is God, who also sealed us and gave us the Spirit in our hearts as a pledge" (2 Corinthians 1:21-22). This anointing indicates being set apart or consecrated for a specific purpose—in our case, to "walk" in "good works" which God has prepared for us (Ephesians 2:10). While Israel's priests were anointed with the "holy oil" in a physical sense, believers are "anointed" with the Holy Spirit in a spiritual one. (Recall our discussion on the anointing of God's people from chapter 3.) Just as the holy anointing oil for the ancient priests and the holy fixtures of the tabernacle was sacred and unique (Exodus 30:22-33), so God's Spirit is sacred and unique: there is no *other* "anointing" that can equal or replace His anointment. Similarly, just as the priests' anointing "will qualify them for a perpetual priesthood throughout their generations" (see Exodus 40:9-15), so our having been anointed with God's Spirit qualifies *us* for a priesthood that begins here on earth (1 Peter 2:9) and extends even into eternity.

Sealed for salvation: The "anointing" and "sealing" processes are intimately related, yet have distinctly-separate purposes. The "sealing" metaphor draws on the ancient practice of sealing an important document with hot wax, then pressing a uniquely-designed stamp or signet ring into this wax. The wax seals the document shut; the signet impression indicates the original source (thus, authority) of the information inside.[103] In the analogy, the promise of God is the "document"; the believer's life is the wax; and the Spirit is the imprint of God upon him. When we are baptized into Christ, having "died with Him" in the watery grave and then raised to "walk in newness of life" (Romans 6:3-4; 2 Timothy 2:11), a new relationship with God is established. We *were* "dead" in our sins, but *now* God has "made us alive together with Christ" by His grace and through the demonstration of our faith (Ephesians 2:1-9). Our lives are then "sealed" with the Spirit, safeguarding the promises of God regarding our salvation and all the spiritual blessings which are found only "in Christ" (Ephesians 1:3). Just as Christ Himself was sealed by the Father with the Spirit (John 6:27), so we are sealed—not for the same ministry as Christ, but certainly by the same *authority*. We are thus sealed with the Holy Spirit "for the day of redemption" (Ephesians 4:30)—the day when our salvation is no longer a matter of faith but will be finally and visibly revealed (1 Peter 1:3-5).

To "seal" something in this manner indicates both *ownership* and *security*. God *owns* those whom He seals; He makes us "a people for His own possession" (Titus 2:14). Likewise, God *protects* those whom He seals; we may suffer the consequences of living in a godless world, but we will never suffer God's direct condemnation *upon* this world.[104] If God has not sealed those who have sought salvation through Him, then we are not identified with Him at all. If this were the case, then He neither owns us nor will He protect us; but this is not the case for those "in Christ." By the authority of God's Spirit we are baptized in water (1 Corinthians 12:13); upon being baptized, we are "clothed" with Christ (Galatians 3:27). Having demonstrated obedience to God on *our* part, God then demonstrates faithfulness on *His* part by anointing and sealing us with His Spirit. Henry Soltau writes on this thought:

> The Spirit of God is also the seal, or stamp of God, upon the believer, proving by His very presence with and in the believer, that he is a child of God—that he is a new creation of God—a deed executed by God—a fiat of God's love and power. The Spirit also is the earnest in the believer's heart of the future glory—a pledge from the right hand of the throne of God—from the risen Christ, of the glorious resurrection which shall be his when Christ returns.[105]

Sanctification: Again, it is sometimes difficult to separate being "sanctified" from being "anointed" or "sealed," but this concept further helps us to understand what the Spirit does for us. To be "sanctified" means to be made holy. Just as God is holy, so must those be who minister to Him (cf. Leviticus 10:3; 11:45; 19:2; et al). Just as the ancient high priests wore a turban with the inscription, "Holy to the LORD" (Exodus 28:36-38), so we are designated by God's Spirit as being holy to the Lord. Just as Jesus was sanctified by God (John 10:36), so we are sanctified by the Spirit of God. When we are made holy in conformity with God's own holiness, then we are brought into God's service. Because of this, we are "enslaved to God" (Romans 6:22)—not for our ruin, as when one enslaves himself to sin (6:16), but for our salvation. Christ is the *embodiment* of our sanctification (1 Corinthians 1:30; Hebrews 10:10), but the Spirit is the *agent* of sanctification (1 Thessalonians 4:7-8; 2 Thessalonians 2:13). It is by His "sanctifying work" that we are identified as the "chosen" of God (1 Peter 1:1-2). In this way, we are collectively being built up as "a holy temple in the Lord...into a dwelling of God in the Spirit" (Ephesians 2:21-22).

It is impossible for men to confer divine holiness upon one another, for we simply do not have the ability or authority to do so. Only God can make men holy; thus, whoever is holy indeed must have been sanctified by God Himself. There is nothing that we can do through our own human effort or piety to equal what God alone can do. On the other hand, we *are* responsible for preparing ourselves for the work of the Spirit within us. We are to be cleansed from the wickedness of this world so that we can "be a vessel for honor, sanctified, useful to the Master, prepared for every good work" (2 Timothy 2:21). Since the Holy Spirit indwells us, carrying out His will through our own physical bodies, we are to "present [our] bodies a living and holy sacrifice, acceptable to God," not being conformed to this world but being "transformed by the renewing of your mind" (Romans 12:1-2). In essence, we are to live as holy people in order to have fellowship with God's Holy Spirit (see 1 Peter 1:13-16).

Pledge: Just as an engagement ring anticipates the actual wedding, so God gives us a promise by which we can anticipate the eternal union of the church (the "bride") with Christ. "Now He who prepared us for this very purpose is God, who gave to us the Spirit as a pledge" (2 Corinthians 5:5). This pledge (or earnest or guarantee) serves to ensure or reserve our "place" in the heavenly kingdom, giving us confidence of our future life with God. No passage in the New Testament brings this out as clearly and succinctly as Ephesians 1:13-14:

In Him [Christ], you also, after listening to the message of truth, the gospel of your salvation—having also believed, you were sealed in Him with the Holy Spirit of promise, who is given as a pledge of our inheritance, with a view to the redemption of God's own possession, to the praise of His glory.

The process of becoming a child of God (and thus eligible for an inheritance) begins when one hears the "message of truth" (the gospel) and responds in faith (Hebrews 11:1, 6). Upon demonstrating his obedience, the believer is then "sealed" in Christ *with* the Spirit, who also serves as the "pledge of our inheritance" (see also Ephesians 1:11). In other words, Christ does not work alone: everything He promises us is guaranteed by the authority of His Father, which is made real to us by the giving of His Holy Spirit. This pledge secures our inheritance with God beyond what we are able to accomplish ourselves; "God's gift of the Holy Spirit is the pledge and first payment for the final inheritance in Christ."[106] However, we also have a responsibility to remain true to the Spirit's gospel message in order to protect our salvation (cf. 2 Timothy 1:14).

Access to the Father: While we have already discussed this previously, we would do well to include this work of the Spirit in this compilation. The apostle Paul is very clear: "through Him [Christ] we both [Jews and Gentiles] have our access in one Spirit to the Father" (Ephesians 2:18, bracketed words are mine). This access is made possible through Christ (Ephesians 3:11-12; Hebrews 4:14-16), but is actually carried out through the agency of the Spirit. The Greek word for "access" is used in the same way in Romans 5:2 (where the New American Standard Bible reads: "we have obtained our introduction by faith").[107] The context there (5:1-5) concerns our justification by faith, which is made real to us "because the love of God has been poured out within our hearts through the Holy Spirit who was given to us" (5:5). Thus, once again we find access to the Father by grace through faith, because of Christ's sacrifice, and by the mediatory work of the Spirit.

Intercession for prayers: It is completely accurate to say that Christ is our Mediator between God and men (1 Timothy 2:5-6), but this does not negate the Spirit's mediation. In the passage just cited, Paul speaks of Christ's sacrificial work on the cross: no one comes to the Father except by the crucified Christ (cf. John 14:6). But Christ is no longer nailed to a cross, and now reigns in heaven as our High Priest. He has since sent the Holy Spirit to those who believe in Him, and He uses the Spirit to carry out His will in His church. Accordingly, Paul speaks of the Spirit's mediation with regard to the prayers of the saints (Romans 8:26-27). Indeed, we are to "pray at all times in the Spirit" (Ephesians 6:18), for the Spirit communes with our spirit in an intimate, profound, and supernatural way that transcends human understanding. Just as the Spirit searches the mind of God (1 Corinthians 2:10), so He also searches our own mind (heart)—not to judge us, but to serve as an Advocate for us.[108] Praying to God for guidance, and then *expecting* a divine response, is nothing short of calling upon supernatural intervention in our mundane lives that exceeds what reading Bible verses will accomplish. We either believe that the Christ—through the Holy Spirit—is actively hearing and responding to our prayers or we do not. We have no use praying to a God who does not hear, cannot answer, or will not help.

Guidance: Once again, we acknowledge Christ as the "Shepherd and Guardian" of our souls (1 Peter 2:25). But Christ employs the Holy Spirit to carry out this guardianship, for we are *led* by Him [the Spirit] according to the will of Christ. Being led by the Spirit (Romans 8:14; Galatians 5:16-17) implies that we have surrendered our will to His, and therefore allow Him to take us where we need to go, or challenge us as He determines is in our best interest. Without the guidance of the Spirit, the Bible is just *words*; it can inform us, but it cannot *lead* us. The Spirit opens our mind to the truths *within* God's Word, brings that Word to life, and thus directly affects our heart. By so illuminating us, He re-educates our conscience, shows us the way in which we should think and live, and exposes those things in our lives which must be removed.[109]

This thought may be unnerving to the very conservative Christian. To him, it may *sound* like, "Just put your Bible aside, for the Spirit will lead you on His own." This is not true; that is not how the Spirit works. One author succinctly summed up the danger of that kind of thinking:

The person [who thinks the Spirit leads him regardless of the written Word—MY WORDS] is not careful about accuracy to what the text says because he thinks the Holy Spirit is giving him understanding. That person is very vulnerable to error. The scriptures provide us with knowledge we do not have in ourselves. God will give wisdom if we ask [cf. James 1:5]. But claims of direct Holy Spirit guidance is [*sic*] Satan's way of turning us away from Bible knowledge to other directions. One who does that goes against Satan one to one, is foolish and will lose the battle.[110]

I agree entirely, as long as by "direct Holy Spirit guidance" he means in some way that contradicts or disregards the written Word. However, if he means that the Holy Spirit is *unable* or *refuses* to guide us except for handing us a Bible, I cannot agree with this simply because the Bible itself does not teach it. The author admits, "God will give wisdom if we ask"—but if whatever wisdom He "gives" is already written down in Scripture, then why ask Him for it?

Strength: We may be able to survive the rigors of this earthly life without asking for God's help; people do it all the time. But we are unable to overcome the many spiritual forces and difficulties that exceed our human strength. As Paul wrote (Ephesians 6:10-12):

> Finally, be strong in the Lord and in the strength of His might. Put on the full armor of God, so that you will be able to stand firm against the schemes of the devil. For our struggle is not against flesh and blood, but against the rulers, against the powers, against the world forces of this darkness, against the spiritual forces of wickedness in the heavenly places.

You and I are simply unable to contend with such "spiritual forces" which seek our destruction; we must rely upon the "full armor of God," which *necessarily includes* the strength and oversight of His Spirit. "He has not promised and He does not give us the power to work miracles, but God in His providence can work behind the scene. He is not so limited that He must work a miracle, or grant us miraculous power, in order to strengthen us and others."[111] It is His strength that works "in the inner man" (Ephesians 3:16)—strength that we cannot see or feel, but which is *real* and *working* nonetheless. In this way, we are "strengthened with all power" (Colossians 1:11), according to the "strength which God supplies" (1 Peter 4:11; see also 2 Thessalonians 2:16-17; 3:3; and 1 Peter 5:10).

Renewal of spirit: There are several New Testament passages which speak of the "renewing" of one's mind (Romans 12:1-2) or the "renewal" of one's "inner man" (2 Corinthians 4:16). In both usages, the renewal process is regular ("day by day") and gradual. Such renewal necessarily requires an external source of power. We cannot renew ourselves, for otherwise we would not need divine help; we must participate in the process, but our own strength is not the process itself. This renewal is in the ever-present tense, the child of God "being constantly renewed with respect to a complete and perfect knowledge which is according to the image of the One who created him."[112] It is not limited to what occurs upon one's baptism, for the context of the "renewal" passages refers to the duration of the Christian life. Because of the onslaught of this sinful world (John 16:33), the war within our soul (cf. 1 Peter 2:11), and our own human frailty, our spirit, left to itself, becomes overwhelmed and exhausted. We need to be refreshed and rejuvenated by a power greater than our own, even greater than the sum of those around us. This is exactly what God promises through the work of His Spirit. *How* the Spirit re-energizes and renews us is not necessary to know; it is sufficient that He does so work.

Confirmation: We who are "in Christ" are not natural children of God, but are adopted as sons of God (Ephesians 1:5). But because we *are* adopted, we are legally entitled to receive an inheritance from God. The fact of this relationship is confirmed by two witnesses (cf. 2 Corinthians 13:1): the testimony of our own sincere heart *together with* the testimony of the Spirit. Our heart testifies that our love for God is genuine; the Spirit testifies that we have been obedient to the Word He has revealed to us (i.e., the gospel). Professor Bales has summarized this well (in his comments on Romans 10:6-17):

> We do not have to ascend to heaven to know that we have been justified. We have to hear, believe, and submit to the gospel. Since we are the ones who do the believing, since we are the ones who confess Christ, we are the ones who know whether or not we have believed in our hearts and sincerely confessed with our lips what is in our hearts.[113]

Thus, "the Spirit Himself testifies with our spirit that we are children of God, and if children, heirs also, heirs of God and fellow heirs with Christ" (Romans 8:14-16; see also Galatians 4:4-7). Someone asks, "To *whom* does the Spirit testify this?" It would seem (from Galatians 4:6) that this is to God; however, His testimony is also manifested to *us* through the "fruit of the Spirit" that is made evident in our lives. The Spirit indwells those who *are* "sons," not those who merely have internalized instructions of Scripture on how to *become* sons.[114] Thus, the Holy Spirit is both defender and prosecutor: He defends those who belong to Him and exposes those who do not. The criteria for either case are determined by what He has already revealed to all men in the written Word.

Fruit of the Spirit: We have already discussed this in a previous chapter; suffice it to say here that it would be impossible for us to produce this "fruit" (cf. Galatians 5:22-23) without the *power* and *activity* of the Spirit in our lives. Once again, we cannot have it both ways: we cannot hope to produce *fruit* of the Spirit by denying the active *work* of the Spirit in the life of the believer. Not only is this illogical, it is also unbiblical.

Summary Thoughts

This is an impressive array of the Spirit's work. This only includes the general activity defined by Scripture; it does not even begin to describe that which *actually happens* but that remains beyond our ability to see or comprehend. Nonetheless, such details lead to a positive and joyful conclusion: "The activity of the Spirit on our behalf points to the ultimate security in God of those whom He has chosen."[115] However, we should also consider the negative implications of all of these works in order to reinforce the positive points that have been made. If the Spirit does *not* work in the life of the Christian, then:

- ❏ We are not anointed for service to God.
- ❏ We are not sealed for salvation.
- ❏ We are not sanctified—thus we are not holy people.
- ❏ We have no pledge from God—even though He promised that we do.
- ❏ We have no access to God.
- ❏ We have no intercession for our prayers.
- ❏ We have no divine guidance; we have the Bible and absolutely nothing else (which makes all prayerful appeals meaningless and contradictory).
- ❏ We are dependent only upon our own strength to overcome things that are admittedly more powerful than we are.
- ❏ We have no confirmation from God that we really *are* His children.
- ❏ We cannot produce the "fruit of the Spirit," but we can only produce our own fruit which (by itself) is simply unacceptable to God.

Thankfully, these points are not true for the genuine believer! Yet the above list illustrates just how *needed* the Spirit is in the Christian's fellowship with God. Again, we are not minimizing the intercessory work of Christ as we focus our attention upon the Holy Spirit. We have also previously established that Christ does not work *apart* from the Holy Spirit, but that the two work in seamless cooperation.

The intention of this study is to bring to light what the New Testament teaches concerning the Spirit's essential work in a Christian's life. What is revealed to us was never meant to answer all our questions or satisfy all our curiosities, yet it is sufficient for our needs. Because of all that He does for us, we would do well to accommodate the Spirit's work.

We do this by submitting to the will of Christ, clinging to that which is good, abstaining from whatever is evil, and prayerfully entreating God for the divine help He has promised to believers. It is through the power of God, which is carried out through the Spirit of God, that we will be "preserved complete"—body, soul, and spirit—in Christ (1 Thessalonians 5:23).

Chapter Nine
The Work of the Spirit in the Church

So then you are no longer strangers and aliens, but you are fellow citizens with the saints, and are of God's household, having been built on the foundation of the apostles and prophets, Christ Jesus Himself being the cornerstone, in whom the whole building, being fitted together, is growing into a holy temple in the Lord, in whom you also are being built together into a dwelling of God in the Spirit.
Ephesians 2:19-22

The New Testament epistles teach that the Holy Spirit is quite active in the lives of individual Christians. Take His work out of the picture, and a believer's spiritual life completely implodes, for there is no longer anything to keep it alive or functional. Only by the life, energy, activity, and guidance of the Spirit are we able to perform as God's servants. This does *not* mean—and this is the fear of some—that the Spirit acts in *contradiction* to the Word, or that He acts *instead* of us. Rather, it means that the explicit details of His work exceed what is described only generally in the New Testament and that *our* work is incomplete without *His.*

Now we will turn our attention to the Spirit's work in the church of Christ as a whole organism rather than focusing only on the individual believer. By "church" in this context, we mean the entire body of believers everywhere, as the word is used in Ephesians 1:22-23.[116] The church does not (and is not expected to) address everything with which *God* is concerned. God's work—through the Holy Spirit—goes far beyond whatever we are able to see, know, or confirm through physical evidence. What the Spirit does *outside* of the church is virtually unknown to us; He has not told us (and is not required to tell us) every aspect of His divine activity. We can necessarily infer (as we will do so shortly), but there are obvious limitations to our inferences.

We should, however, be concerned with what the Spirit does *within* the church, since this directly affects all of us who are "in Christ." By way of the Spirit's working within the body of Christ, we fulfill the three major areas of the church's mission: evangelism (both within and without the body); edification of the brotherhood of believers; and benevolence (or charity) towards those who are in the body. Certainly these are very broad categories, and often overlap each other, but everything that Christ requires of His church will be defined by one of these three groups. What is important to remember, then, is that we (the church) are not alone: we do not act alone; we do not choose our own direction; we are not truly self-sufficient. This is comforting to know, since men—when left alone—naturally gravitate toward the abuse of power, selfishness, and the corruption of any good thing that God has given us. Christians are not immune to such corruptions; we are in desperate and constant need of divine guidance *away* from these. Only when we refuse the Spirit's guidance and teachings do we begin that long, gradual descent into moral darkness and human depravity (as graphically depicted in Romans 1:18-32; 1 Timothy 4:1-3; 2 Timothy 3:1-9; and 4:3-4).

The Mission of Christ's Church

Christ's primary concern for His church does *not* involve debates about brotherhood "issues," church protocol, finely-crafted sermons, or physical buildings. Some *Christians* may find their time and energy consumed with these things, and this is most unfortunate. Christ's primary focus is always on saving souls from their self-inflicted destruction. Jesus said Himself, "For the Son of Man has come to seek and to save that which was lost" (Luke 19:10). Thus, our primary concern must also be the salvation of lost souls. Everyone who is in the church was once lost but now has been found; we should never lose sight of this. Jesus also accepted whatever personal losses were required to achieve this objective: "For even the Son of Man did not come to be served, but to serve, and to give His life a ransom for many" (Mark 10:45). Thus, we also—individually *and* collectively—should be prepared for service and to suffer incidental losses in order to accommodate the Savior's will. His mission, then, becomes the mission of His church: whatever detracts from this mission is unauthorized; whatever does not directly advance this mission is deemed expendable.[117]

The work of the *body* of Christ is not identical with the work of the individual *member* of that body, although the two may admittedly overlap. The human body provides an ideal analogy here: the mission of the entire human body is to not necessarily the same as its individual components. The mission of the human body is to survive against the elements, find sufficient food and water, reproduce, and so forth. The mission of the lungs, however, is to provide respiration; the mission of the heart is to pump blood; the mission of the foot is to provide mobility; and so forth. Both the corporate body *and* the individual members answer to the head (brain), but for different objectives.

Similarly, the individual Christian is not bound to the exact same expectations as the entire community of believers. What an individual believer does with his time, money, and resources is not bound by what the entire body of Christ does with *its* time, money, and resources. Christ owns the individual Christian just as He does His church (1 Corinthians 6:19-20; Colossians 1:18), but His church is governed as a collective entity rather than an individual one (just as the entire human body is governed by the brain differently than are its individual parts). For example, if a believer wishes to donate his own time and money to feed impoverished people who refuse Christ's gospel, then that is his choice. But neither the entire church nor individual congregations are given permission to do this; the *collective* saints are only to support fellow saints, not those outside of the body of Christ. The New Testament does not teach or offer examples otherwise.

We are focusing on this point because it affects people's perceptions of the work of the Spirit. If Christ's church is expected to feed the poor, one will assume this must also be the Spirit's objective, which distorts the New Testament message. Jesus never asked His church to take care of the world's poor people, but expected *individuals* to rise to the occasion and take care of this (Matthew 19:21; Mark 14:7; Luke 14:13; et al). The Spirit Himself is not unconcerned about the poor; indeed, He works to have the gospel preached to them (Matthew 11:4-5; Luke 4:18; 7:22; et al). But the mission of Christ's church is to address people's *spiritual* needs; once they become "family" ("sons of God through faith"; Galatians 3:26-28), then His church may help them also with their physical needs (as in Acts 4:32-37).

Most certainly the Spirit of God has been involved in the church from the beginning. It was the *power* of the Spirit that first opened the door and invited men to come *into* the church. (We will return to this thought shortly.) This does not mean, however, that the Holy Spirit was never *utilized* or *needed* until this time, for we have already examined His work among the prophets and in the ministry of Christ. Rather, it means that the Spirit had never been identified to believers until then: men knew that He existed, but they had never before known Him as Advocate, Helper,

Comforter, or Guide. Even today, while our understanding of the Spirit is limited, we realize nonetheless that He is inextricably *involved* with the church, since the entire Godhead seeks the objective of the church's existence: the salvation of souls.

In John 7:37-38, Jesus "cried out" on the last day of the Feast of Booths, "If anyone is thirsty, let him come to Me and drink. He who believes in Me, as the Scripture said, 'From his innermost being will flow rivers of living water.'" We have previously linked this to John 4:13-14, where Jesus said to the woman at the well in Samaria, "Everyone who drinks of this water will thirst again; but whoever drinks of the water that I will give him shall never thirst; but the water that I will give him will become in him a well of water springing up to eternal life." This "living water" is given to us *by* Christ, but He is not the water itself. We know this because John himself declared (John 7:39): "But this He spoke of the Spirit, whom those who believed in Him were to receive; for the Spirit was not yet given, because Jesus was not yet glorified." The "water" is the Spirit; the One from whom the water flows is Christ. This is parallel to the Old Testament account of Moses striking the rock in the wilderness to produce water (Exodus 17:6). Paul later says that "the rock was Christ" (1 Corinthians 10:4)—not literally, of course, but this is what the rock symbolized. Likewise, the Spirit is not literal water in the body, but He is symbolized in this way. Christ is the Rock of our salvation; the Spirit is the Water of Life.

The *implementation* of this system—with Christ as Savior of the church and the Spirit as its living essence—had not yet occurred when Jesus spoke about this "living water" in John 7. The Spirit was not yet "given," that is, He was not yet sent by Christ to perform in this capacity. Jesus promised His disciples that the Spirit ("Helper") would be given to them in due time, once He had been "glorified" or exalted to the right hand of God (John 14:16-17; 16:7; Acts 2:33). Christ's ascension to the right hand of His Father indicates the legitimate, successful transfer of power from the Father to the Son,[118] so that the *kingdom* of God is now overseen by the *Son* of God. The reason for this transfer of power is so that Christ can serve as Redeemer: He has the ability (as High Priest) to reconcile us to God; He has the authority (as King) to render eternal decisions concerning our souls. In order to fully and legitimately serve as our Savior, Jesus Christ was given full control of His Father's kingdom.

All of this necessarily had to be accomplished before Christ could "build" His church. Christ could not build without the proper authority; He could not redeem a single soul until He had shed His blood for this very purpose. When His blood was "poured out" (Mark 14:24) for the forgiveness of our sins *and* His Person was exalted to the right hand of God (Acts 2:33), only then could Christ's church be established. This is why no one was baptized in the name of Jesus Christ into His church until Acts 2. Prior to this, Jesus' church had not yet existed because His authority had not yet been given to Him. (Jesus' statement in Matthew 28:18 anticipates this, however, just as John 20:22 anticipated the "power" that would come upon His apostles after His ascension; see also Luke 24:49.)

Once He took His rightful place in the heavens, Jesus sent the Holy Spirit into His church, to give life to it. Just as our own body is dead without our spirit to give it life (James 2:26), so Christ's "body" (church) must be filled with the Spirit of God. Otherwise, the church would have existed, but only as a lifeless construction. God "breathed into [Adam's] nostrils the breath of life; and man became a living being" (Genesis 2:7); likewise, Christ breathed the Holy Spirit into His church, and it became a living, God-breathing organism. When we are baptized into Christ's body (church), we are not brought into a lifeless, empty chamber, like a church building or a mere holding pen. Rather, we are made a part of an *animate body* that pulses with the blood of Christ and breathes with the Spirit of God. Each soul that is brought into this body is made a functional member of it (Romans 12:4-5); together with Christ and the Spirit, this living body serves a living temple of God (Ephesians 2:19-22; 1 Peter 2:4-5).

The Spirit's Power in Christ's Church

Again, the Spirit has been necessarily involved with Christ's church from its beginning. He has been actively and inseparably involved in its establishment, organization, evangelism, and success.[119] He works to secure the fellowship of believers as well as provide the gospel for unbelievers. H. Leo Boles has said it well: "Christ is the authority *over* the church, and the Holy Spirit is the authority *within* the church."[120] Initially, the Spirit's work (or "power") was manifested through Christ's apostles, for it was these to whom this power was promised. The "apostles whom He [Christ] had chosen" were the "you" to whom Jesus said, "… You will receive power when the Holy Spirit has come upon you; and you shall be My witnesses both in Jerusalem, and in all Judea and Samaria, and even to the remotest part of the earth" (see Acts 1:2-8). The apostles were not only given the ability to remember all that Jesus taught them, but also the discernment for the proper *application* of that knowledge *and* of prophetic Scripture (John 14:25-26). We see this exhibited in Peter's several sermons to the Jews in Acts 2 – 5.

The Spirit's *visible* power—though His power certainly is not limited to that which is visible—was also manifested through the "spiritual gifts" (*charisma*) that were imparted to the church through the laying on of the apostles' hands. (We will discuss this further in chapter 10.) These gifts were given and distributed by the Spirit as He deemed appropriate for the "common good" of the church (1 Corinthians 12:4-11). These gifts were not given to everyone, and they were not intended to be perpetuated throughout the church's history. Once the *fact* of the Spirit's presence in the church had been sufficiently established, then it was no longer necessary to continue "proving" what had already been irrefutably proved. It is not as though the gospel lost its power (cf. Romans 1:16), but it was no longer necessary to prove the *source* of its power.

The Spirit also served as a witness of the work and authority of Jesus Christ. Jesus predicted this before His death (John 16:8-11), and Peter acknowledged this himself: "And we [apostles] are witnesses of these things [i.e., the death, resurrection, and ascension of Christ]; and so is the Holy Spirit, whom God has given to those who obey Him" (Acts 5:32, bracketed words are mine). Later, the apostle John also says (1 John 5:6-8)[121]:

This is the One who came by water and blood, Jesus Christ; not with the water only, but with the water and with the blood. It is the Spirit who testifies, because the Spirit is the truth. For there are three that testify: the Spirit and the water and the blood; and the three are in agreement.

Jesus' ministry began with water (His baptism), and ended in blood (His crucifixion); but it is the Spirit who accompanied Him all along, and bore Jesus' testimony to and on behalf of the early church.[122] This "testimony" was given in the form of prophetic utterance, interpretation of Scripture, the working of miracles, and ultimately the written record of all these things. This record is necessary for all who were not physically present to see these things, including us. We do not *have* to see these things in order to believe, for the divine witness of the Spirit is sufficient (1 Timothy 3:16).

The book of Acts offers some details on how the Spirit oversaw and prompted the evangelistic efforts of the early church.

❑ In Acts 6 – 7, it was the Holy Spirit's power and inspiration that were behind Stephen's passionate efforts. This man's martyrdom ignited a raging persecution in Jerusalem and beyond, led by none other than Saul (Paul) himself, which effectively spread the gospel throughout all of Palestine (Acts 8:1-4).

❑ In Acts 8, Philip brought the gospel to the Samaritans, who received it gladly. Because of the many Samaritans who believed and were baptized into Christ's body (8:12), the apostles sent Peter and John from Jerusalem to lay their hands on these people so that they would also be given the visible, miraculous manifestations of the Spirit (8:14-17). The gospel *message* there was first supported by the miracles which Philip performed (8:5-7), but the Samaritans *themselves* were supported by God through the Spirit's gifts. In other words, the Spirit was directly involved in this evangelistic work from beginning to end.

❑ Also in Acts 8, "an angel of the Lord" instructed Philip to go to a certain desert road, where he met the entourage of the court official of Candace, the queen of the Ethiopians.[123] There, the Spirit told Philip to join the man's chariot, which ultimately resulted in the man's conversion (8:26-38). Immediately after this, "the Spirit of the Lord snatched Philip away; and the eunuch no longer saw him, but went on his way rejoicing" (8:39). As has happened countless times afterward, the Spirit was directly instrumental in bringing together both the *messenger* of the gospel and the *hearer* of it (Romans 10:14-15).[124] The Spirit does not force what happens when these two are united; but He does provide the opportunity for the gospel to be preached.

❑ In Acts 9, Saul was converted to "the Way" (9:2) through Christ's miraculous appearance to him on the road to Damascus. Upon being baptized, Ananias told Saul that he would "be filled with the Holy Spirit" (9:17), which inspired Saul to speak boldly in Damascus and later in Jerusalem. This being "filled" refers to what *all* believers enjoy, not the ability to perform miracles. (We do not see Saul performing miracles until after he has met with the apostles, as recorded in 9:27.) While it was Christ who personally convinced Saul to become His disciple, it was the Spirit who guided and inspired him to carry out the ministry for which Christ had set him apart (9:15-16). As a result, "the church throughout all Judea and Galilee and Samaria enjoyed peace, being built up; and going on in the fear of the Lord and in the comfort of the Holy Spirit, it continued to increase" (9:31).

❑ In Acts 13:2-4, the Spirit Himself commissioned Barnabas and Saul to conduct what we know familiarly as the first missionary journey. This journey, which led to the establishment of several churches and the conversion of many people, was thus authorized and prompted by the Spirit, who also oversaw its great success. Thus, the disciples who were the fruit of that effort "were continually filled with joy and with the Holy Spirit" (13:52).

❑ In Acts 15, the church wrestled with a major doctrinal issue, that is, whether or not the Law of Moses should be imposed upon Christians everywhere (15:1, 5). After much debate, a letter was proposed by James (who is believed to be the physical brother of Jesus) stating in effect that the Law could *not* be so imposed. The Holy Spirit provided the evidence for this decision (15:7-11), and also gave His consent to this letter (15:28). In other words, the Spirit oversaw the entire event, and guided the apostles and elders toward His intended objective through a means that served everyone's best interest.

❑ In Acts 16:6-10, on Paul's second missionary journey, the Spirit prevented Paul and Silas from going where *they* had intended and instead directed them to where *He* needed them. Through the means of a vision, the Spirit communicated to Paul that he was to go into Macedonia; this is our first record of the gospel being brought into the European continent.

Given such examples, we have no reason to believe that the Spirit is any less *active* or *interested* in promoting evangelism today. While this is not accomplished through (or accompanied with) the working of visible miracles as it was at first, nonetheless the Spirit is *by necessity* involved in all forms of evangelism of the genuine gospel of Christ. "From these examples [in Acts] we gather the character and scope of the work of the Spirit, which he does independently of the word he has inspired. They develop also a solid reason and necessity for the Spirit's continued presence with the church."[125] After all, it is the Spirit who continues to invite men into fellowship with God, to "take the water of life without cost" (Revelation 22:17). Or, consider what Paul wrote (2 Thessalonians 2:13-14): "...God has chosen you from the beginning for salvation through sanctification by the Spirit and faith in the truth. It was for this He called you through our gospel, that you may gain the glory of our Lord

Jesus Christ." The Bible, as a mere book, cannot "call" to people. It is the Spirit who calls people *into* Christ *through* His living Word—the dynamic message contained *within* the Bible. And who is in need of calling? It is not those already *in* the church, but those who are yet *outside* of Christ.

Someone asks, "Yes, but *how* does the Spirit do this?" No person is able to answer this, nor does it need to be answered. There are many things that God does that remain mysterious and unexplained, including much of what His Spirit does in the lives of men. A Christian is not any more privileged to know these mysteries than is anyone else. Yet when we refuse to believe in God's activity on the basis that He has not yet explained it to us (often, to our personal satisfaction), we are no longer exhibiting faith but *unbelief.* We are essentially demanding full explanations of God before we will *believe* in Him, tacitly insinuating that God is intentionally holding back information that is rightfully ours to know—or similar implied accusations. Such reasoning is not befitting of Christians, but is exactly that of the atheist and agnostic, who refuse to believe *anything* unless it is proved according to their own expectations.[126]

It is presumptuous to think that *we ourselves* are God's only hope for a lost and dying world. It is equally presumptuous to think that the Spirit has left us alone, leaving it up to our strength, our efforts, and our talents—or perhaps sheer luck or coincidence—that the lost soul happens to hear the gospel of his salvation. On the contrary, God has a great interest in the wayward souls of men (as illustrated in Luke 15); and while most of the world rejects Christ's atoning sacrifice, Christ still died *for* the "whole world" (John 3:16; 1 John 2:2). God's desire for man's salvation is not a passive one, but is active (Isaiah 55:10-11; 1 Timothy 2:3-6).

Evangelism is God's business, and He will see that it is accomplished. God does not leave the fate of men's souls in the hands of men, but "calls" to each man in whatever way is sufficient. Christians most certainly are *expected* to participate in evangelism—through prayer, preaching, giving "an account for the hope that lies within" us (1 Peter 3:15), our good works (Matthew 5:16), etc.—but the Spirit oversees all evangelistic efforts. We are His tools in the process, but we are not "the process." This is one of the primary messages of Acts; this also makes sense, given the supernatural character of Christ's church.

The Inter-relationship of the Church

Wherever God the Father is, God the Spirit is also present. If God "abides" in us (1 John 4:13, 15), then certainly the Spirit abides in us. If Christ "lives" in us (Galatians 2:20), then certainly the Spirit lives in us. If the body of Christ is filled with the Spirit of Christ, then certainly it is filled with the Spirit of God.

The body of Christ is not made up of congregations, and certainly not of a variety of "faiths," man-made churches, or physical structures.[127] Rather, Christ's church is composed of individual believers: the Living God dwells within a living organism (the body of Christ), which is animated by a Living Spirit. As each member of Christ grows, is strengthened, and is inspired to do good works (cf. Ephesians 2:10), so the entire body grows, is strengthened, and is inspired. Just as Solomon's temple was constructed board by board, brick by brick, and stone by stone, so God's holy temple is built soul by soul. Each congregation serves as a microcosm of the entire body; just as the Spirit of God dwells in each identifiable group of believers (1 Corinthians 3:16), so the Spirit dwells in the entire group.

Once again, we would do well to appeal to Ephesians 2:19-22:

> So then you are no longer strangers and aliens, but you are fellow citizens with the saints, and are of God's household, having been built on the foundation of the apostles and prophets, Christ Jesus Himself being the corner stone, in whom the whole building, being fitted together, is growing into a holy temple in the Lord, in whom you also are being built together into a dwelling of God in the Spirit.

The context here most certainly deals with the entire body of believers and is in no way limited to a single congregation in Ephesus. Even though every Christian in the body of Christ participates individually by contributing his personal strengths, talents, and efforts, it is through the corporate body that we are all inseparably linked. In Christ, we have one fellowship: He is the One who makes such fellowship possible. This fellowship is sanctified and guarded by the Holy Spirit: He is the One who oversees the "building" process of the "holy temple." In the above passage, Paul uses three expressions to describe our relationship to the body of Christ—and each relationship is defined as being "in the Spirit":

❑ **"fellow citizens":** Christians are members of a heavenly community, a spiritual society, and an otherworldly kingdom that does not conform to the manner of this world. We are all "fellow heirs," "fellow members," and "fellow partakers" of the promises of God *in the Spirit* (compare Ephesians 1:13-14 with 3:6).

❑ **"God's household":** Christians are members of a heavenly *family*, which makes us all brothers and sisters ("brethren") in Christ. Earthly families are united by blood; God's spiritual family is united by His Spirit, which transcends all earthly ties.[128] Since we are all connected through our common faith in Christ, we regard one another with much greater distinction than mere participants in a religious organization (see, for example, Matthew 12:47-50 and 1 Timothy 5:1-2).

❑ **"holy temple":** Temples are intended to serve as meeting places between men and their gods. Likewise, the ancient tabernacle of God among the Israelites—and later, Solomon's temple that replaced this—served as a sanctuary for God among His people (Exodus 29:43-46). Now, the holy temple is no longer one that has been constructed by men, but by the Lord (Hebrews 8:1-2); it is no longer made of earthly elements, but is composed of "living stones" (1 Peter 2:4-5). Just as the Spirit of God filled the ancient tabernacle with the "cloud" of His presence (Exodus 40:34-35; see also 1 Kings 8:10-11), so now His Spirit fills the church with His presence. In a very real sense, the physical church serves as a sacred intersection between heaven and earth.

Thus, we see three different *kinds* of relationships: community, family, and priestly. The Holy Spirit is inseparably involved with each one of these. We are not fellow citizens apart from having been "sealed" by Him; we are not God's household apart from His indwelling of each of us; and we are not a holy temple apart from His having sanctified us for this very purpose.

Preserving the Unity of the Spirit

Since the Holy Spirit is so intimately involved with Christ's church, all those who are *in* this church have a moral responsibility to conduct themselves accordingly. No disciple of the Lord has a right to "walk" in whatever way he chooses, for in having *died* with the Master in baptism, he is to *walk* with the Master "in newness of life" (cf. Romans 6:4-7). This is not an imposition upon the Christian, but something that each of us has voluntarily chosen. "For this is the love of God, that we keep His commandments; and His commandments are not burdensome" (1 John 5:3). God, through His Spirit which *helps* us to keep these commandments, is not burdening us but is liberating us from an empty and useless life. Walking by the Spirit leads us to where we truly wish to go; we are unable to go there otherwise.

There are at least two passages in the New Testament that succinctly and beautifully characterize the kind of "mind" expected of those who are being led by the Spirit. The first of these is Philippians 2:1-5:

> Therefore if there is any encouragement in Christ, if there is any consolation of love, if there is any fellowship of the Spirit, if any affection and compassion, make my joy complete by being of the same mind, maintaining the same love, united in spirit, intent on one purpose. Do nothing from selfishness or empty conceit, but with humility of mind regard one another as more important than yourselves; do not merely look out for your own personal interests, but also for the interests of others. Have this attitude in yourselves which was also in Christ Jesus....

Those who have "fellowship of the Spirit" are not to have personal agendas, preferential love, contradictory attitudes, or a conflicting purpose. We are to be of "the same mind," which means we are to think, live, and treat one another as those trained by the same *Spirit*, for indeed that is what Christ expects of us. Being of the "same mind" does not allow man-made doctrines, sectarianism, or religious denominationalism to divide Christ's holy church: the Holy Spirit will *never* endorse such worldly, man-made impositions. Instead, we are to have the mind of Christ, which is in absolute agreement with the Spirit of God.

Certainly men can be united in spirit while still working against the Lord. Jesus spoke of those who were united amongst themselves, but antagonistic to Him (Matthew 7:22-23); those who murdered Stephen did so "with one impulse" (Acts 7:57); even demons can cooperate together for their sinister work (Matthew 12:45; Luke 8:30). We should not think that unity *alone* (i.e., amongst ourselves) is sufficient for being united with God's *Spirit*. The spirit of denominationalism begins with the assumption that we can be *united in God* in our *diversity of beliefs (or faiths)*. This "unity in diversity" concept will work if we are discussing different talents of believers being brought together for one purpose (as in Romans 12:4-8), but it is unworkable when applied to uniting opposing faiths or religions within one "body."

If we are united by God's Spirit, then we will be united with one another in the way that God desires. In fact, no other *kind* of unity is acceptable to Him. Furthermore, whoever purposely destroys this unity stands condemned by God and is to be avoided by us (1 Corinthians 3:17; Romans 16:17; Titus 3:10-11, et al). Just as God's Spirit is one, so we who belong to God are to be one *in* His Spirit.

This brings us to the second passage to which I referred earlier (Ephesians 4:1-6):

> Therefore I [Paul], the prisoner of the Lord, implore you to walk in a manner worthy of the calling with which you have been called, with all humility and gentleness, with patience, showing tolerance for one another in love, being diligent to preserve the unity of the Spirit in the bond of peace. There is one body and one Spirit, just as also you were called in one hope of your calling; one Lord, one faith, one baptism, one God and Father of all who is over all and through all and in all.

While many "walks" exist among men, there is only one "walk" that is worthy of our calling, just as there is only one "narrow way" that leads to life (Matthew 7:13-14). Christ *is* "the way" (John 14:6), and we are to walk according to Him (1 John 2:6), but it is the Spirit who guides us in this walk. Just as it is impossible to be united with God without being united by His Son, so it is impossible to be united as one church without being united by one Spirit. This "unity of the Spirit" will not be forced upon us; God will not twist our arms to obey Him. Rather, *we who are in the church* have the moral responsibility to "preserve" this unity amongst ourselves. (If we choose not to do this, then the Spirit will also withdraw His fellowship from us. He will not be party to division, rebellion, or indifference.)

This "unity of the Spirit" must manifest itself with certain visible characteristics: love, humility, gentleness, compassion, patience, tolerance, forgiveness, cooperation, selflessness, and whatever is like these virtues. These are the "fruit of the Spirit": we can only bear such "fruit" if we are united with God's Spirit. If we are controlled by a different spirit, then this will also be evident: we will not have these virtues.[129]

Likewise, our *teaching*—i.e., the doctrine upon which the Christian's beliefs are based—must also be "one" with the Spirit. Once again, religious error is the fruit of man-made teachings; "sound doctrine" can only come from God Himself, having been inspired and preserved by His Spirit (1 Timothy 4:6, 6:3-5; 2 Timothy 1:13-14; Titus 1:9; et al). It is impossible to claim "oneness" with God while advocating any doctrine which we *know* His Spirit has not authorized. We have the gospel given to us in full; it has been "once for all delivered" to us (Jude 3); we have no need for further "gospels." In fact, Paul has laid one of the most strongly-worded curses of the New Testament upon anyone who would tamper with what he was authorized by the Spirit to give (Galatians 1:8-9). On the other hand, if we maintain the "unity of the Spirit" *of* the gospel, then this will naturally produce an intelligent, consistent, and universally-applied doctrine by which every person may walk in fellowship with Christ. By submitting ourselves to this teaching, we act in our own best interests, we serve the greatest needs of others, and we "sanctify Christ as Lord" in our hearts (1 Peter 3:15). In other words, the Spirit's *one doctrine* is not meant to cause us trouble, but to save us from our own error.

The apostle Paul then emphasizes the unity of the Spirit by the unity of His teaching (Ephesians 4:4-6). There are not many churches of Christ, but one; there are not many paths to heaven, but one; etc. There is only ONE:

- ❑ Body of Christ—Christ died for only one church, and He built only one church.
- ❑ Spirit of God—just as you yourself have only one spirit.
- ❑ Hope of your calling—that in which the Spirit has called you through His gospel.
- ❑ Lord—one Savior of men, Jesus Christ.
- ❑ Faith—that which is based upon the teaching of the gospel that God has provided us.
- ❑ Baptism—that which is required of *us*, which is immersion in water.
- ❑ Father—just as we have only one earthly father, so there is only one spiritual Father who presides over all of His Creation.

These are seven distinct and critical teachings which all serve to "preserve the unity of the Spirit." Because we are all at different levels of maturity in our walk with Christ, we will also be at different levels of understanding concerning these facts. However, our *attitude* must be one which embraces whatever God's Word says is *true* (and denies whatever the Word says is *false*); this is what Christ expects of those who "walk in a manner worthy of the calling with which [we] have been called" (Ephesians 4:1). The revealed truths of God's gospel must become our own personal convictions. "This is good and acceptable in the sight of God our Savior, who desires all men to be saved and to come to the knowledge of the truth" (1 Timothy 2:3-4).

Summary Thoughts

Christ is unquestionably the head over His body; He is Lord over His church. The Spirit of God is the dynamic influence *of* that church, and always serves its best interest. There is no competition or interference between Christ and the Spirit, for they work together in seamless, flawless cooperation toward the same goal: the salvation of men to the glory of God the Father. We might understand this better by drawing on a familiar relationship: the elders and ministers of a given congregation. The elders' primary responsibility is the oversight of the "flock" (congregation); the preacher's primary responsibility is the accurate handling and proclamation of the Word. Nonetheless, these two parties must work together in cooperation, since both serve the same Lord and work toward the same over-arching objective. Sometimes the elders and ministers' efforts will overlap—since they all function as "shepherds" and "preachers," in a sense—without compromising their individual responsibilities. So it is with Christ and the Spirit: both have separate responsibilities, but work together in perfect unison. Christ oversees His church as its Chief Shepherd (1 Peter 2:25; 5:4) and the Spirit sees to the success of the Word (1 Peter 1:12); their work will necessarily overlap, since it is impossible to make either work exclusive of the other. Nonetheless, neither Christ nor the Spirit compromises His individual responsibility by collaborating with the other.

Christ and the Father are one (John 10:30); Christ and the Spirit are one (2 Corinthians 3:17); the believer and the Lord are one (1 Corinthians 6:17); and Christ's church is one with the Spirit of God (Ephesians 2:22). The church works in conjunction with the Spirit, but never apart from Him; indeed, the church is an unproductive, inert, inorganic concept except for the *life* and *energy* that the Spirit breathes into it. Everything the church does—in evangelism, edification, and benevolence—is overseen by the

Spirit according to the will of Christ. Even those who are outside of the church are being called (invited) by the Spirit through the gospel *and* whatever means He chooses to use. We do not have to know *how*; we only need to believe that He *does*.

If we are in Christ, then we have a moral responsibility to conduct ourselves rightly before God and each other. Just as Jesus always pleased the Father (John 8:29), so we should strive to do the same. The Spirit seeks this same objective, and thus leads us heavenward in ways which exceed our understanding but are nonetheless *real* and *effective*. Preserving the unity of the Spirit means to conform to the doctrine (teaching) of the Spirit, which has been revealed to us in the written gospel. By obediently honoring the doctrine of God, we honor the God of that doctrine, which always translates to grace and blessings to us.

Much more could be said on all of these sub-topics, but the intention here is not to go beyond what is necessary to establish the main topic— namely, that the Holy Spirit is most certainly at work in Christ's church. This is a matter of supreme importance for an accurate understanding of the cooperation of the Godhead, the definition of the church, and our moral responsibilities as Christians. All of these subjects directly *affect* our salvation and what we teach *concerning* salvation. Thankfully, these are matters of great interest to *you*; would that these could be of great interest to Christians everywhere.

Chapter Ten
Miracles and the Holy Spirit

After it was at the first spoken through the Lord, it was confirmed to us by those who heard, God also testifying with them, both by signs and wonders and by various miracles and by gifts of the Holy Spirit according to His own will. Hebrews 2:3-4

It is now necessary to turn our attention to a subject that we have so far only mentioned in passing: the belief among many people—Christians and non-Christians alike—that God is still performing miracles in the world today.[130] Among Christians in particular, this refers to the belief that the Holy Spirit continues to perform miracles as a means of providing credibility to the ministry, preaching, and authority of those who promote His Word.

Ten Premises

The persistence of miracles is popularly supported not only among charismatic groups who passionately defend it, but many other traditional religious groups as well. Not everyone who believes in miracles, however, is on the same page: some believe that the gospel is propagated through the use of miracles; others believe that God performs miracles only when He deems necessary, but that the power of the gospel is sufficient otherwise. Where these beliefs generally agree is detailed in the following ten premises:

1) Since the early church performed miracles by the power of the Holy Spirit, therefore the modern church should be able to do so as well.
2) Since God *has* performed miracles in the past and is *expected* to perform miracles in the future (i.e., the resurrection of the dead; 1 Thessalonians 4:13-18), therefore it stands to reason that He is *presently* performing them as well.
3) The Holy Spirit has chosen miracles as His means of manifesting Himself to the church; there is no reason to think that He would discontinue this practice today.
4) Since the Spirit manifests Himself through miracles, therefore

the absence of miracles would necessarily imply the absence of the Holy Spirit.

5) The power to perform miracles is always given directly by the Holy Spirit, and therefore is not dependent upon any man or group of men to transfer it from one person to another.

6) Denying the (contemporary) miracles of God is tantamount to denying the *ability* of God, since the two must be evidenced simultaneously.

7) Any contemporary preaching that is unaccompanied by miracles lacks authority, authenticity, and (thus) credibility; therefore, it cannot be "the truth." (Not everyone who believes in modern miracles will agree entirely with this statement, however.)

8) Miracles are God's way of getting people's attention and drawing them into fellowship with Him; the mere preaching of the gospel is not always sufficient or is altogether insufficient for this.

9) The gospel of Christ needs to be regularly updated to accommodate a changing world that is considerably different (and more advanced) than the world of the early church. This is accomplished through contemporary revelations of the Spirit. (Again, not everyone who believes in miracles will agree entirely with this statement.)

10) There is no conflict between contemporary revelations of the Spirit and those given to the ancient church, since the same Spirit authorizes and provides both.

Some of these premises are based upon honest misunderstandings of what the New Testament teaches concerning both miracles and the work of the Spirit. However, it is here proposed that none of the above premises are actually supported by Scripture. At the same time, it is also admitted that perhaps *no* amount of explaining, discussing, or biblical citations may convince every person of this. This subject is as emotionally-charged (on both sides) as it is theologically-debated; therefore, it is not an easy one for any of us to approach with detached objectivity. Some of the arguments used to support *or* deny modern miracles are based upon necessary inferences and not "Thus says the Lord" citations. Not everyone understands this kind of reasoning, and even those who do are not always convinced of it—especially when the conclusions run counter to what they already believe to be true.

This does *not* mean that the Christian fellowship of every person who holds to any of the above premises, however, is immediately questionable. Nowhere in the New Testament does it state that our fellowship with God is wholly dependent upon our "position" on modern-day miracles. Indeed, some may have accepted these premises as matters of fact without having even thought to investigate them. Others may have put a great deal of trust in their preachers and church leaders concerning these matters, and do not feel adequate to question such men. Regardless, our present discussion involves what the Bible teaches *and* the conclusions drawn from these teachings, not a blanket judgment against any given person(s).

On the other hand, *every* Christian has a moral responsibility to base his or her beliefs on *God's truth* and not simply someone else's (or a church's) version of it. I know from personal experience that it takes much time and effort to become familiar with the Bible, and subjects like the Holy Spirit are particularly involved and demanding. Yet the Word of God has been revealed so that we would "read and understand" (cf. 2 Corinthians 1:13), not so that others could tell us what to believe.

"Miracle" Defined

The discussion of miracles requires the definition of one. The word "miracle" in the New Testament is from *dunamis*, from which we get "dynamic"; it means power, strength, force, or work. The context defines such "works" as being of supernatural origin or power, as in Mark 6:2 or Acts 2:22. A "sign" (*semeion*) is an indication or token of something; it describes miraculous action when the context demands this (as in Mark 8:11 or John 6:2). "Wonder" (*teras*) refers to something that inspires awe, dread, or terror. Thus, miracles refer to supernatural works themselves; signs indicate (or signify) the source of such power; and wonders appeal to the human imagination, provoking deep respect and even fear. Sometimes these are used together (as in Acts 5:12 or 2 Corinthians 12:12) to convey the full impact of God's presence in the natural world.[131]

A miracle is, by necessary implication, an event or activity that supersedes the physical laws or abilities of nature. A miracle describes an action that is not just unlikely, rare, or phenomenal, but is *impossible* in the context of the physical universe. A miracle cannot merely defy our personal expectations; it must defy the human and natural limitations of our world. "A miracle is by definition an exception" and not the rule; it is a temporary suspension of the rules.[132] A miracle changes (or interrupts) the natural world for the duration of the event, but it does not permanently alter the laws of nature. Just because God parted the Red Sea for Israel (Exodus 14) does not mean that from now on we should expect seas to part in order for us to cross them. What God did in that instance was interrupt the system of nature; He did not impose upon it any lasting change.

That which is breathtaking or fortunate is not necessarily miraculous. Anyone who has witnessed the birth of a child, for example, would be inclined to use the word "miraculous" to describe the experience, but childbirth is a rather natural, ordinary, and fixed part of human life. Even childbirth under difficult or life-threatening conditions is not miraculous. (A woman giving birth to a child without having been impregnated by a man, however, *is* miraculous, since it is beyond all *natural* means; Matthew 1:18-25). In another example, if someone loses control of his car and would have driven off a cliff had it not been for a large tree that he hit instead, it is not a miracle that the tree was there. Trees are a natural part of this world; they can grow just about anywhere. It is extremely *fortunate* that a person's car hit a tree rather than disappear over a cliff, but it is not miraculous. (Now, if that tree had not *been* there a moment before, but then suddenly appeared—*that* would have been miraculous!)

That which is unexplainable is not necessarily miraculous. For example, we do not know all there is about the human body's ability to fight cancer; when someone's cancerous tumor disappears over time, it is presumptuous to think that a miracle had to have occurred. If a cancer is said to be incurable, and yet the body cures it on its own, then "incurable" is an incorrect diagnosis and "miracle" is unwarranted. It is certainly *rare* and *fortunate* when this happens, but it does happen, and we cannot automatically assume supernatural intervention when it does. Similarly, just because a person survives a lightning strike, a fall from a high place, being trapped in an underground mine for days, or any other hostile, life-threatening situation, does not mean a miracle has occurred. We are prone to exclaim, "It's a miracle!" when these things happen—and indeed, these are profound situations—but to insist that such people have been spared *supernaturally* is to deny what is actually naturally possible. In a modern example, on January 15, 2009, US Airways Flight 1549 made an emergency landing on the Hudson River in New York without a single fatality. This incident has been dubbed "the miracle landing" by the media, and many agree with this. But commercial jets are designed to make water landings; the emergency procedures for such landings are designed to save human lives. In other words, it is not a miracle when what was *expected* to happen actually happened.

On the other hand, Jesus performed genuine, bona fide miracles: He did things that were impossible to happen, not just unlikely or inexplicable. Walking on water, for example, is not just a rare event, but it is an *impossible* event, given the natural laws of physics and human abilities. So is instantaneously healing a man born deaf, blind, or lame; sufficiently feeding 5,000 men with a few loaves of bread and a couple of fish; or raising oneself from the dead. Such things simply cannot happen apart from external, supernatural intervention. This is why Jesus pointed to His miracles as proof positive of His divine nature:

❑ Matthew 11:2-6, Jesus told John the Baptist's disciples to tell John of the miracles they witnessed as proof that He was "the Expected One" (i.e., the Messiah).

❑ John 3:2, Nicodemus rightly observed that "no one can do these signs that You do unless God is with him"—in other words, Jesus' works were not of men, but divine origin.

❑ John 5:36, Jesus declared that "the works which the Father has given Me to accomplish—the very works that I do—testify about Me, that the Father has sent Me."

❑ John 10:37-38, Jesus admitted that His own testimony *by itself* was insufficient to prove that He was the Son of God; but the works He performed served as irrefutable proof of this.

We could cite a number of other passages, but the point is this: Jesus performed miracles indeed, works that were impossible by any other explanation. He did not use sleight-of-hand, strategically-placed props, or financially-lucrative "miracle crusades" to do these. When He healed people, He did not employ a troop of stage hands to weed out those with obvious deformities or truly incurable situations, like "faith healers" commonly do today. Jesus was not making what He did *look* real, but it *was* real—and impossible, if not for the Spirit of God working in Him.

Even after Jesus' ascension, the apostles—and later, others as well—performed miracles in the midst of the people. When the apostles spoke in tongues, for example, they spoke in known, recognizable, interpretable languages; they did not babble incoherently and then claim that this was an angelic language.[133] These actions confounded even the harshest critics. With regard to one particular event, even the Jewish leaders who jailed the apostles admitted, "…The fact that a noteworthy miracle has taken place through them is apparent to all who live in Jerusalem, and we cannot deny it" (Acts 4:16). Peter declared that it was not by his own power that this was accomplished, but that this had been done "on the basis of faith in His [Jesus'] name" (Acts 3:16). It was by the Holy Spirit's power, according to Jesus' authority, that these works were performed.

Once again, *power* is the hallmark of the Holy Spirit's work among Christians and in Christ's church generally. It is impossible for us to exceed our human limitations; likewise, we are unable to overcome the natural laws that have been imposed upon us. But the Spirit has no such limitations, and He (as God) is above all man-made or physical laws. If it is true that the Spirit is no longer performing such visible works *among* Christians, this does not mean that He has lost all such power to work *within* Christians. One is a visible, event-oriented work in the world; the other is an invisible and spiritual process in the heart. The Spirit is still *capable* of performing both; but it is only *necessary* that He works on the heart rather than continue to produce signs and wonders in the world.

The Purpose of Miracles

Any serious Bible student realizes that God does not do *anything* without deliberate intent and purpose. In God's world, there are no such things as accidents, coincidences, happenstance, or luck. From creating the world to establishing Christ's church to ushering in the end of time, God's work is methodical, systematic, purposeful, and completely logical. Everything He does works toward a known and ideal objective; He does not deter from this. His Word always fulfills His will (Isaiah 55:10-11); His will always seeks the ultimate good of all parties involved (James 1:17), and especially of those who believe in Him (Romans 8:28).

Since this is true, it stands to reason that miracles were performed— by the prophets, Jesus Christ, the apostles, and the early church—for a specific purpose. To say that these were just random, spontaneous works of God defies the very *nature* of God, for He is neither random nor spontaneous. To say that these were done *without* a clear purpose or intention also denies God's nature, for He is a God of clear purpose and intention.

In the case of Israel, God performed many miracles through His servant Moses. He carried out the ten plagues against Egypt, safely liberated

Israel from "the iron furnace" (Deuteronomy 4:20), and supernaturally provided for them for forty years in the wilderness. This latter provision included daily manna, water (as needed), and the preservation of their shoes and clothing (cf. Exodus 17:6; Deuteronomy 8:2-4). Besides all this, God manifested Himself as a cloud above the tent of meeting by day and a pillar of fire by night (Exodus 40:36-38).

God did not supernaturally provide for Israel perpetually, however; it is apparent that this was never His intent. In fact, as they neared the end of their forty year wandering and anticipated their entrance into Canaan, God informed them that things were going to change. Once in the Promised Land, the Israelites would eat the food of the land (instead of manna) and would have to dig their own wells for water (cf. Deuteronomy 8:7-9; Joshua 5:12). The *purpose* of God's having wrought miracles among Israel was to prove that He was Jehovah God, the Keeper of the covenant originally made with their fathers Abraham, Isaac, and Jacob (Exodus 6:2-8). Once this was established—once God had sufficiently and irrefutably proven His power among the people—it was unnecessary to continue doing this. In fact, after Israel came into Canaan, God did not repeat or re-enact these miracles, but simply called their attention to what had already been done. Israel was supposed to *remember* these things as an act of faith, for faith is all about things that are unseen and hoped for, not things that are seen in fact (cf. Hebrews 11:1-2). As it was, Israel did not remember the miracles of God, and thus was judged to be unfaithful: in the absence of actual miracles, the people simply would not believe.[134] Later (in the time of Christ), their hearts had become so hardened that even in the *presence* of such miracles, many refused to believe.

Someone says, "Yes, but God *did* perform miracles after Israel came into the Promised Land." There is no denying this, and this is where the analogy between the era of ancient Israel and the era of the church breaks down. In the Old Testament era, Israel's Messiah had not yet come; His "once for all" work had not yet been accomplished; therefore, a point-for-point comparison will not work. For example, God once "overlooked the times of ignorance"—"times" prior to a complete and universal gospel—yet He does this no more (Acts 17:30-31; see also Ephesians 3:1-12). Likewise, the fact that God performed unprecedented signs through His prophets after the Law was revealed (think of Elijah, for example) does not mean that He will (or even needs to) raise up modern-day prophets to perform contemporary signs for us. The inauguration of the nation of Israel *is* comparable to the inauguration of Christ's church;

but whatever God did for Israel thereafter *is not* necessarily comparable to what God does for Christians today. God responded to Israel's situations as needed—sometimes with visible miracles—because He promised them that He would (Deuteronomy 28:1-14, et al). Yet He gives no promise to us that He will respond to *our* situations with these same kinds of works.[135]

The point here is this: God is certainly capable of taking care of His people without performing visible, event-oriented miracles. He *begins* this process with miracles to prove this fact; after this is established, He expects His people to *remember* what He has done in the past. Appropriately, then, the establishment of the covenant with Israel was surrounded with miracles, signs, and wonders; this was necessary in order to convince Israel that God was completely able to fulfill His part of that covenant. Likewise, the inauguration of the *new* covenant (i.e., the gospel of Christ) was surrounded by miracles and wonders. Such works were never intended to be a permanent fixture of the church, but were to convince men—Israelites and Gentiles alike—that Jesus Christ saves by the power of God, having overcome every obstacle *to* salvation. Once this fact had been confirmed, it was unnecessary to continue confirming it perpetually. We cannot believe in what is *unseen* until it is evidenced sufficiently through what is *seen*. Miracles provided this evidence: if God can perform supernatural work upon the earth (i.e., in the human domain), then certainly He is capable of performing supernatural work upon the human soul (i.e., in the spiritual domain). The miracles of Christ and the apostles provided visible confirmation of Christ's authority *and* the work of the Spirit in the church (bracketed words are mine):

- ❑ (Matthew 12:28) "…If I [Jesus] cast out demons by the Spirit of God, then the kingdom of God has come upon you."[136]
- ❑ (Luke 4:36) "And amazement came upon them all, and they began talking with one another saying, 'What is this message? For with authority and power He [Jesus] commands the unclean spirits and they come out.'"
- ❑ (Mark 16:20) "And they went out and preached everywhere, while the Lord worked with them, and confirmed the word by the signs that followed."
- ❑ (John 7:31) "But many of the crowd believed in Him; and they were saying, 'When the Christ comes, He will not perform more signs than those which this man has, will He?'"
- ❑ (John 20:30-31) "Therefore many other signs Jesus also performed in the presence of the disciples, which are not written in this book;

but these have been written so that you may believe that Jesus is the Christ, the Son of God; and that believing you may have life in His name."

❑ (Acts 1:3) "To these [apostles] He also presented Himself alive after His suffering, by many convincing proofs, appearing to them over a period of forty days and speaking of the things concerning the kingdom of God."

❑ (Acts 2:22-24) "Men of Israel, listen to these words: Jesus the Nazarene, a man attested to you by God with miracles and wonders and signs which God performed through Him in your midst, just as you yourselves know—this Man, delivered over by the predetermined plan and foreknowledge of God, you nailed to a cross by the hands of godless men and put Him to death. But God raised Him up again…."

❑ (2 Corinthians 12:12) "The signs of a true apostle were performed among you with all perseverance, by signs and wonders and miracles."

❑ (Galatians 3:5) "So then, does He who provides you with the Spirit and works miracles among you, do it by the works of the Law, or by hearing with faith?"

❑ (Hebrews 2:3-4) "After it [the gospel] was at the first spoken through the Lord, it was confirmed to us by those who heard, God also testifying with them, both by signs and wonders and by various miracles and by gifts of the Holy Spirit according to His own will."

Once the gospel was confirmed as "good news" which had come from God, it was no longer necessary to keep confirming this. From that point on, "we walk by faith, not by sight" (2 Corinthians 5:7), no longer having to physically *see* all that the Spirit had done at first, but believing it nonetheless because of the New Testament record He has preserved for us. (Remember what Jesus said to Thomas [John 20:29]: "Blessed are they who did not see, and yet believed.") Jesus is under no obligation to perform again all the miracles He wrought in Israel just so that we can believe. It is enough that they were *once* performed, and that we have a credible record of them that has been substantiated by many witnesses. Likewise, the Holy Spirit is under no obligation to continue to work miracles among the church; it is enough that He *once* did this, and that we have a credible, substantiated record of it.

The *purpose* for miracles has been fulfilled: It has been proved that Christ has the power of God *and* that the Holy Spirit has been given to all those who believe in Christ. "All the extraordinary gifts of the Spirit must cease with their necessity, and the necessity for them ceases when the object for which they were given is attained."[137] Just as God expects us to believe He is the Creator "by faith" (Hebrews 11:3), so we are to believe that we are a "new creation" in Christ by faith (2 Corinthians 5:17). The work of the Spirit upon the human soul is indeed miraculous; but we do not need a visible miracle to confirm this. The fact has already been confirmed; to expect further confirmation is pointlessly redundant and implies doubt, not faith.[138]

Miracles, while being profound and supernatural works in themselves, are still limited in duration. They are also limited in what they are able to accomplish. For example, miracles were never intended to remove all of the world's problems. It is clear that Jesus healed many people while He was here on earth (Matthew 4:23-24), but when He ascended into heaven, He left behind a world still filled with hunger, sickness, disease, deafness, and blindness. He had the *power* to eradicate all of these from the world, but this was never His purpose. Even today, the wiping out of man's physical problems would still not necessarily turn more hearts to God, no more than did God's miracles fully convict the heart of every ancient Israelite.

The purpose of miracles was never to reduce the amount of friction and conflict between believers and unbelievers. Even though Christ performed many miracles—and His strongest critics could not deny this (cf. John 11:45-47)—His own countrymen still charged Him with blasphemy and crucified Him. Even th ough the apostles later performed irrefutable miracles, the powers-that-be still persecuted them, even to the point of martyrdom. We should not think that if God *did* perform signs among us today, then the world would be any kinder toward Christians. In fact, it might have just the opposite effect.

The purpose of miracles was never to *replace* the gospel message but only to accompany it. It is through the miraculous work (grace) of God that we are saved; but we are not saved by miracles. There is no record in the New Testament of anyone being saved *by* a visible miracle, but miracles only led people to the *source* of salvation (as in Acts 5:14-16; 8:6-12; 13:12; 19:11-12; and 19:18-20). Even with all the miracles performed by Christ and His apostles, many witnesses of these still did not believe in Him (John 12:37).[139] Jesus admitted in His account of the rich man and Lazarus that some men will not believe even if God raises someone from the dead (Luke 16:30-31). Indeed, Jesus raised *Himself* from the dead, and proportionately few people in the world today listen to Him.

The purpose of miracles was never to take the place of the work of the individual Christian or the collective church. We can (and must) defer to the written record of miracles in the Bible to support the authenticity of the gospel message. However, we still must preach this message ourselves; miracles cannot do for us that which we have been commissioned to do (cf. Matthew 28:19). Likewise, one's spiritual growth, maturity, and fellowship with God could never be improved by the working of a visible miracle, but only by his diligent effort toward his own faith (cf. 2 Peter 1:5-11). Most certainly the Holy Spirit makes our growth possible, just as He makes our salvation possible, but this is accomplished *through* our own initiative and commitment, not apart from these.

Thus the purpose of miracles is *not* to: be a permanent visible feature of the church; remove the problems of this world or the physical human condition; remove the conflict between good and evil; replace the gospel; replace our individual or collective efforts *in* the gospel. The purpose of miracles, according to the revelation of the Spirit Himself, is to confirm the authority, authenticity, and power of the gospel message (Mark 16:20; Hebrews 2:4). We have the gospel message in full (cf. Galatians 1:8; Colossians 1:23; Jude 3, et al); this gospel has been proved genuine by the miracles that accompanied its deliverance to us. If miracles still *needed* to be performed in order to substantiate the gospel, then this would necessarily imply that we do not *have* the full gospel, even though the gospel itself says otherwise.[140] This would call into question the integrity and finality of the gospel: Maybe we do not have the final draft?[141] Perhaps what we *thought* was true about Christ's work, the ministry of the Spirit, and the doctrine of salvation really has yet to be clearly defined? How can we know anything of the Spirit's words for certain? Or perhaps the Spirit did not think that those first miracles were convincing enough, and that He must continue to amaze men with others?

This does not make sense, and contradicts the nature of God as depicted in the Bible record. Furthermore, if the Holy Spirit must keep proving over and over what has already been established, what does this say about the credibility of the original message? For example, suppose I tell you some profound yet allegedly true fact about myself, and I come back to you at every opportunity and say, "But it's true! But it's true! But it's true!" You would not be *more* convinced that what I said was true, but it would not take long for you to begin to *doubt* it altogether. It would seem that I have something to hide that would render my message *un*-true. I would cast suspicion, not reinforce credibility. So it would be with the Spirit if He had to continue "convincing" us of His gospel after having already revealed it. His actions would inspire doubt, not faith; we would wonder of what He does *not* want us to know rather than what He has made known.

As it is, the task of proving the gospel has already been accomplished; the purpose of miracles has been fulfilled; it is unnecessary to go on "completing" a completed work. To expect anything further is to read into Scripture that which simply isn't there, and to assume something that the Spirit never promised. The Spirit has said what is true; now it is up to each one of us to either believe it or not.

In 1 Corinthians 13:8-10, Paul wrote:

> Love never fails; but if there are gifts of prophecy, they will be done away; if there are tongues, they will cease; if there is knowledge, it will be done away. For we know in part and we prophesy in part; but when the perfect comes, the partial will be done away.

This is a significant passage, especially since it is in the midst of a discussion on spiritual (miraculous) gifts. The Corinthians desired certain gifts over others, and showed preference to those who had such gifts. Paul then declared that *everyone* has one "gift" which excels above all others: the gift of love. Everyone can practice godly love; it is a timeless, boundless, unhindered gift that will *never* be "done away." However, miraculous gifts (of prophecy, tongues, supernatural knowledge, etc.) *will* be "done away." These gifts are "the partial"; they were never meant to last forever. These spiritual gifts had a specific purpose, and once that purpose was fulfilled, then they were no longer needed. At what *time* did this happen? Paul already stated this: "when the perfect comes." This serves as a universal principle which includes the present subject but is not limited to it. Everything among men begins with an immature stage; once maturity is reached, then the immature stage is gone forever.[142] Thus, when Paul was a child, he acted like a child; but when he became a man, he "did away with childish things" (1 Corinthians 13:11). Likewise, consider the construction of a building: while the structure is being built, its scaffolding remains; once the structure is complete, the scaffolding is permanently removed. It is not as though the scaffolding was unimportant, for it served a critical purpose. But no one leaves the scaffolding up once the building is complete; the *building itself* was the real objective, not the scaffolding.

So it is with the miraculous gifts of the early church. While the church was in its infancy—a "child," so to speak—it was necessary for the Spirit to provide it with the miraculous tools necessary to bring about its maturity. These miracles supplemented doctrines and instructions in the absence of the finished gospel. Once the gospel was fully revealed and permanently recorded, however—in essence, once "the perfect" had come—these tools were no longer necessary.[143] We (the church) have grown past the need for visible signs; now we walk by faith, and live according to the "hope of righteousness" through the Spirit (Galatians 5:5). To claim that the church still needs "signs" to support its message is to say that it has never matured past infancy, that it is still a child and not a "mature man" (cf. Ephesians 4:13), that it is still only "partial" and not a fully-formed, completed organism. This is not only unflattering, it defies all natural and spiritual expectations of the body of Christ. In effect, it is a great insult against Christ *and* the Holy Spirit.

We are speaking, of course, only of *miraculous* gifts. The *non*-miraculous gifts of the church still remain: teaching, ministering, hospitality, pastoral work, evangelism, exhortation, giving, compassion, mercy, faith, and so on.[144] These are the virtues of a mature church; they are the characteristics of a finished building, so to speak. The scaffolding which was necessary to construct a church capable of such gifts has served its purpose; it has since been taken down. To leave it standing would offer no useful function; in a very real sense, it would be a hindrance and a distraction to the real mission of the church.

The Transference of Miraculous Ability

A further insuperable condition that prevents men from performing miracles in the church today is the manner by which such ability was transferred. In the church's beginning, it was only through the apostles themselves that miracles were performed. These were the ones to whom Jesus promised such "power" (Acts 1:5-8). When this power was first manifested (Acts 2:1-4), it was not given to the entire "hundred and twenty persons" that regularly gathered in the "upper room" (Acts 1:15), but to the twelve chosen apostles. Not only is this grammatically accurate in the text,[145] but it also makes sense: Christ chose *twelve men* to oversee the gospel's deliverance to Israel. When one of these original twelve (Judas) "turned aside to go to his own place" (1:25), then He replaced him with another (Matthias). These twelve representatives of Christ—twelve signifying a heavenly perspective of an earthly assembly[146]—brought the gospel *first* to the twelve tribes of Israel. We must remember that the "kingdom of God" was originally the fulfillment of God's promise to Israel; thus it was essential that they received an invitation into the kingdom before Gentiles (cf. Matthew 10:5-6; Romans 1:16). It was only after this was accomplished that the apostles (and the church) turned their energies to proclaiming the gospel to Gentiles.

The point is this: the ability to perform miracles was not automatically or indiscriminately given to all believers. It *is* true that the Spirit would be "poured out" upon *all* believers, regardless of status, gender, or nationality (Acts 2:17-18); it was *not* true that this would be accomplished without due process. The church itself did not choose this process, nor did the apostles, but it was the Holy Spirit who provided the manner in which the ability to exercise miracles was given: the laying on of the apostles' hands.

As was said, the apostles alone performed miracles at first. After they laid their hands upon others, then those people could do the same (Acts 6:5-6, 8). Philip, one of those on whom the apostles had laid their hands, took the gospel into Samaria and supported that message through the exercising of miracles. Many of these people were baptized into Christ—that is, they had become *Christians*—yet they were still in need of the Spirit's visible power, and Philip was unable to confer this upon them. Thus, Peter and John were dispatched to Samaria to lay their hands upon them so that they, too, could exercise miracles to accompany this newly-delivered gospel (Acts 8:4-17). Likewise, Saul also, after being converted, received the Spirit in this same way: through the laying on of the apostles' hands when he visited Jerusalem.[147] After Saul (Paul) was ordained *as* an apostle[148] then he also was able to impart the ability to perform miracles to others by the laying on of his own hands (Acts 19:6; 2 Timothy 1:6).

As discussed before, the case of the apostles on Pentecost (Acts 2) and that of Cornelius (Acts 10) are the only two occasions after Christ's ascension where the Spirit imparted miraculous ability other than through the laying on of hands. There was a valid and specific *purpose* for this; these were most special events. Before the Spirit could minister among the two groups (Jews and Gentiles, respectively), He personally had to *invite* them into fellowship; He needed to identify them as acceptable candidates for entrance into the kingdom of God. There are no other such instances; the Spirit did not need to keep approving these two groups; what was done was done once for all. Thus, for someone today to use this argument ("The Spirit came upon so-and-so today in the same way that He did the apostles on Pentecost!") would indicate a gross misunderstanding of the *purpose* and *distinctiveness* of those two events. Furthermore, since the Spirit acted on His own in these two occasions, these cannot be cited as a precedent for the *transference* of miraculous power, for indeed the Spirit is the *source* of such power, and not merely a conveyer of it.[149]

So then, the only means of transference for the power to perform miracles from man to man is through the laying on of the apostles' hands. This begs the question, "Are there genuine apostles today?" If the answer is yes, then one could make a logical argument for this transference of power and thus for miracles themselves. If the answer is no, then to argue in favor of men performing modern miracles is a pointless exercise.

"Apostle" has two uses in the New Testament. The first is a generic one which refers to "one (who is) sent" to fulfill a certain work or mission. The word (*apostolos*) implies both *conveyance* (of something) and *representation* (of someone). Thus, an apostle is generally one who conveys a message provided by the one whom he also represents. We can see this generic usage in such passages as Luke 11:49; John 13:16 ("one... sent"), Acts 14:14; 2 Corinthians 8:23 ("messengers"); and Philippians 2:25 ("messenger").

The other sense in the New Testament is that of an *office*, for which one is "called" and "set apart" (Romans 1:1). This does not describe only what certain men *did* (in conveying and representing), but also the authority which such men *possessed*. These men collectively are known as "the" apostles, designating a specific group of hand-picked ambassadors (Matthew 10:2-4). When Judas abandoned this calling, he was replaced by another whom the Lord Himself also selected (Acts 1:23-26).

The apostles of Christ—all hand-picked, God-appointed men— were led directly by the Holy Spirit to carry out their responsibilities

(John 14:26). This did not make them infallible (as Galatians 2:11-13 indicates), but it gave them the ability to speak and act in the *name* of Jesus Christ (Acts 3:6; 16:18; 1 Corinthians 1:10; 5:4, et al). This is why Paul often referred to himself as an apostle rather than only as a minister or evangelist: he taught, rebuked, and rendered decisions with the authority of God, since he was chosen by Christ *and* directed by God's Spirit.

Christ chose His own apostles; no man could nominate or declare himself to be an apostle otherwise. We have no record of men making other men apostles equal to those whom Christ chose. This appointment was understood to be permanent, unless the man "turned aside" to something else. (We have only the case of Judas to draw upon here; since he took his own life, it is impossible to speculate how he would have been dealt with if he had continued to live.) The original twelve apostles were personally selected by Christ out of all the many disciples who followed Him (Luke 6:13-16). After this, only Matthias and Paul were added to this unique and distinguished group. Matthias was added to complete the "twelve" just prior to their unveiling of the gospel of Christ to the Jews. Paul was added as an ideal ambassador to the Gentiles (Acts 9:15-16; Romans 15:15-16). These men all had the same *authority*, even though one could well argue that both Peter and Paul had certain *responsibilities* that differed from the others. Nonetheless, "the signs of a true apostle" must be confirmed "by signs and wonders and miracles" (2 Corinthians 12:12).

The choosing of Matthias shows the unique criteria required for apostolic succession. The candidate had to have accompanied Jesus' earthly ministry from His baptism to His ascension; of necessity, then, he had to be a physical witness of His resurrection. Obviously, no such candidate is possible today (Acts 1:21-23). (Even though Paul did not historically meet all these requirements, it is entirely possible that he "saw" these things through the revelations provided to him during his long absence from the chronicles of the New Testament [Galatians 1:11-12]. Regardless, Christ selected him by His own sovereign authority, which supersedes any selection process that would require human involvement.)

When these apostles died (as in Acts 12:2), they were not replaced: we have no *record* of this; there was no *need* for this; and thus we have no authority to *impose* such a replacement. These apostles joined "the prophets" in providing the doctrinal authority and miraculous proof for the foundation of the gospel (Ephesians 2:20, 3:5; 2 Peter 3:1-2). Just as the church needs only one cornerstone—Jesus Christ (1 Peter 2:6), so it needs only one foundation. This foundation has been once for all established; it needs no further additions or embellishments. If we *do* need a continual succession of apostles, it would only imply that this foundation has *not* been established, which would call into question the salvation of every Christian.

Thus the church's apostles have died out and their office has not been succeeded by anyone else. We have no reason or authority to appoint any apostles to replace them, and yet their legacy is extended to us in the written gospel of Christ. The Holy Spirit does not *need* apostles today, since He works through the established church differently than what was needed when it was still in the *process* of being established. Since there are no apostles today, there is no more laying on of the apostles' hands. And since this laying on of hands is impossible, it is also impossible to have the power to perform miracles transferred from one person to the next.

This also means that the *only* means by which God would perform a miracle today would be through the Spirit's own divine decision—one which we cannot assume into existence or demand through adjuration. In other words, if the Holy Spirit chooses to work a visible miracle among men today, He is certainly *capable* of doing so. But He will *not* do so unless there is sufficient reason for this, and He has not revealed to us such a reason. We have the gospel of Christ; if men will not listen to the gospel, then neither will they be persuaded if the Spirit performed a miracle for them. To *bring* God's revelation to man did require miracles; but "it requires no miracle to preach it now, or to believe and obey it."[150]

Summary Thoughts

Once again, a miracle is not something spectacular that we *want* to happen or think *has* happened. It is something that is *impossible* to happen apart from supernatural intervention. The modern "faith healer" relies upon sleight of hand, a cast of stagehands, and other performers to rig the setting of his "miracles"—not to mention the emotional susceptibility of his audience.[151] He *never* produces a visible miracle which can be verified in any definite or incontestable sense; his "miracles" are nothing more than one's subjective interpretation of whatever it is that just happened. (For example, the power of persuasion can affect *eventual* changes in the human body's fight against sickness and disease, but not *naturally impossible* ones.) If these statements are not true, then it would only require that the "faith healer" produce miracles on par with what Christ and the apostles produced to refute them.

The *purpose* of miracles is to provide a convincing testimony for the power of God among men. This is absolutely necessary if God wishes fallen human beings to believe in His power to save them from ruin. Once this testimony has been substantiated, it is no longer necessary to continue reinforcing it; in fact, it is counterproductive to do so. Just as Jesus is not required to re-enact His crucifixion for every generation in order for us to believe in Him, so the Spirit does not have to reproduce all the miracles of the first century. The entire concept of "faith" is rendered useless if we insist on *seeing* everything first. Having faith in God means that He does not literally have to *show* you and me what He does before we can *believe* in Him.

Except for two necessary events in which the Spirit performed miracles through men specially, the only means of transferring this power is through the laying on of the apostles' hands. Since there is no continuous succession of the apostolic office, there are no such apostles today; thus, there can be no laying on of hands for this purpose. This is very clear and straightforward in the gospel, and we cannot invent offices or impose human authority to have it otherwise.

If there *are* miracles being performed among men today, then this should be undeniably evident to us; "Miracles are the subject for demonstration, not just argumentation."[152] As it is, "there is nothing in Scripture, reason, or experience to prove that speaking in tongues is for today"[153]—or any other kind of visible, demonstrable miracle as recorded in the New Testament. This is one of the strongest arguments against miraculous events today: we simply do not see them. This is not to say that God will not or cannot perform them; rather, it *is* to say that what are *claimed* as miracles are not convincing, which is nothing like the genuine miracles recorded in the New Testament. The Holy Spirit never hid the effects of His power in obscurity, nor did He ever use His power as an opportunity to generate revenue for the church.

Of course, not everyone who believes in modern miracles supports the claims of the modern "faith healer." Some people—Christians and non-Christians alike—simply *want* to believe that God still performs miracles today, but have not necessarily considered the implications of this belief. Others may remain unconvinced of the arguments put forward above—

and that is their choice. Again, this subject has been discussed because it bears directly upon the work of the Holy Spirit, and not to serve as a "test of fellowship" with Christ. This is not to say that one's understanding of this subject is harmless or unimportant; it only means that one's salvation does not hinge upon this subject alone.

In any case, it remains the individual Christian's responsibility to know the truth, handle it accurately (cf. 2 Timothy 2:15), and not fall prey to the deceptions of men (Romans 16:17; 1 Timothy 6:3-5). The truth will not only set us free from such deceptions, but will also usher us into deeper, more fulfilling, and profitable fellowship with God through His Holy Spirit.

Chapter Eleven
Do Not Quench the Spirit

*Do not quench the Spirit; do not despise prophetic utterances. But
examine everything carefully; hold fast to that which is good; abstain
from every form of evil.*   1 Thessalonians 5:19-22

Many of us are probably familiar with what is known as "Stephen's
defense" in Acts 7. Stephen is introduced as being "full of faith and of the
Holy Spirit" (Acts 6:5) and was chosen to serve a specific need in the
church in Jerusalem. After the apostles laid their hands upon him, Stephen
was able to perform miracles as well (6:8). The Holy Spirit also provided
him with irrefutable arguments against opponents of the gospel (6:10).

These opponents did not just melt away because their arguments
were soundly defeated, however. It has been said that when logic and
reason fail, men will resort to violence and murder; indeed, the assault
against Stephen is a classic case in point. Certain Jews rose up against
Stephen with false charges and misrepresentations, and he was promptly
hauled before the Jewish Council (6:9-15). The men of the Council had
already been humiliated by Peter and John's refusal to obey them (Acts
4); a miraculous escape from prison had further exposed their inability to
silence the twelve apostles (Acts 5). Now they surrounded Stephen like a
pack of wolves surrounds a lone caribou that has been separated from the
herd, virtually salivating over the opportunity laid before them.

It was in this setting that Stephen made what he likely knew would
be his last stand. The high priest was probably Caiaphas—the same man
who conspired against Jesus (John 11:49-53) and who later condemned
Him to death (Mark 14:61-64).[154] But Stephen was not alone, for the
Spirit continued to inspire his words. Because of this, the record of his
testimony exudes as much wisdom and power today as it did when Stephen
first uttered it.

Stephen began his defense (Acts 7) by recounting the long
and bittersweet history of the Jews, beginning with God's promises to
Abraham. God knew that Abraham's descendents would be oppressed
by other men (Egypt), but He never abandoned them. In fact, God raised

up a savior (Joseph) for His people, but they betrayed him and sold him into slavery (7:9). Later, when God was ready to deliver His people, He raised up another savior (Moses), but they rejected him at first, and later continued to resist him (7:35, 39). Nonetheless, Moses promised that yet another Savior was coming, one whose authority as a lawgiver would even exceed his own (7:37). Yet by the time the promise to Abraham was to be fulfilled in Christ, the Jews revered their physical temple even at the expense of their Savior.[155]

Having exhibited a pattern of rejecting those whom God had sent to save them, the Jewish nation brought upon itself an irrevocable curse (cf. Luke 19:41-44). This curse was not imposed only because they had killed the Son of God—which is sufficient reason by itself—but also because they also had rejected the Spirit of God. "You men who are stiff-necked and uncircumcised in heart and ears are always resisting the Holy Spirit; you are doing just as your fathers did," Stephen boldly accused the Council (Acts 7:51).[156] They *claimed* to be God's people, but they did not *act* like God's people (Nehemiah 9:30). Their hearts were obstinate and unconverted; they refused to listen to the Father, Son, or Spirit; they had rejected God over and over.

Their response to Stephen's blunt but accurate assessment? Humility of heart? Tears of godly sorrow? Repentance and confession of sins? No, but they "with one impulse" rushed upon Stephen and dragged him to the place of his execution. They could silence the messenger, but not the message: everything Stephen said was true, since it was the testimony of the Spirit Himself (cf. Matthew 10:17-20). In due time, God would silence *them* because of their refusal to listen to *Him* (cf. Luke 19:12-14, 27).

This lengthy introduction is intended to make a most important point: as powerful as God's Spirit is, men can still reject His teaching and influence. The Jews did this for centuries before Christ; certainly many men after them have done the same thing. The Holy Spirit is like a fire to those who believe—full of energy, burning with zeal, providing illumination, and refining the human soul. Yet to the one who will not believe—one whose neck is unyielding and heart is unconverted[157]—it is like pouring water on the fire and rendering useless everything that the Spirit has to offer him.

Paul said succinctly in 1 Thessalonians 5:19, "Do not quench the

Spirit." To "quench the Spirit" would be to stifle or suppress His will in the heart of the believer. It seems that Paul referred specifically to the *miraculous work* of the Spirit (because of 5:20, "And do not despise prophetic utterances"), but this principle also works outside the context of miracles, as we will see. As we think more deeply upon what it means to "quench the Spirit," let us not forget those hard-hearted Jews before whom Stephen courageously stood. They thought themselves to be pleasing to God, even though they resisted His Spirit (see John 16:2-3). Unfortunately, Christians are capable of doing this same thing.

Scripture Is What the Spirit Says to the Churches

In 2 Timothy 3:16, Paul wrote, "All Scripture is inspired by God...." That phrase "inspired by God" (*theopneustos*) literally means "God-breathed." Just as God breathed life into man (Genesis 2:7), and the Spirit breathes life into the church (John 6:63), so God has breathed His gospel of salvation into the world.[158] The Spirit of God is directly involved in this process. In an earlier chapter, we examined how the Spirit spoke through the ancient prophets, and how He has also "preached the gospel" to us all (1 Peter 1:10-12). All Scripture has been revealed through the Spirit of God. While God has come to us in the flesh (John 1:14), the Spirit has appeared to us (so to speak) in the form of an inspired message. The gospel, then, is not merely a book of doctrinal instructions and spiritual encouragement; it is *first* to be regarded as the divinely-spoken words of God's Spirit, as the oracles of God Himself.

Since this is true, no wonder there is a curse laid upon anyone who would tamper with this message (Galatians 1:8).[159] Scripture is to be understood as the voice of the Holy Spirit to God's people (and to those who seek God in faith; Hebrews 11:6). This is not something to be treated lightly; we must have proper reverence for what "the Spirit says to the churches" (Revelation 2:7, et al). Everything the Spirit has communicated to us must be kept and read in its proper context. We cannot read the Bible like a novel, because it isn't one; we cannot study it like a treasure map, because it is not so simple; we cannot preach it like a theological treatise, because it is much more personal than this. The Spirit's message to us is a message of love and hope for a fallen people. God the Father is the source of this message; God the Son made it real to us; and God the Spirit has recorded it for the entire world to read and understand.

It is not uncommon for people to invoke the Holy Spirit as the source of their inspiration. It is true that anyone who is inspired by the gospel of Christ is inspired by the Holy Spirit, but such inspiration is indirect (non-miraculous), not direct (miraculous). In *this* (indirect) sense, all Christians should be inspired by the Holy Spirit! Of course, being inspired by the Spirit cannot mean that one is no longer required to follow the pattern that was established by the apostles (cf. Philippians 3:17). One cannot ignore apostolic authority and at the same time be led by the Spirit who guided the apostles into "all truth" (John 16:13). Some believe that whatever they "feel" in their hearts, so the Spirit has led them to believe; yet this describes an emotional experience and not a genuine revelation. James Bales says of this:

> There are some individuals who seemingly think it is too mundane, too prosaic, and too commonplace to study the Bible and to walk by its precepts and principles. ...Instead they want something direct and mysterious. They ask the Lord to guide them and then they wait for an inward impulse or impression. They get some sort of feeling, as one is bound to get as he waits for some sort of impression, and they interpret this as God's means of guiding them. In reality they are trusting [in] their own impulses instead of trusting in God and His Word. ... [Others] have assumed that their so-called guidance of the Spirit frees them from any obligation and concern with reference to any detailed study of the Word.[160]

Another observer, Dave Miller, sees the problem similarly:

> Attributing thoughts that pop into the mind to the Holy Spirit, or feeling that the Holy Spirit is leading one to do something, are convenient ways to do what one chooses to do and still feel justified. Crediting the Holy Spirit with one's thoughts and acts allows the individual to feel his decisions are out of his control and under the guidance of the Spirit. The resulting euphoria and sense of freedom is a recipe for disaster.[161]

Whenever "worship" descends into an opportunity for self-expression, self-gratification, or self-exaltation, it ceases to be worship of *God* and becomes worship of mere *men*. We must do our best to avoid succumbing to this increasingly popular manifestation of religion.

We cannot allow men's attempts to re-invent the gospel rob us of passion and respect for the inspired Word. Even in the apostles' day, men were maligning the gospel for their self-serving interests (2 Timothy 4:3-4; 2 Peter 2:1-3). Others were simply "untaught and unstable" in the faith, and thus distorted the integrity of the message (2 Peter 3:14-17). In 1 Thessalonians 5:19-22, Paul wrote, "Do not quench the Spirit; do not despise prophetic utterances. But examine everything carefully; hold fast to that which is good; abstain from every form of evil." This should be understood as one unbroken thought, not several different instructions. The Spirit had provided miraculous gifts to the church in Thessalonica (including gifts of prophecy and knowledge), but some were not taking the inspired revelations of the Spirit seriously. Paul's response was firm and clear. In essence, he said:

- ❏ "Do not suppress the truth!"—and thus provoke the wrath of God (Romans 1:18).
- ❏ "Do not disrespect the Spirit's authority!"—since His authority far exceeds that of men and even angels (2 Peter 2:10-11).
- ❏ "You *know* the standard of 'good'—do not abandon it for anything else!"—since every good thing can only come from God (James 1:17).
- ❏ "Do not even entertain any human motive!"—for whatever is not of God is worldly, unspiritual, and satanic (James 3:13-17).

Those who purposely malign the gospel of Christ to accommodate personal agendas are most certainly quenching the Spirit of God. They refuse to submit themselves to the Spirit's leadership; they will not listen to what the Spirit says to the churches. They may *call* themselves Christians, but they are not acting like Christians. They are throwing water on the fire, so to speak—the same fire by which they claim to warm themselves! The Spirit did not reveal the gospel of Christ merely so that we could sit around and share our opinions on it. Rather, He revealed this gospel so that we could learn from it, obey it, and thus be transformed by its transcendent message.

We cannot disregard what the Spirit has said to the early church just because we are no longer receiving "prophetic utterances." There is no need for a "that-was-then-but-this-is-now" attitude toward Scripture. What Christians needed to know *then* for living righteously is exactly what we need to know today. Moral behavior—a reflection of God's holy nature—does not change, even though cultures, customs, rituals, and even religious ceremony may change. Peter, for example, admonishes us to "remember the words spoken beforehand by the holy prophets and the commandment of the Lord and Savior spoken by your apostles" (2 Peter 3:1-2). This puts apostolic authority on par with ancient prophetic authority. This is because the same *Spirit* spoke through both groups (1 Peter 1:12), and all that He has said must be received with a "sincere mind." We know more today than did ancient Israel, but that should make us more humble and reverent toward Scripture, not less.

Becoming a More Spiritual People

Of course, it does not matter how reverently one *claims* to treat Scripture if he is unwilling to *obey* it. The Spirit has revealed Scripture to us so that we would come to Christ—not just in ceremonial ritual, but with the full surrender of our heart. The Jews of Jesus' day were experts at reading, parsing, commenting on, and arguing over Scripture, but they still failed to grasp its full objective: to bring them to obedience to Christ (John 5:39-40). This sounds a lot like some *Christians* who render profound interpretations of Scripture but fail to internalize its essential message: *come to Christ*. The Spirit did not bless us with the gospel of Christ just so that we could become students of the gospel. Rather, He gave us the good news of Christ so that we could embrace the Christ of good news!

So then, we should examine ourselves in light of that which we are studying. We may examine the Spirit's message every week, but are we being transformed by that message? And if so, then into what exactly are we being transformed? We pray to God in the Spirit; we read the revealed words of the Spirit; our bodies are a sanctuary for the Spirit; but are we becoming more *spiritual*? Having all these advantages, are we truly drawing near to God (James 4:8) *because* of the Spirit's work, or are we simply becoming better churchgoers and more eloquent teachers?

Having such privileged access to the Father as we do through the Spirit, we ought to live as "children of God above reproach in the midst of a crooked and perverse generation, among whom you appear as lights in the world" (Philippians 2:15). It is not enough that we make bold professions of faith or claim to handle the Word more accurately than others (cf. 2 Timothy 2:15). It is necessary that we also surrender ourselves fully and completely to the will of Christ, which is expressed through the Spirit's gospel. After all, it is not an idle message, nor can it be disregarded without consequence. As Paul wrote, "For our gospel did not come to you in word only, but also in power and in the Holy Spirit and with full conviction; just as you know what kind of men we proved to be among you for your sake" (1 Thessalonians 1:5). In other words, whatever kind of disciple the Spirit led Paul to become, He expects *us* to become as well. We would do well, then, to pay attention to the Spirit's instruction.

If we resist the teachings of the gospel, then we resist the One who (through the apostles) imparted to us those teachings. In reality, we quench the Holy Spirit in our heart. Whereas His presence in our life ought to kindle within us a bold and brilliant flame of zeal, we may instead be dousing that fire with legalism, formalism, worldliness, irreverence, or sheer indifference. Christians have the responsibility to know what such resistance looks like:

- ❑ "If we live by the Spirit, let us also walk by the Spirit" (Galatians 5:25). When you submit yourself to the Spirit's guidance, you give Him full consent to "lead" you wherever He wants you to go. You may not immediately *like* the direction He takes you, but must trust that He will not lead you astray or abandon you (cf. Hebrews 13:5-6). Paul's point is logical as well as it is scriptural: if the Spirit is the source of your *spiritual* life, then He must also have controlling interest over your *earthly* life. If you *live* by His power, then you are expected to *walk* according to His counsel. If you *walk* by the Spirit, then you will do your very best to internalize the teachings of His gospel and live accordingly. Otherwise, you quench His influence and oversight: while *claiming* that He is the source of spiritual life, you will not trust His Word to lead you day by day.

- ❑ "...If you are living according to the flesh, you must die; but if by the Spirit you are putting to death the deeds of the body, you will live. For all who are being led by the Spirit of God, these are sons of God" (Romans 8:13-14). A person either lives according to the Spirit of God, or he lives according to some other spirit; there are no other choices. Paul purposely contrasts here *life* and *death*: in order for the Spirit to generate *life* in you, you must *put to death* whatever contradicts the holy nature of God (see also 1 Peter 1:13-16). However, if you resist putting to death the deeds of the flesh (i.e., those born of human will and desire), then you cannot be a son of God. All genuine sons of God have within them the Spirit of God. One who quenches this Spirit by resisting His will forfeits the privileged relationship offered to him by the Father through Christ.

- ❑ "Do not grieve the Holy Spirit of God, by whom you were sealed for the day of redemption" (Ephesians 4:30). If you choose worldly lusts and ambitions over the purity and righteousness of the Spirit, you bring Him sorrow and disappointment.[162] Paul lists in this section (Ephesians 4:20-31) several practices among Christians that would cause the Spirit grief: failure to lay aside "the old self," falsehood, prolonged anger, giving Satan "opportunity," stealing, unwholesome speech, bitterness, wrath, clamor, slander, and "all malice." Those practices which bring Him joy, however, include: putting on the "new self," righteousness, holiness, truth, quiet industriousness, words of edification, kindness, tolerance, and a forgiving heart. Which list best describes *your* conduct? Are you yielding to the Spirit, or are you quenching His work in you?

❑ "...God has chosen you from the beginning for salvation through sanctification by the Spirit and faith in the truth. It was for this He called you through our gospel, that you may gain the glory of our Lord Jesus Christ" (2 Thessalonians 2:13-14). You are called by the Spirit for a specific objective: to be sanctified (or made holy) in order to enter into service to God. By submitting to the Spirit, you agree to do whatever is required of those who serve the King. This means that you must refuse to live a double life or engage in secret, worldly behavior while professing to walk in the light (see Ephesians 5:7-13).

❑ "Guard, through the Holy Spirit who dwells in us, the treasure which has been entrusted to you" (2 Timothy 1:14). The word translated "treasure" here literally means "good deposit," "sacred trust," or "precious thing." The idea here is that the Spirit has made an *investment* in you which needs (and deserves) to be protected. If one's body is a temple of the Holy Spirit (1 Corinthians 6:19-20), then that person does not have permission to do anything he desires with his body; "you are not your own." This is why a Christian cannot engage in immoral practices with his physical body (1 Corinthians 6:15-18). The *principle* here may also bear upon other subjects like smoking, alcohol, recreational drugs, body piercing, tattoos, and perhaps even extreme sports—any practice or recreation which causes unnecessary harm to your "temple of God." "...We should not by our own neglect, and even mistreatment of the body, cripple our opportunities for the most effective service possible for us."[163] "You have been bought with a price": Christ's blood has redeemed your soul for service to God. "You are not your own": God's Spirit expects to use your body for His service. If indeed you are a Christian, then you must take these facts very seriously.

❑ "...The time already past is sufficient for you to have carried out the desire of the Gentiles" (1 Peter 4:3). Christians purposely give up illicit human desires and worldly indulgences in order to become servants of the King. The Spirit has gladly made this servitude possible, having sanctified us for this very purpose. But you would bring great sorrow and disappointment to Him if you resisted His guidance and chose instead to pursue that which you once left behind. The Spirit knows the awful consequences that men will suffer if they continue in such foolishness; He also knows what wonderful things await those who listen to Him. The choice is yours, but you would do well to choose wisely.

Summary Thoughts

Our objective in praying through the Spirit and studying the message of the Spirit is to become a more spiritually-minded people. It is possible, of course, to be very "spiritual" without being obedient to God, so *spiritual* in the context of our present discussion necessarily implies *obedience*. Jesus lived in obedience to God's Spirit; we are expected to strive to do the same. The Holy Spirit never fails, disappoints, or forgets; but we can do all of these things, and therefore we must actively resist succumbing to them.

This admonition applies to a group of believers as much as it does an individual believer. A congregation may be very good at singing, preaching, holding meetings with well-known speakers, and offering classes, and still be *devoid* of the Spirit. In such a case, those people show no real concern for the lost; they put no real energy into spiritual growth; they are content to remain just as they are because it is comfortable and familiar to them. They are untouched and untransformed by the Spirit, since they have suppressed His work among them. This group just goes through the motions for now, but in due time it will cease to exist altogether.

If we submit to Him, the Spirit produces within us a fire of zeal, determination, diligence, and faith. In fact, we need His guidance to lead us into this; we depend upon His energy to fuel this fire. "Indifference, lukewarmness, and idleness all hinder the work of the Holy Spirit. To discourage the work of the Lord is to quench the Holy Spirit who prompts and guides in this work."[164] It is not as though the Spirit Himself would be in any way diminished if we were to resist Him, but *we* would suffer.

While He would be grieved at our foolish decision, the Holy Spirit remains who He is.

So then, *do not quench the Spirit.* Do not be like those Jews who tried to stare down Stephen—those who claimed to be God's servants but killed His prophets and spokesmen. Do not be like those rebellious, stiff-necked men who proudly boasted in their badge of circumcision but whose hearts were untouched and untransformed. Do not resist and blaspheme God as they did, such that He turned away from them and gave His gifts to others who would appreciate them (Acts 18:6).

Instead, "put on the full armor of God" and resist the evil that fills this world (Ephesians 6:13). "Resist the devil and he will flee from you" (James 4:7), for he is no match for the power of the Spirit. Resist Satan, "firm in your faith," knowing that you are not alone in this struggle (1 Peter 5:9). There are most certainly entities and forces that we must resist and quench in this world; the Holy Spirit is not one of them.

If you *have* been quenching the Spirit, then it is time to "kindle afresh the gift of God which is within you" (2 Timothy 1:6-7). While Paul may have referred specifically to a miraculous gift in that passage, we nonetheless also have a gift entrusted to us—one that should be burning hot with zeal, passion, and the determination to do what is right no matter what the cost. The gift of the Holy Spirit's presence in our lives is priceless and all-important, and it ought to be our solemn endeavor to make full use of that gift for the glory of God.

Chapter Twelve
Being Filled with the Spirit

And the disciples were continually filled with joy and with the Holy Spirit.
Acts 13:52

We now need to turn our discussion toward something we use all the time, but to which we may not always give serious attention. This thing drives all of our loves, hates, passions, and convictions, yet seldom receives much direct acknowledgment. This is something that the secular world tells us to follow and ignore all at once. Most people long to share this thing with one another, but few actually know how to do so—and fewer yet know how to do so expressively. This is something Satan wants to disconnect from our relationship with God—and God wants connected with Him more than anything.

I am talking, of course, about *the heart of man.*

The heart is the seat of all intellect and reasoning. It is the sanctuary of emotions, affections, and passions. It is the source of will and desire. These things are the most powerful driving forces in our life, so it is imperative that we take great care of this very special part of us. "Watch over your heart with all diligence," we are instructed, "for from it flow the springs of life" (Proverbs 4:23). Our physical heart is filled with blood, but our *spiritual* heart is supposed to be filled with "the springs of life"—in essence, *living water.*

This should sound familiar to us by now. The Holy Spirit *is* the Living Water that fills the heart of the believer. Not everyone's heart is filled with living water; some men's hearts are filled with evil thoughts, murders, adulteries, fornications, thefts, false witness, and slandering. These are the things that defile the heart; they do not promote life, but always lead to death (cf. Matthew 15:15-20). We are interested in that which leads to life, however, and "it is the Spirit who gives life" (John 6:63). Our desire, then, should be for a heart that is filled with the Spirit.

Jesus promised that the Spirit would fill a person's "innermost being" with "rivers of living water" (John 7:37-39). If this refers only to the exercise of miracles, this severely distorts the scope and context of

147

what Jesus said. If this refers only to the learning of Bible passages, then this underestimates the power and work of the Holy Spirit.

What do *you* think it means?

Taking Your Heart Seriously

People often inspire others by saying, "Follow your heart!" There's certainly nothing wrong with this, unless of course your heart has no idea where it is heading. If one's heart is lost, then his soul will also be lost. God says that the heart, left to itself, "is more deceitful than all else and is desperately sick; who can understand it?" (Jeremiah 17:9). We have a hard enough time making sense of what is going on all around us; it is an even greater struggle to understand what is going on *within*. The heart can delude itself into thinking a person's soul is very healthy even when in fact it may be spiritually sick.

When God searches and tests the human heart (Jeremiah 17:10), He is not hampered by human limitations and His discernment is flawless. "The word of God," which is portrayed as an intelligent personality and not a collection of chapters and verses, "is living and active and sharper than any two-edged sword, and piercing as far as the division of soul and spirit, of both joints and marrow, and able to judge the thoughts and intentions of the heart" (Hebrews 4:12). Like a finely-honed knife, the Spirit shaves away all the façades, pretensions, delusions, and other human defects of the heart. It peels back any false veneer that we might have used to disguise our heart and exposes us for what we really *are*. It penetrates that thick skin of pride, self-righteousness, and self-protection with which we may have encased our heart, pricking the very core of our true identity. When we give ourselves over to the Lord's keeping, the Spirit simply will not allow us to remain as we are. It is both His responsibility *and* desire to transform us into something much better than that.

People often do not give their heart priority. The everyday struggle to survive—the "rat race" and other grueling ordeals—and the pressing yet mundane calls of duty compel us to put our attention elsewhere. There is so much going on in our lives, and yet so much of it is petty and irrelevant. A hundred years from now, no one will care about what may fill your plate today—and neither will you. Yet if you ignore your heart and its spiritual needs, then a hundred years from now—even though you will then be in a place where there are no years—this will occupy your full attention.

Many of us—and I'm lumping myself into this group—are thick-headed and slow to learn. We may *know* what is all-important and all-consuming, but we may still put off doing anything about it. There are always "issues" to deal with, kids to take care of, problems to resolve, bills to pay, and doctors to visit. There's always *something* that fills our time, *something* that robs us of our attention, *something* that "comes up" just when we think we've got everything taken care of—there's always SOMETHING. We seek money, attention, sympathy, and possessions, but we may spend relatively little time seeking what is in our heart's best interest. We may spend even *less* time seeking to fill our spiritual heart with Living Water.

We work, to be sure, but we don't always work toward that which is productive or important. We think that working a *career* is as beneficial and satisfying as working out our salvation (cf. Philippians 2:12). We talk to our spouses, but our communication may be stunted and mundane. We talk about the kids, getting the car's tires rotated, fixing the leaky faucet, getting our taxes done, and dinner plans, but we may rarely talk about our hearts. We sit down to coffee with friends, but we end up talking about silly, banal topics—or maybe we slide into criticism, gossip, and character assassination. After all, this is an easy if not strangely gratifying thing to do. Yet we may rarely sit down with someone and truly, honestly, and unguardedly share our heart. We just don't trust people enough to do this; maybe we don't trust ourselves.

In the process of hectic, everyday life—and life can *feel* hectic even when we are in the quiet of our own sanctuary—we are silently and gradually being indoctrinated. This indoctrination is not from God, for it leads us away from Him. The message we are internalizing may be subtle beyond any conscious perception; yet it is real, powerful, and deadly. In whatever form it comes to us, the message is always the same: "Your heart really isn't that important. These other pressing issues—*these* are what should occupy your life." This, of course, is not true, but many people are persuaded by its propaganda. Then we may unconsciously take this to the next step: "If my *heart* is the defining element and driving force of who I am, and yet my heart is not that important, then *I* am not that important." Some take it even a step further: "If *I* am not that important to *me*, then I must not be important to God, either."

The lives of such people are thus reduced to mere survival. They do not live with any real purpose or joy; they just exist. Whatever joys they do experience are artificial, shallow, and fleeting. Having sacrificed their heart for something so much less important—which is anything in this world—they have also abandoned all hope of meaningful *completion*. Life is tenuous, unfulfilling, and desperate. They are terrified of death, since they are not prepared for what comes after it, but they also anticipate it as an end to their empty, soulless lives. In the hereafter, some suppose that they will throw themselves at the mercy of God, not realizing that only in this life does God show mercy. In the life to come, there is only justice.

It is this broken, disfigured, and cynical life that Satan wants us to experience. He wants us to feel like there's really nothing we can do to make things better except to enjoy a little worldly joy or guilty pleasure every now and then. He smiles when people ache with emptiness as they succumb to the idea that *life itself* is empty and without meaning. He loves it when people turn to vice and addiction to soothe the anguish of their heart. He is thrilled when people give up all hope, curse God, and die.

Just as devastating as dwelling on despair, however, are apathy and indifference. How many people have you met who are simply disinterested in spiritual concerns? Or who treat "spiritual life" like they do holidays: they get real serious about it only a couple of times a year, while the rest of the time is swallowed up by work, "plans," bills, and the endless drone of day-to-day existence? These people appear happy and will talk about being "fulfilled," but if you scratch the surface of their lives, what you will see is frightening. Their heart is cold, black, and ghoulish. It is not beating with life; it has no fellowship with the Source of life; it has long since shriveled up for lack of Living Water.

"And you were dead in your trespasses and sins, in which you formerly walked according to the course of this world, according to the prince of the power of the air…" (Ephesians 2:1-2). This passage suddenly takes on new meaning, doesn't it? The heart that is cut off from Living Water drinks instead from man-made wells; these hold no water, but are filled with lies and poison (cf. Jeremiah 2:13). Those who drink from these do not "walk by the Spirit" (Galatians 5:16), but they walk "according to the prince of the power of the air." Think about that: the power of the *air*—no substance, no fulfillment, nothing definable. That is all Satan has to offer; yet many choose to "walk" according to him. Such people may well "[indulge in] the desires of the flesh and of the mind" (Ephesians 2:3), but this offers them no benefit. Once the heart is corrupted, it is just a matter of time before whatever else remains of those people is also ruined. After all, they are already *dead*.

The Spirit's Call to the Human Heart

Regardless of what Satan thinks or does, God is supremely interested in the condition of the human heart. He wants it above all else; only He can save it from its own death. Jesus often spoke about the heart of man in His teachings and parables. The parable of the lost sheep, for example (Luke 15:4-7), is all about seeking the heart that has lost its way. The *message* of the parable is that God is deeply concerned with rescuing the human heart—a message underscored by heaven's joy over that which was lost but now has been found. The parable of the sower, for example (Matthew 13:3-9), describes four different responses of the human heart. The *message* of the parable is that the divinely-powerful Word of God requires the right kind of heart in order to bring about salvation *and* a productive, fruit-bearing life.

The gospel calls to the heart of man; its message is designed to appeal to it. Jesus taught that the highest objective in this world is to love God with all your heart (Luke 10:25-28). He knows that if your heart is consumed with love *for* God, then your soul will be preserved *by* God. This is exactly what Jesus wants: the salvation of your soul. Satan, on the other hand, wants you disconnected and isolated from God. He really does not care if you read the Bible, go to church, say a few prayers, or do a few good deeds now and then—as long as your *heart* is not in it.[165] Religion by itself is no replacement for loving God with all of one's heart; Satan knows this, and so should you and I.

In contrast, Jesus does not want religious piety, casual interests, or lukewarm commitments. He wants your *heart* more than anything else. Jesus did not come into this world to give us yet another religion; He came to rescue men's hearts from certain ruin. He did not die on the cross to redeem our self-serving lives, nor to rescue us from the rat race; He died to redeem our *heart* from God's condemnation. He did not give us the Holy Spirit to make us comfortable with human misery; He gave us the Spirit to fill us with light, life, and hope *despite* whatever we must face in this life. In essence, He gave us the Spirit to fill our heart—not just to lead us in a certain direction, but to improve, enlighten, and inspire us. The heart that is filled with the Spirit is no longer black, shriveled, and dead; God has nothing to do with death. Rather, it is healthy, pulsing with energy, and respiring with the breath of life.

To gain an even further perspective on this, we should consider yet another Old Testament "type" beyond the holy anointing oil and the oil used for the candelabra within the tabernacle, which we discussed in chapter 3. In Exodus 40:34-35, upon the completion of the physical tabernacle in the wilderness and all the consecratory sacrifices required for putting it into service, we read:

> Then the cloud covered the tent of meeting, and the glory of the LORD filled the tabernacle. Moses was not able to enter the tent of meeting because the cloud had settled on it, and the glory of the LORD filled the tabernacle.

The Israelites saw the same cloud-like phenomenon upon the dedication of Solomon's temple (1 Kings 8:10-11). In later rabbinic writings, this "cloud" was referred to as *shekinah*, which is most closely translated "that which dwells." In this context, it depicts the divine presence of God as a cloud—an ethereal, formless manifestation that (like liquid) can adapt to any surroundings and yet cannot be reproduced as a graven image. The ancient rabbis thus called this *shekinah* "the glory of Jehovah" or "the word of the Lord."[166]

It is not hard for us to draw a parallel between what the Israelites literally saw filling the tabernacle and what we "see" (by faith) as filling our own bodies. Just as the presence of Jehovah filled the ancient tabernacle, the Spirit fills our "earthly tent" (cf. 2 Corinthians 5:1). Indeed, God's presence is always intimately associated with His Spirit: where the one is, there will the other be. Just as our bodies cannot be separated from our spirit except through death, so God—who never dies, but exists in an ever-present, perpetual state of being—cannot separate Himself from His Spirit. Our physical bodies serve in the same capacity as the ancient tabernacle (or temple): as an intersection between heaven and earth. This is the essence of 1 Corinthians 6:19: "Your body is a temple of the Holy Spirit who is in you." Just as the physical temple was declared holy because of God's presence, so our bodies are declared holy because of God's presence (Spirit) in *us*.

In order for the Spirit to indwell our *body*, He must first fill our *heart*. God's *shekinah* would not have filled the temple of an unfaithful people; He had to be in their *hearts* before His glory could fill their *temple*. (When His people ceased to remain faithful, then God's glory departed from His temple. This is depicted in visionary form in Ezekiel 8 – 10. Likewise, if a Christian decides to "go on sinning willfully," then he insults the Spirit of God and forces Him to separate Himself from that person; Hebrews 10:26-31.) Once we are made "sons" of God through the redemption and intercession of Jesus Christ, then the Spirit fills our heart (Galatians 4:4-7). Once the Spirit is in our heart, then we give Him controlling interest, so to speak, over our body as well. Whatever controls the *heart* of a person also controls the *life* of that person.

For those who remain faithful to the Lord, our "hope [in God—MY WORDS] does not disappoint, because the love of God has been poured out within our hearts through the Holy Spirit who was given to us" (Romans 5:5). In other words, our hope is made real because we are filled with the Spirit and have *fellowship* with Him (2 Corinthians 13:14). Even though our earthly "tent" (body) will not last forever, nonetheless we will be given a spiritual body wherein we can dwell with the Lord (1 Corinthians 15:44). "Now He who prepared us for this very purpose is God, who gave to us the Spirit as a pledge" (2 Corinthians 5:5). The assurance that we are *prepared* for that future life with God is evidenced by the *Spirit* who fills our heart in this present life. This "pledge" indicates that there is more to come—and that what is coming is guaranteed to be given.

Letting the Spirit Fill Our Heart

The human heart has three major dimensions to it. First, there is its intellect, which includes knowledge, the power of reason, and its ability to discern between two things against an objective standard. Second, there is will (or volition), which provides the driving force behind all that a person does. Third, there is desire, which includes passion, emotions, and intense spiritual longings. These three real but invisible aspects—intellect, will, and desire—are intertwined and continuously affect each other. For example, as one's knowledge increases, his will to pursue a life consistent with his newfound beliefs is inspired, which directly affects his emotional response toward that which he believes to be true. More specifically, his increasing knowledge directly affects his will to follow his beliefs; this in turn inspires his joy and passion for the object of those beliefs.

The heart is the engine of a person's life. Just like an automobile engine, it needs regular maintenance and attention. Sometimes, its problems are beyond what a minor tune-up will fix; it needs a major overhaul. This is what one's conversion to Christ is: a major overhaul. In a sense, it is like a complete engine rebuild, since upon one's commitment to Christ he is given a new heart (2 Corinthians 5:17; see also Psalm 51:10-11, in principle). His conscience being cleansed by the blood of Christ (Hebrews 9:13-14), the believer's heart is filled with the Spirit of God. This is to his advantage, of course, since anyone whose heart is filled with the Spirit is most certainly in fellowship with God and has no reason to fear divine judgment.

Satan also knows the human heart—not necessarily what is *in* it, but certainly what makes it work. We give Satan too much credit in assuming that he can read our every thought, but we do not credit him enough for knowing the dynamics of our heart better than we do. Being well aware of the heart's weaknesses and limitations, he takes advantage of our ignorance and preys upon our doubts. He counts on our blindness, self-dependence, and vanity in order to accomplish his will in us. We say things like, "I'm in control!" even while Satan is in fact steering us toward disaster.

We may think that being in the company of believers or having access to God will prevent our heart from being deceived, but this is not true. Judas was in the company of the Son of God for three years, and yet he allowed Satan to enter into his heart (John 13:2, 27). Ananias and Sapphira were surrounded by the apostles' teaching and the influence of many good Christians, yet they allowed Satan to enter into their hearts so as to lie to the Holy Spirit (Acts 5:3). Such sobering examples ought to remind each of us how *close* we also are to succumbing to Satan's temptations. Regardless of how close we are to God, Satan is always within our reach, testing the integrity of our armor, waiting for a moment of human weakness.

Because of this—and because of the fellowship He craves from us—God cannot be reduced to a mere influence in our lives. His Spirit is not like a passing parade—one which delights and captures our attention for the moment, but then recedes into the noise and busyness of everyday life. He is not to be limited to an incidental encounter, like when we meet an old friend and have a brief but intense conversation, but soon realize that we really have little in common anymore and we quickly look for a reason to leave. He is not to be "read" like a well-written novel, which enthralls us for the duration of our reading, but is replaced by another book once we have finished "reading" Him.

Consider another approach: perhaps you have been to a Costco, or some other megastore where they provide samples of food at the ends of the aisles. We (consumers) will test, taste, and even savor these samplings, but we won't necessarily buy that which is being advertised. The samples are free, and we are not forced to commit to anything. The truth is that we are often shopping for something else; the samples are merely a pleasant diversion, an incidental opportunity to experience something we may not have tried otherwise. There is no crime in this, of course; for many (myself included!) it is an anticipated part of that shopping experience.

Yet I see an analogy here between this passive nibbling and how some people may regard the Holy Spirit. Some are content to sample the Holy Spirit while shopping (in essence) for something else. The world is their Costco; they are busy looking here for the things and pleasures which will satisfy their souls. Every now and then, they will come upon a particularly tasty morsel—a sampling of God, if you will—and they savor it for a moment, slowly nod in approval, but then resume their search for something else. That sampling may be in a sermon, a passage of the Bible, a small but intense period of spiritual insight, or a profound deliverance of some kind which they attribute to God. But after the sampling is gone, even while the taste of that goodness is still in their mouths, they turn their attention to the shelves and pallets of worldly merchandise, and quickly forget what it was that they had tasted.

This defines "Christianity" for many churchgoers. Such people are allowing their hearts to be filled with the world while nibbling on spiritual truths. This is not what God ever intended for us; this will never satisfy our souls. God wants us *filled* with His Spirit, not just experimenting with spiritual appetizers and samplings. We cannot be *led* by His Spirit if we refuse to be *filled* with His Spirit. Only when we allow the Spirit to fill our heart is He given control of our life. Once we surrender this control, then He will lead us in the narrow way that leads to God (Matthew 7:14). This is not only in our *own* best interest, but it is also in *God's* best interest, since this ushers us into an eternal fellowship with Him.

Giving the Spirit Control of Our Lives

Being "filled with the Spirit" is a phrase that does not always mean exactly the same thing. In the New Testament, it often indicates a temporary but necessary surge of assurance, conveyance of power, or disclosure of information by the Holy Spirit. In fact, this is the meaning of the phrase in the following passages:

❑ Luke 1:41-45, Elizabeth (mother of John the Baptist) was "filled with the Spirit" and thus began to speak prophetically to Mary.

❑ Luke 1:67-79, Zacharias (father of John the Baptist) was "filled with the Spirit" and thus prophesied concerning his son and the Christ.

❑ Acts 2:4, the twelve apostles were "filled with the Spirit" on Pentecost and thus miraculously spoke in tongues.

❑ Acts 4:8, Peter was "filled with the Spirit" and thus spoke boldly before the Council which had had him arrested.

❑ Acts 6:8, Stephen, "full of grace and power" of the Spirit, spoke irrefutably before his accusers and also performed "wonders and signs" (see also 7:55).

❑ Acts 4:31, the apostles (and others) were "filled with the Spirit" and thus began to "speak the word of God with boldness."

❑ Acts 13:9, Saul (Paul) was "filled with the Spirit" as he confronted the false prophet Elymas on the island of Cyprus.

These citations have specific reference to miracles or miraculous help from the Spirit, as evidenced by their contexts. In such incidents, the Spirit miraculously guided or emboldened believers to face a particular trial or confrontation. Not every usage of the phrase necessarily involves miracles, however. In some cases, being "filled with the Spirit" indicates a person whose heart is given over to God's will and is consequently controlled by God's Spirit. Such examples include:

❑ Luke 4:1-13, Jesus was filled with the Spirit, but not only for the purpose of performing miracles; in fact, in this passage, He *refused* to perform any miracles for Satan.

❑ Acts 6:3-5, the men chosen to serve as deacons for the church in Jerusalem were full of the Spirit, but this refers to the character of their *heart* and not to any miraculous abilities.

❑ Acts 9:17, Saul (Paul) was filled with the Spirit upon his conversion to Christ, but as we have discussed before, this was nothing different in itself than what any convert would experience.

❑ Acts 11:24, Barnabas was a man full of the Holy Spirit, which is why he was considered "a good man" apart from any reference to miracles he might have performed.

❑ Acts 13:52, the disciples at Antioch of Pisidia were "filled with joy and the Holy Spirit," but this depicts their character and change of heart, not their ability to perform miracles.

❑ Romans 15:13, Paul prayed that the Roman Christians would be filled with the power of the Spirit, but for the purpose of joy and hope, not to perform miracles.

Certainly these characterizations can be applied to believers today, if indeed our own hearts are "filled" with the presence of God's Spirit and the influence of His power (Romans 8:9). Again, there is no need to describe this as a demonstrable miracle, although the Spirit's *nature* is most certainly miraculous, as we have discussed previously. Since His nature is miraculous (by definition), then whatever He does for us, in us, and through us cannot be fully explained in the natural (physical) world. If one's heart can be filled with evil (Matthew 12:34; Acts 5:3), then one's heart can also be filled with God.

In Ephesians 5:18, Paul wrote: "And do not get drunk with wine, for that is dissipation, but be filled with the Spirit...." There is nothing in this context to suggest that Paul was urging the performance of miracles among the Ephesians. Instead, this is something he would say to *all* Christians on *any* occasion. Whether a man is filled with wine or God's Spirit ultimately is his own choice, based upon his response to God's gospel. "Be filled with the Spirit" actually indicates an ever-present admonition: there is not a time when we should *not* be filled with the Spirit.[167] This is not an occasional "filling," or one that carries us until the next "filling," but anticipates a constant action in response to that which is always needed.

We need to be filled with the Spirit continually not because *He* becomes exhausted or needs to be recharged, but because the human *heart* does. The heart is not a perfect vessel; it is not an intact container. It is closer to a sieve than a flask, for whatever we put into it is subject to "loss" because of our weakness (of resolve), forgetfulness, and the bombardment of earthly distractions. (Apply this analogy carefully, for it is not a perfect one, and dares not to suggest that the Spirit Himself is in any way reduced because of our human frailty.) This is why we cannot be "filled" once and then are done with the matter. To tweak the illustration a bit: it is not being suggested that the Spirit is "leaking out" of our heart, but that there is so much else *rushing in*. Left to ourselves, we will be inundated and overwhelmed by the deluge of worldliness that continually surrounds us.

Jesus said, "Where your treasure is, there your heart will be also" (Matthew 6:21). One's desire for a particular "treasure" will master that person's heart, which will control that person's life, and will ultimately determine his eternal destiny. One cannot be filled with two opposing "spirits" or seek two opposite "treasures" all at once; "No one can serve two masters…" (Matthew 6:24). If one's heart is filled with the spirit of the world, then he cannot be filled with the Spirit of God (1 John 2:15-17). However, if one's heart is filled with the Holy Spirit, then his soul will be mastered by God and will transcend the emptiness and futility of this world (Colossians 3:1-4). Accordingly, Paul wrote, "For we through the Spirit, by faith, are waiting for the hope of righteousness" (Galatians 5:5).

Remember, the heart of man involves his rational mind, his will, and his emotions. The control (or mastery) of every dominion of his heart must be given over to the Spirit, not just one dominion or the other. It is necessary, then, that we consciously subdue each facet of our heart and relinquish control of it to the Spirit's providential oversight. It is not enough to subdue only one aspect of the heart while maintaining personal control over another. For example, we cannot merely say, "God, I *think* about You," for we also need to share His passion for righteousness. We cannot merely say, "God, I share Your *passion*," for we also need to cooperate with His will. And we cannot merely say, "God, I submit to Your *will*," for we also need to internalize the right kind of thinking—i.e., the doctrinal truths of His gospel.

If we are filled with the Spirit, then we cannot be "filled" with anything else. There is no room, then, for "deeds of the flesh" if indeed you wish to produce "fruit of the Spirit" (cf. Galatians 5:19-23). There are numerous places in the New Testament where the Spirit instructs us to "put aside" the things of this world so that we might be filled (in essence) with *Him*: Ephesians 4:20-32; Colossians 3:5-11; Titus 2:11-14; 1 Peter 2:1-3, et al.[168] If our heart is filled with anything *but* the Spirit, then we are not under His control; He is not leading us; we are not drawing near to God. "If we live by the Spirit, let us also walk by the Spirit" (Galatians 5:25), meaning: if the Holy Spirit is the source of our spiritual life (John 6:63), then He must dictate the direction of our *earthly* life. We cannot be led heavenward otherwise.

The Mysteriousness of the Spirit's Presence

So far, there may be little doubt that the Holy Spirit is to fill the Christian's heart. The question everyone wants definitively answered here is: *how does the Spirit do this?* There is no way I or any other mere mortal can answer this. God works in mysterious ways, and His Spirit is most certainly mysterious in all that He does. This, of course, bothers the one who insists on thoroughly knowing everything God does before He ever does it, as if this were a necessary requirement. Some might even think that to defer to the mysteriousness of the Spirit is to sidestep the issue entirely. Yet what remains shrouded in mystery to us is not a good reason (by itself) to doubt whatever is truly being accomplished. The exact description of the human soul—its nature, operation, and passion—is mysterious, yet we do not doubt that it exists and is animating our physical body. So it is with justification, sanctification, fellowship with Christ, the love of the Father, and God Himself. There are many things we cannot fully understand, but God is not asking us to fully understand them. He is asking us to *believe* in Him because of the indisputable evidence He has provided toward this end.

The human heart is in fact aroused by the mysteriousness of God's presence. When it comes down to it, our heart is not stimulated by facts, figures, or scientific data. We are not compelled to draw near to God only because of the knowledge of Scripture, Bible classes, church services, or eloquent sermons. Please don't misunderstand: we *need* these things to substantiate what is real and true, and to steer us in the proper direction, but these are not the source of our *inspiration*. Rather, the human heart is inspired by poetic expression, symmetry and balance, beauty of design, ethereal majesty, uninhibited intimacy, sublime otherworldliness, and *mystery*. Such abstract, intangible, and immeasurable wonders are what the Spirit represents to us: He *is* to us all of these things. This is why we are at once so attracted to Him *and* unsure of what to do with Him. When we begin to understand the full scope of what He does for us, He nearly overwhelms our senses. To those who accept Him for who He is, this is rewarding, rejuvenating, and exhilarating. To those who are afraid of relinquishing control of their heart until they have every detail explained to them, this is disturbing, dangerous, and untenable.

Those whose hearts are filled with the Holy Spirit enjoy an intimacy with God that others simply will not understand. These people are not just "happy" to have God in their lives; they are *enthralled* with the experience. Knowing that the Spirit is guiding their hearts, helping them to overcome the trials and temptations of this life, and leading them heavenward is exciting, reassuring, and liberating all at once. These people do not sit around just quoting Bible verses to each other or gushing euphorically about the "awesomeness" of God. They are instead *drawn* to God through the intercession and influence of His Spirit, and they find the experience to be indescribably pleasurable.

This is a huge contrast to those who have become "bored with church." People *may* become bored with a church service, preacher, sermon, old songs sung like funeral dirges, and stiff, mechanical prayers. These are external "fixtures" of worship; these represent what men do to religion, not what true religion can do for men. This scenario does not describe people who are filled with the Spirit, but those who are filled with emptiness, hopelessness, and the futility of formality. Christians who are touched by Christ and filled with His Spirit are *never* bored with what it is they are called to do. A meaningful relationship with God is far too wonderful an experience to ever become boring.

People who find themselves trapped in a useless religion often try to spice things up by addressing only their external perceptions of what religion is in the first place. Some churches apparently believe that if their services are more entertaining and their preacher is more animated, then the church will become more *spiritual*. They assume that feeling "spiritual" is equivalent with being filled with the Holy Spirit. Anyone can "feel" spiritual, regardless of his relationship with God; but only those who are in fellowship with God can be filled with the Holy Spirit.

"Feeling spiritual" is a characteristically human approach to drawing near to the Divine. It provides no lasting benefits; it does not satisfy the human soul; it misrepresents the gospel of Christ. If the human heart is unaffected and unchanged by what it seeks after, it is just a matter of time before it becomes thirsty for something else. The wells of man-made religion cannot provide living water (cf. Jeremiah 2:13). The emptiness of entertaining congregations cannot replace the need for worshiping in spirit and truth (cf. John 4:23-24). Inevitably, members of those churches will say something like, "Something is still *missing*," but that "something" is not what they think. The "something" is God, but they may think it to be a fresher innovation of some kind. In reality, the "something" is what would bring the human soul to its completion: to be filled with the Spirit of God.

One must directly *address* a problem in order to *fix* it. An automotive body shop cannot just spray paint over a car's rust in order to make it go away. Likewise, we cannot just paint over the old, unconverted, untransformed heart in hopes that it will change into something better. One cannot become more Christ-like by simply dressing up the religious environment around him. The problem is still there; his heart is still not led by the Spirit; he remains what he *is* despite what he *does*. Religion, by itself, is no safeguard for the soul. Likewise, sound doctrine is no replacement for zeal and desire for God. We cannot just throw religion (or Bible verses) at the human heart and expect God-given results.

Once again: your heart is incomplete, inadequate, and unprepared to draw near to God without being filled with the Spirit. As we have seen, being filled with the Spirit is not something you can accomplish in your own way, by your own power, or according to your own preferences. It is only accomplished by your surrender to Jesus Christ, obedience to His gospel, and submission to the Spirit of God who leads you.

Summary Thoughts

Someone has said, in essence, that only two things pierce the human heart: beauty and affliction. The "affliction" of fear, loss, pain, and suffering certainly does get our attention, but this cannot be the only thing that provokes action. We certainly do suffer the consequences of our own poor decisions, but we cannot only look to God as the Great Fix-It Being in the Sky. Jesus did not die to make us comfortable; God does not impart His Spirit to absolve us of earthly afflictions. There must be more to God's presence in our lives than the alleviation of pain.

It is also necessary, then, to let the beauty of God pierce our hearts. He wants us to look upon Him not only with wonder, but also with profound appreciation for who He is and what He is able to accomplish in us. His glory, majesty, excellence, and power ought to elicit our deepest admiration and compel us to draw nearer to Him. It is His presence in our lives—as represented by the Spirit who indwells us—that ought to generate desire, stimulate passion, and arouse our awareness *for* that fellowship. The more we allow His Spirit to direct us heavenward, the greater the anticipation of being with the Father who is *in* heaven becomes.

We will never find the beauty of God in a church building, hymnal, or sermon. The traditional trappings of religion can never *by themselves* draw us closer to the spiritual intimacy that God expects us to have, seeing as we are made "in His image." When we are filled with the Spirit of God, however, we are able to transcend the fixtures and props of religious liturgy and can "know the love of Christ which surpasses knowledge, that you may be filled up to all the fullness of God" (Ephesians 3:19). Christ has bridged the gap between us and God through His supreme sacrifice.

It is the Holy Spirit, whom the Father has given to us *because* of Christ's work, who ushers us into the heavenly perspective.

Satan wants us to be content with the plastic pleasures and mediocre stimulants of this world. He wants us to be satisfied with the trivial, the meaningless, and the mundane. He wants us to believe that if we gratify our *senses*, then this will satisfy our *heart*. The Holy Spirit, however, desires to give to us what gratifies the heart and satisfies the soul. Through the ministry of Christ, and because of the great love of the Father, the Spirit longs to bring us to completion (1 Peter 1:2, 5:10).

Chapter Thirteen

A Critique of the "Bible Only" Position

For the word of God is living and active and sharper than any two-edged sword, and piercing as far as the division of soul and spirit, of both joints and marrow, and able to judge the thoughts and intentions of the heart. And there is no creature hidden from His sight, but all things are open and laid bare to the eyes of Him with whom we have to do. Hebrews 4:12-13

Throughout this book, I have been alluding to the "Bible only" position without fully defining either that belief or my obvious disagreements with it. It seemed advantageous to address this only after having already discussed what the Bible teaches on the Holy Spirit, since earlier chapters have already laid the groundwork for what will be said here.

Many good Christian men and women subscribe to this position—some of them deliberately, others unknowingly. My critique of a *position* here is in no way a question of those Christians' *standing with God.* This critique is practical, not personal. Thus, I am *not* making this a "test of fellowship," as though one's relationship with God was determined by his stand on this issue.

At the same time, it is possible that Christians can be mistaken in their religious beliefs, even those concerning the work of the Spirit. You may not have even been aware of this position (or its controversy) prior to reading this. The point here is not necessarily to make you familiar with the position itself as much as it is to expound even further on what the Bible teaches (and does not teach) concerning the Holy Spirit.

The Position Stated

The "Bible only" position[169] maintains that there is no divine activity among Christ's church other than what is accomplished through the written Word, the Bible. This initially begins with a line of reasoning that I myself maintain: What is often referred to as the "immediate" or "direct operation" of the Holy Spirit—i.e., visible miracles performed among Christians—ceased soon after the first century. Those miraculous powers could not be conferred upon anyone without the laying on of the apostles' hands, and that power could not be perpetuated beyond those who received it. For these reasons, and others that we have discussed in an earlier chapter, the miracles that were performed among the early Christians are no longer being performed today.

After this, however, the "Bible only" view takes a different direction and begins to lose credibility. Since the Spirit's miracles have ceased, it is argued, therefore the Spirit's personal *activity* must have also ceased. The Holy Spirit would not have given us the written New Testament if we needed Him any longer. The fact that He has supplied us with "everything pertaining to life and godliness" in Scripture (2 Peter 1:3) indicates that we simply no longer require His services otherwise. The Spirit's work is done; we have the written gospel; its information is sufficient for guiding us heavenward. The Bible itself is "all-sufficient" for whatever we need.

Some adherents claim that this description misrepresents their position. They say, "Of *course* God's Spirit is still active among His church!" But when pressed to define this activity, they inevitably rehearse the same premise: "Anything that the Spirit does for us is now accomplished through the Word (Bible)." Translation: The Spirit works *through* the Bible; thus His activity is confined to whatever is specifically expressed *in* the Bible. Here are some statements which clearly articulate this position:

- ❑ "...The Spirit works today, but it [*sic*] works through the Word, and separate and apart from the Word there cannot be any work done by the Holy Spirit."[170]
- ❑ "In the time when there were miraculous gifts for the revelation of the Word, 'spiritual' had a different significance than today where we have the WORD, not in the man, but in the BOOK."[171] (I will address this view—namely, that all New Testament references to "spiritual" meant "miraculous gifts"—below.)
- ❑ "Since revelation and confirmation have ceased, the faith has been once for all delivered to the saints. What would reception of the Spirit provide today? What the reception of the Spirit one time furnished miraculously and directly is now furnished through the written Word."[172]
- ❑ "No single action of the Spirit directed to man is attributed to the Spirit apart from the Word of God. The Word is the medium through which the Spirit operates today."[173]

❑ "It is here proposed...that whatever influence is ascribed to the Holy Spirit *within us* in the New Testament is affirmed also of the Word of God. From this vantage ground we proceed to prove that the Holy Spirit operates upon and within the heart of man *only through the Word*."[174]

This position maintains that it is impossible for the Spirit to do something apart from performing a miracle; "non-miraculous" activity of a supernatural Spirit is a contradiction of terms. While the Spirit doesn't do anything *directly* or *immediately* for God's people, He still provides for our spiritual needs through the Bible. Thus, if the Spirit works through the Bible, then that is not miraculous; but if He works apart from the Bible, then that is a miracle. Since God is performing no miracles today, the Bible is His only medium for activity.

This seems to be a safe argument. It denies any claims to genuine, visible miracles being performed today, limiting God's activity to the words of Scripture alone. At the same time, this allows (or appears to allow) for God's continued presence among His church: He leads, guides, provides, sanctifies, prepares, corrects, and completes us through His Spirit. Of course, what is really meant by "His Spirit" is what the Spirit performs through the written Word, since He cannot perform "immediately" or "directly." This view was strongly promoted in the 1960s and 1970s, when charismatic religion (specifically, neo-Pentecostalism) became very popular in America. While the "Bible only" position was most clearly *stated* in those decades (thus, the dating of many of the citations used in this critique), the position itself is alive and well among many of the more conservative Christians across the country.

I am *not* advocating the exact opposite of the "Bible only" position, and what has already been discussed in this book ought to be evidence of this. I agree that the Spirit is no longer providing new revelations to anyone; whatever God needed to reveal to man has already been accomplished through Christ and His "once for all delivered" gospel (Jude 3). Whatever miracles God needed to perform in order to authenticate that revelation have already been performed; we have no need of anything else in the way of *proof for* or the *substance of* God's gospel. But this is where such beliefs and the "Bible only" position diverge. The Bible—the same one that the Spirit revealed to us—sufficiently argues in favor of the Spirit's very active and dynamic presence among Christ's church today. At the same time, the Bible does *not* support a position that limits the

Spirit's work to, or only allows the Spirit to operate through, the literal words of Scripture.

The Book and the Living Word

A fundamental error in advocating a "Bible only" position begins with confusing two subjects: the literal, physical Bible (a book) with the spiritual, divine message (the "living word of God"). While often assumed to be the same thing, these are not necessarily interchangeable terms or subjects. One (the book) exists only in the realm of man; the other (the Word)[175] exists only in the realm of God—that is, in the spiritual context. There are no physical Bibles in God's world; likewise, the living Word is not something that can be confined to words of ink on a page in a book.

Someone gasps, "Then you are saying that we don't *need* the Bible!" I would never say this. The Bible *book* is a written record of the living *Word* of God to man. No one has ever been saved apart from the words that God has revealed from heaven; at the same time, no one has ever been saved by words alone. The gospel which we have received through Christ's apostles (Ephesians 2:20; 2 Peter 3:2; Jude 17; et al) was *delivered* as a spiritual "Word"—a divine revelation—but was *recorded* as a written revelation—a divine source of authority. The once-mysterious gospel of God "has now been manifested to His saints" (Colossians 1:26) through divinely-inspired men who wrote down this message for everyone to read and understand (see Ephesians 3:4-5 and Revelation 1:1-3, for example). Thus, the Bible is the only authentic and authoritative record of what God has revealed to man for the purpose of his salvation. First God reveals, *then* man understands—and always in this order ("Hear, and understand…," Matthew 15:10; Mark 7:14, et al).[176]

Having said this, it is now necessary to recognize some distinctions between the *nature* of that revelation and the written *record* of it. It may seem at first that these are petty semantic differences and nothing more; this is not the case, and these differences bear directly on the discussion at hand.

❑ First, the spiritual Word of God is timeless, universal, singular, and immutable; the written revelation, however, can be expressed in more than one way. The Bible has been translated into over 200 languages, even though the Word of God (His truth) is unchanged and universal. We do not have over 200 *gospels*, for there is only one; yet we may well have that many *accurate expressions* of the one gospel.

❏ Second, a Bible can be created or destroyed by men; the "living and enduring word of God" (1 Peter 1:23) is beyond man's reach. The written Bible is translated by men; it is then printed and bound by a book publisher. The Word, however, is spoken by the Holy Spirit, and transcends human agencies or machinery. Men can malign the text of the Bible, but they cannot corrupt the eternal message of God. We can restrict the availability of the Bible, but we cannot imprison the Word of God (cf. 2 Timothy 2:9). We can destroy a Bible, just as we can destroy any man-made book, but no one can destroy the Word of God. (I have had Christians tell me that "the Bible will endure forever," citing Matthew 25:35. Yet what they meant to say was that the *Word of God*—God's revealed truth—will endure forever. Your Bible does have a finite existence.)

❏ Third, the Bible is a static, non-living, inanimate record; the Word, however, is "living and active" (Hebrews 4:12), "living and enduring," and is able to *perform* actions. A book cannot do anything; the divine Word of God, however, is able to bring into existence things that formerly did not exist (Hebrews 11:3; 2 Peter 3:5). We are not "born again" of the Bible (a book), but we are most certainly "born again" of the "living and enduring word of God" (1 Peter 1:23). The Bible cannot make you into a child of God anymore than an encyclopedia can make you into a college graduate, but the Word of God "performs its work in you who believe" (1 Thessalonians 2:13) and is able to reconcile you to God as a "new creature" (2 Corinthians 5:17-19). The Bible cannot make you free, but the *truth* will (John 8:32). The Bible (book) *teaches* us what God needs us to know, but the Word of God (His truth) *transforms* us into what we need to be.

❏ Fourth, the Bible is the written record of what the Spirit has revealed, whereas the "living and active word of God" is in essence the power *of* the Spirit.[177] Words can *lead* us to life, but the soul is not regenerated by words alone; only God Himself can bring life from that which is dead. Jesus *spoke* words to the people, but it was only because of the Spirit who *gave* those words that anything was accomplished (John 6:63). Likewise, Peter *spoke* words by which Cornelius would be saved (Acts 11:14), but it was only because of Cornelius' obedient faith *coupled with* the Spirit's divine regeneration (i.e., grace; see Titus 3:4-7) that

Cornelius was saved. Paul wrote, "The kingdom of God does not consist in words but in power" (1 Corinthians 4:20), which has a dual meaning: the power of the kingdom cannot be reduced to empty boasts (like what the Corinthians were hearing from false apostles), but neither can it be reduced to words of an epistle.

❑ Fifth, in every case in Scripture, we *can* interchange the "living word of God" (or similar phrases) to the activity of the Spirit Himself, since the divine *revelation* of the Spirit and the divine *action* of the Spirit speak of the same thing. This does not mean that the Spirit has revealed everything that He does, but that whatever He does is in complete agreement with what He has revealed. The Word is "living" in the same sense that the Spirit is (perpetually) living; even after every Bible has been destroyed at the end of time, the Word of the Spirit will continue eternally just as the Spirit of God who gave it is an eternal Being. The Bible is not the Spirit, but the Word of God is inseparable from the Holy Spirit in the same way that salvation is inseparable from God Himself.

❑ Sixth, we cannot ascribe to the Bible (a book) attributes or actions which are only possible with a divine being (God). A book cannot add you to the body of Christ, forgive your sins, sanctify your soul, provide for you a "way of escape" (1 Corinthians 10:13), or do more abundantly than all that you ask or think (Ephesians 3:20-21). However, the "living and enduring word of God" can do all these things, seeing as how the Word of God is inseparable from the Spirit Himself. The gospel is recorded in the Bible, but the power *of* the gospel exceeds what the Bible alone is able to accomplish (Romans 1:16). One can believe in the gospel record (John 20:31), but that record itself is incapable of responding to that belief; God's Spirit, however, most certainly does respond to the believer and can sanctify that person's soul (1 Peter 1:2). The Bible is not Deity in book form; the Spirit has never been reduced to mere words on a page anymore than Jehovah was reduced to a tablet of stone.[178]

❑ Seventh, because the Bible is not Deity, we must regard it for what it is: a book. This may come across as blasphemous at first, unless one thinks it through logically. If a Bible is worn beyond repair, or if you spill a cup of coffee on it, then you dispose of it and get another one. If you leave it on the roof of your car and lose it when you drive off (I speak from experience), you purchase another one. Holy things cannot be purchased at a book store;

neither do we dispose of them in a very unholy way. The holy *revelation* that the Bible contains cannot be worn out, ruined, or lost; it is timeless, perfect, and indestructible, just as the Spirit Himself is all of these things. The Bible itself is just a book, not a thing to be worshiped. This does *not* mean that we should treat a Bible carelessly or consider it expendable; it is to be valued above all other books since it contains God's instructions for your salvation. It remains the most important, special, and unique book that has ever been assembled. Yet when all is said and done, the book *itself* cannot be considered equal to the Spirit who inspired that book.

"Bible only" advocates do operate according to a very legitimate concern: they do not want the gospel to be misused or abused, even though they cannot prevent this from happening despite their best efforts. They also deeply respect the written text itself, and thus do not want people to extract something from the message that really isn't there. I certainly agree with—and applaud—such efforts, for in order to show reverence to God, we must also respect His message. However, their major premise— "Whatever the Spirit does for the believer is accomplished through the Word (in this case, the Bible)"—is itself conspicuously absent in the New Testament. Some have cited Romans 8:2 to support this view, where Paul speaks of "the law of the Spirit of life in Christ Jesus."[179] This passage does state that the one "in Christ" is guided by the Spirit (see 8:14); however, it does not state that the Bible replaces the Spirit's guidance.

The Concern over Miracles

"Bible only" advocates are also very concerned over the subject of miracles. Once again, they are insistent that since spiritual gifts have ceased within the church, therefore the Spirit has also disappeared from view. If the Spirit were among us, then He would be performing miracles (or so it is assumed); since miracles are not being performed, therefore He is not present. Yet what of the genuine miracle of a "dead" soul being reborn as a "new creature" upon one's conversion to the Lord? Is there not something miraculous in an otherworldly God forgiving one's soul of its sins, even though the human soul, the stain of sin, and God Himself are all invisible to us? When we are "transformed" into something better than what we are capable of doing on our own, does this not require miraculous intervention?

If we rob Christ's church of *all* miracles, then we rob ourselves of what God's power accomplishes for us in the spiritual realm. We also deny the very purpose of His church, which is to provide a spiritual sanctuary wherein spiritual gifts are found (Ephesians 1:3).[180] Jesus did not build His church only so that we would have something to "join" or "identify with," as though mere membership or association could heal us of our spiritual diseases. Just as Jesus healed people when He was here upon this earth, so He heals us today: the *same power* (Spirit) that performed then continues to perform today. Just because His power is invisible to us, and is performed upon invisible human souls and not human bodies, does not make the Spirit any less real, powerful, or active. We have no divinely-expressed purpose or actual proof of visible miracles being performed today.[181] However, we *do*—in fact, we *must*—see the evidence of miraculous power being performed upon the human heart, if indeed anyone is no longer conformed to this world but is transformed by way of spiritual renewal (cf. Romans 12:1-2; Colossians 3:9-10). The obvious effects of this transformation are in the form of the "fruit of the Spirit," as discussed in an earlier chapter. We cannot claim that God is active in His church while simultaneously denying His very real activity in our own lives. He *is* active among us—which *necessitates* unseen yet miraculous activity—or else the church is lifeless and inactive. We cannot have it both ways at once, that is, zero divine activity *and* a living and active church. These are incompatible states of being.

Some "Bible only" advocates (certainly not all of them!) believe that New Testament passages that speak of the Spirit's work in the church refer only to those who received miraculous gifts of the Spirit. When considering a passage like Romans 5:1-5, for example, they argue that this *must* be dealing only with the *charisma* of the early church and not our present situation. The Holy Spirit was given to *them*, but not to *us*; all the other facts of that passage apply across the board, but not *that* fact. In another example, Acts 2:38 is said to be only partially relevant to us today: yes, we need to repent and be baptized, but since the "gift of the Holy Spirit" only refers to miraculous abilities (so it is claimed) we really cannot teach this today. Now whenever we cite Acts 2:38 with regard to one's response to the gospel, we are to believe that *we* do not receive the same "gift" that *those* Christians received.

In light of all that we have studied so far, does this make sense?

The New Testament does not *naturally conclude* that the Spirit is absent from the Christian's day-to-day walk. It does not teach that we receive a book where the early church received the living Spirit of God. Granted, the early church was provided with visible manifestations of the Spirit in lieu of the written word, but now that we have the written word, are we no longer in need of the Spirit? Suppose we saw this in a different light: the early church received the Holy Spirit *and* spiritual gifts, whereas today we receive the Holy Spirit *and* the completed gospel (i.e., the Bible). In both cases, then, *all* of Christ's church—whether today or 2,000 years ago—receives the Holy Spirit as a "gift" of God, which is exactly what Peter taught in Acts 2:38. Also, in both cases, *all* of Christ's church—whether today or 2,000 years ago—receives the revelation of the Spirit: where once this was received directly (by inspiration), we now receive this indirectly (in the Bible), but we *all receive the same revelation*.

If we teach otherwise, we unintentionally support a theology foreign to the New Testament: salvation by works. If we claim that the only thing that God provides us with is a Bible—nothing else!—then our salvation is predicated upon our infallible understanding of that Bible, our infallible handling of that Bible, and our worthy obedience to that Bible. Thus, we are resting upon our *own* effort for salvation. Someone objects: "But God's Spirit *gave* us this Bible—that is His part!" This is nothing different than what the Pharisees believed: "God *gave* us the Law—that is His part!" They (wrongly) believed that the rest was up to their own efforts. These men did not rely upon God's grace, for they believed that they were justified by their own piety and acts of law-keeping (e.g., Luke 18:9-14; Romans 10:2-4; and Galatians 5:1-4.) A Christian succumbs to this self-justifying mentality when he depends upon God for his conversion, yet afterwards relies on his own knowledge, effort, good works, and self-righteousness in order to bring him to completion. Some "Bible only" advocates have expressed this very thing:

> Our salvation is in our hands. There is nothing more that God will do for us other than presenting the opportunity to obey. He sent His Son. He sent His Spirit with a message. ...Now it is up to us. We accept the favor or mercy of God, believe on Jesus Christ, and obey the commandments contained in the message of the Spirit [i.e., the Bible]. If we do that, we can truly say that we have been saved by grace through faith. The Spirit's part in converting us was accomplished through the Word.[182]

According to this position, whatever one needs from God can be found in Scripture, and it is that person's responsibility to locate relevant passages and comply obediently. Grace is something God does at baptism, but obedience to Scripture is what justifies that person to God.

To the contrary, the Bible teaches that "by grace you are saved through faith; and that not of yourselves, it is the gift of God; not as a result of works, so that no one may boast" (Ephesians 2:8-9). We cannot be saved *once* by grace, and then by works from that point forward. This is *exactly* what Paul countered when he asked rhetorically, "Are you so foolish? Having begun by the Spirit, are you now being perfected by the flesh?" (Galatians 3:3). Yet the "Bible only" position forces this upon us: God acts upon the human heart at the point of one's conversion—allegedly without a miracle being performed!—and from then on, it is up to us to perfect ourselves by being excellent Bible students. "Faith comes by hearing, and hearing by the word of Christ" (Romans 10:17) is often quoted to defend this, but this means faith is predicated upon the gospel and not an automatic result of hearing it. It does *not* mean—as "Bible only" advocates imply—the written "word of Christ" *is equal to* or *replaces* the divine work of God.

Similarly, the ancient Jews identified themselves as the "people of the book," and virtually idolized the written Torah (Law);[183] but righteousness was not achieved through the Torah (see John 5:39-47; Acts 13:38-39; Romans 10:1-4; et al). Likewise, we can be students of the Bible without having come to the righteousness of God *if* we deny the very real and continuous power *of* God that He exercises upon the soul *in response to* our human faith. That "power" is divine grace, which really is the work of Christ *through* the agency of the Holy Spirit. Even atheists can learn and understand Scripture; yet because they do not have faith, therefore God's grace does not help them. The words are there; these words lead to the source of life; but no life is given because Christ is not made Lord in their hearts (1 Peter 3:15) *and* the Spirit does not perform His work upon them. Likewise, Israel heard the good news of God, but this information did nothing for those who did not believe in it (Hebrews 4:2). While the Bible is available to anyone, the "living and enduring word of God"—in essence, the activity of the Holy Spirit—is only given to those who trust and obey what is written *in* the Bible. The Spirit uses the Bible as His tool to convince men of what is true in order to provide a reason to believe in Christ, but what He offers the believer is more than mere statements of truth and convincing reasons.

Trying to Avoid the Unavoidable

The "Bible only" position dismisses, but does not answer, the real issue concerning miracles. In other words, advocates of this position are adamant that no miracles can be performed today by way of human agency, but they seem to have no problem with a book (the Bible) performing works upon the human soul. "Anything that the Spirit does for us is now accomplished through the Word (Bible)" is a standard refrain, and yet it contradicts their *other* standard refrain: "The Holy Spirit is not performing miracles among men today."

One advocate of this position states: "To deny that the Holy Spirit is operating miraculously today is not to deny that the Holy Spirit operates. Before the New Testament was written, the Holy Spirit operated through inspired men. Now He operates through the inspired Book [the Bible—MY WORDS]."[184] This imposes a self-determined limitation upon God's Spirit: He can only perform through men or books. It presumes that the Spirit is unable (or unwilling) to work in any other manner, through any other means. It also presumes that unless God has spelled out for us *how* He works, therefore He does not or cannot work. Certainly God held ancient Israel to the Law of Moses; this was His revelation to them; it was binding and non-negotiable. At the same time, *it is obvious* that God's work of grace, mercy, and divine providence toward Israel superseded what was specifically written in the words of that Law. Sometimes this manifestation of providence appeared as visible miracles (Deuteronomy 8:3); more often, however, it was invisible and unexplained—yet real all the same (8:4).

As defined before (in chapter 10), a "miracle" is when God performs His work apart from an earthly medium, superseding all natural laws and expectations. Yet (it is argued) if He performs His work through the Bible, then no miracles are being performed.[185] This is just a manipulation of words. It avoids the immediate problem (of modern-day miracles), but it creates another one: *how* does the Spirit work through the written Word without performing a miracle? There is no rational or biblical explanation of this. "The Holy Spirit operates (works) in conversion and sanctification through the Word"[186]—but what exactly does this mean? Does just reading a Bible passage change my soul? Am I converted to Christ simply by reading and obeying Scripture (as some maintain)?[187] If I read James 1:5, for example ("But if any of you lacks wisdom, let him ask of God, who gives to all generously and without reproach, and it will be given to him"), is it *God* who gives me wisdom, or the *Bible*? There is no doubt that the Bible can make one wise; there is also no doubt that the Spirit is its Author. If the Bible alone can impart wisdom, then why do I need God any longer?—I already have His book. Furthermore, why would I pray to God for something that I already have? This also does not follow. On the other hand, if God really does provide wisdom *in a manner that exceeds what is accomplished through mere Bible reading* (or any other natural means), then isn't that miraculous in nature?

We do not see God performing visible, event-oriented miracles like what the early Christians beheld and enjoyed, but God's intervention on behalf of the believer is miraculous in nature. In this spiritual context, God *is* performing miracles today: He regenerates human souls; He renews human hearts; He forgives sins, restores us to fellowship, leads us away from overwhelming temptation, and imparts wisdom to the heart. *How* He performs these works is not something we can answer definitively; but as God, He is *capable* of doing this, we can *ask* Him to do this, and we must believe He *will* do this. In his comments on Ephesians 1:13-14, T. W. Brents concurs: "If we are now sealed with the Holy Spirit, as those Ephesians were, it takes place *after*, and is *something more than hearing, believing, and receiving the Word.*"[188]

"The Spirit only works through the Word (Bible)" is like saying, "Your broken-down car will be repaired only through the car manufacturer's repair manual." The statement is correct to a point: the manual identifies the problem and offers the solution. It is clear, however, that the manual cannot fix your car by itself. The actual repair work requires a third party: a mechanic. Likewise, the Bible identifies the problems of the human condition and explains the solution, but the Bible itself cannot *heal* the corrupted human soul of its problems. This requires supernatural, divine intervention—a power beyond the words of the Bible itself: Christ's intercession *and* the Spirit's activity.

Does God's activity today supersede what the Bible *says*? Let's be very careful here. God's miracles upon the human heart do supersede what the Bible (a book) can do, but *never* what the Bible teaches. The "living and abiding word of God"—the activity of the Holy Spirit upon the hearts of men—most certainly can perform where pages and ink cannot. Yet the Spirit cannot and will not contradict Himself. The Spirit does not show partiality, but He is most certainly *powerful*, and is able to "equip you in every good thing to do His will, working in us that which is pleasing in

His sight, through Jesus Christ" (Hebrews 13:21). The "you" here really means *all of us* who are saved through the blood of Christ.

The Implications of Prayer

The final point in this discussion is perhaps the most obvious: If God is not directly, supernaturally, and actively involved in the lives of Christians, then why do we pray to Him? One "Bible only" advocate writes: "Did God hear and answer prayer before the Christian Age? If yes, then the personal indwelling and operation of the Spirit apart from the Word is not essential to God's hearing and answering prayers."[189] But we must ask: how has God *ever* answered prayers without necessarily involving some supernatural action on His part? This skirts around the problem but fails to address it. This seems to assume that the Spirit has not ever been involved in answering prayers at all, except through what He has provided through written revelation.

Prayer necessarily implies two things: *our* faith in God's activity and *God's* active response to our faith. When we pray to God, we ask for Him to perform *beyond* what the Bible is able to do. Yet if we pray to God and His answer is always the same—"Go read your Bible; it is all-sufficient for your needs"—then doesn't this render prayer useless? If God's work is now limited to whatever Scripture literally says, then why are we asking Him for help? We are to "let [our] requests be made known to God" (Philippians 4:6), but what's the point? We are to cast all our anxiety upon Him (1 Peter 5:7), but what's the use? If the Bible is all-sufficient for our needs, then what else is there to receive? Once again, why should we pray for that which we already have?

Communion with God is not entirely defined by reading and understanding Scripture. There is more to the Christian life than just knowledge and information. Being filled with the Spirit is much more than just being filled with Bible verses and book citations. God does not *actually* or *verbally* speak to the human heart, but He most certainly does *communicate* with it. If He does not do this, then the very act of praying to Him is pointless and hopeless. We pray to God not only so that He would hear us, but also so that we would hear *Him*. We "listen" to His answers, even though they are not in the form of audible words; we follow the direction of His Spirit, even though we cannot see Him. Our prayers are offered up "in the Spirit" (Romans 8:26-27; Ephesians 6:18; Jude 20), which means that the Spirit is always listening to *us* as a result of our having been filled with *Him*. When we pray for things that are according to His will, then He responds to us in whatever way seems best to Him (1 John 5:14-15). If we ask, seek, and knock, then the Spirit works to answer, enlighten, and open doors (Matthew 7:7-8). God will "give what is good to those who ask Him" (Matthew 7:11)—this is not empty rhetoric, but is His *promise* to those who believe. Jesus Himself said, "And all things you ask in prayer, believing, you will receive" (Matthew 21:22). If we pray without such belief, then we are unstable, doubting, and double-minded people who will receive nothing from the Lord (James 1:6-8, in principle). We would no longer be believers in a God who answers prayers, but only churchgoers who think that the mere *act* of praying somehow justifies us before God.

"Bible only" advocates claim that Scripture is "all-sufficient," and therefore if God operates outside of Scripture, it negates the all-sufficiency of the Bible.[190] Yet *prayer* is outside of Scripture, and even "Bible only" advocates believe that God hears our prayers and responds in whatever way He chooses.[191] What they *mean* to say is that with regard to *doctrine*, which is God's revelation to man concerning the terms and conditions of our fellowship with Him, Scripture *is* all-sufficient and God does *not* need to reinforce it with ongoing miracles. Scripture is sufficient for the purpose for which it was given, just as the Law of Moses was sufficient for an earlier purpose. There is one gospel for all men; it cannot be amended or redefined (Galatians 1:8). We pray "according to His will" (1 John 5:14) which means we should never ask God to do anything that would violate the Spirit's revealed gospel. The Spirit does not speak out of both sides of His mouth: He does not support the gospel *and at the same time* endorse a prayer that defies that same gospel.

Scripture *teaches* us everything that needs to be done (by God *and* His people), but it does not *do* everything that needs to be done. Scripture is for man, not God; the Spirit does not need to consult the Bible to know what He has already revealed to us. He does, however, perform in ways that are "beyond all that we ask or think," which is in complete agreement with the Scripture He has given us (Ephesians 3:20).

Summary Thoughts

I am in no way impugning the *motives* of those Christians who hold to the "Bible only" position. It would be presumptuous—and malicious— for me to suggest any deliberate misrepresentation on their part. However, I do believe their *methods of argumentation* do not work and that some of their conclusions are not only forced but also mistaken.

The "Bible only" position has also had serious negative effects upon many believers today. Several generations of Christians have been trained to discount any real activity of the Holy Spirit in their own lives *or* the body of Christ. The Spirit has been reduced to a ceremonial vestige of the ancient church, but has no appreciable effect on the contemporary believer. Scripture—the literal Bible itself—has been elevated to the point of virtual deification: where once the Spirit performed His work, now the Bible performs instead. The "living and enduring word of God" has been erroneously made equal to the literal, book-chapter-verse Bible. Being "led by the Spirit" has been reduced to "read your Bible," which inadvertently invalidates the need for prayer or divine intervention. The access that we have through the Spirit (Ephesians 2:18) has been reduced to the enlightenment we receive entirely through Bible reading.

I am not—and would never!—dismiss the value of reading, meditating upon, and being enlightened by Scripture. Once again, "All Scripture is inspired by God and profitable for teaching, for reproof, for correction, for training in righteousness; so that the man of God may be adequate, equipped for every good work" (2 Timothy 3:16-17). This has not changed, and I personally believe it without reservation. My appreciation and respect for Scripture is enormous. I have profusely appealed to Scripture throughout the entirety of this book in order to arrive at the conclusions stated here; there is no greater authority to which I could appeal. However, "all Scripture" teaches me *how* and *why* I need to be equipped to serve God; it is not the *power* which equips me (Hebrews 13:20-21). All Scripture teaches me *how* to be justified, but it is God who justifies me through Christ (Romans 3:23-26; 5:1-2). I cannot be saved by reading the Bible alone; my faith must ultimately be in Jesus Christ, not only in Scripture.

My intention here is to more accurately define fellowship with God *and* Christians everywhere through an objective appeal to the Scriptures. At the same time, I strongly urge advocates of the "Bible only" position to look again at the structure of their arguments. Even if their conclusions do not change, it will have been worth the time and effort invested. The subject of the Holy Spirit is far too important to approach only once or twice. The more we learn about Him and His work, the better appreciation we have for Christ and *His* work, and for the grace of God which we all so desperately need.

Conclusion

Jesus told Nicodemus, "The wind blows where it wishes and you hear the sound of it, but do not know where it comes from and where it is going; so is everyone who is born of the Spirit" (John 3:8). We know the wind exists, we can see its effects, and we can measure its speed; but we cannot *see* it. Likewise, there is something unseen and otherworldly about those who are "born of the Spirit." It is not something we can observe literally, but it is evident nonetheless. It is also not something we have done to ourselves, but is something God has done for us in response to our faith in Him. We are made to be spiritual people because of the Spirit whom He has given us.

Being "*born* of the Spirit" necessarily implies the *work* of the Spirit. We are no longer merely born of the flesh or human desire. Now, if indeed we are "in Christ," we are "born again to a living hope" through the same power with which Christ raised Himself from the dead (1 Peter 1:3). Not only this, but the Spirit has sealed us for the day of redemption (Ephesians 4:30). This is no ordinary birth; it is as unnatural as any miracle; it is nothing we can duplicate here on earth (John 1:12-13). This is because the Holy Spirit is not of this world and is miraculous in nature, and yet He most certainly works *in* this world and *through* those who belong to Christ.

What this means is: the Spirit is too powerful to be constrained by our own personal beliefs or preferences. In Luke 5:36-38, Jesus taught a parable about wineskins (leather flasks) and cloth. Old wineskins cannot accommodate new wine, since through fermentation the new wine expands beyond the elasticity of the old skins. Likewise, a new patch cannot be used on old cloth, since the patch will shrink with washing and will pull away from the old cloth. In both cases, the elements spoken of are commonly *related*, but in the given context they are not *compatible*. The parable concerned neither wine nor cloth, but the message of the otherworldly gospel of God compared to the rigid legalism of the Jews. The two appeared on the surface to be *related*, when in fact they are *incompatible*. The one (gospel) cannot be contained by the other (Judaism); it far exceeds its comprehension and teaching. The one (gospel) cannot be mated with the other (Judaism); one is of heaven, whereas the other is of man (cf. Galatians 4:21-31).

Likewise, while modern teachings on the Spirit and the actual work of the Spirit may seem obviously related in nature, this does not mean they are compatible. The teachings of men—whatever they might be—are simply unable to contain (or comprehend) the work of the Spirit. He is too strong and powerful to be poured into an old system, or into any system which is not of God. There is no duality between the heavenly and the earthly; likewise, we cannot cling to teachings (or fears) that originate from men while seeking spiritual transformation in the kingdom of God. Judaism could not be combined with Christ's gospel, but neither can any other "gospel" be combined with His, no matter how good the intentions are that promote it.

That being said, it is likely that *everyone*—myself included—will have some mistaken views concerning this mysterious member of the Godhead. We should not be passive about this, however; our attitude ought to be one of seeking to expose and correct these errors, not blindly perpetuating them. Through deeper study and understanding of the Scriptures, we ought to come to a clearer and more effective understanding of the Holy Spirit of God. This takes much time, meditation, and research, which is, of course, why so many are content to remain with whatever belief they had first embraced.

On the other hand, there is only so much that we are ever going to know about the Spirit and His work. God has not revealed to us His Spirit as much as He has His Son. There are several probable reasons for this. First, the greater attention must be on Christ the Redeemer, for without Him the Spirit cannot help us in any way. Second, we do not have to fully understand the Spirit's work in order to benefit from it. Third, God has provided a sufficient amount of information in order for us to believe in His Spirit; it is now up to us to believe in (i.e., build our faith upon) the evidence He has provided. Fourth, just as the soul is the mysterious counterpart to human life, so the Spirit is the mysterious counterpart (relatively speaking) to the Godhead. We must wait until we are with God to have all our questions answered concerning our souls *and* His Spirit. Finally, God has His own reasons for what He has disclosed and what He has withheld, and we dare not question His decisions in either case (Deuteronomy 29:29) .

To shrug at this and say, "Well, then, what's the point of pursuing a subject that we will never fully understand?" is to miss the point of God's revelations entirely. The fact is: we will *never* fully understand who God

179

is or what He does—not in this life. Subjects like saving grace, Christ's redemption, and the love of God are as limitless as they are fascinating. Just as God has given us a profound (yet finite) amount of information on these subjects, so He has concerning His Holy Spirit. Who are we to pick and choose which of these we will study deeply and which we will give only a passing glance? Whatever God has revealed to us concerning our fellowship with Him ought to be *supremely important* to us—and this most certainly includes His Spirit and the Spirit's ministry throughout the spiritual body of Christ.

It is my sincere hope that you have found this study not only informative and genuine, but also personally rewarding. Hopefully, you are a more informed Bible student because of your having engaged in this study, even if you have not shared all of my personal views in cases where the Bible has not been specific. It was never my intention to force my convictions upon you; it was my *earnest* intention, however, to confront you with perspectives with which you may not have previously considered. What you do with this from this point forward is up to you.

To those readers who may not have yet been "born of water and the Spirit" (John 3:3-8), then I implore you to act upon the instructions God has provided in His Word (John 20:31). I strongly recommend that you begin by reading the book of Luke in order to learn about the Savior; then read the book of Acts to learn how to respond to the Savior's gospel. It is God's desire that you come to the knowledge of the truth of Christ so as to be saved (1 Timothy 2:3-6); it is also my ardent desire that you be saved through the blood of Jesus Christ.

To those readers who have already been "clothed" with Christ in baptism (Galatians 3:26-27), I cannot think of a better way to end this study than by quoting the apostle Paul, whom the Spirit had inspired to write (2 Corinthians 13:14): "The grace of the Lord Jesus Christ, and the love of God, and the fellowship of the Holy Spirit, be with you all." Amen.

Endnotes

Chapter One

1   "Jehovah" is the Masoretic rendering of Yahweh (from the ancient Hebrew, *YHWH*), the noun form of the verb phrase, "I AM" (as used in Exodus 3:14). Permanent vowels were not added to the Hebrew Bible text until perhaps the fifth century AD by the Masoretic scribes, thus producing Yahweh from *YHWH* (Larry Walker, *The Origin of the Bible*, ed. Philip Comfort [Wheaton, IL: Tyndale House Publishers, Inc., 1992], 215-216). If one wishes to investigate this further, http://apostolic.net/biblicalstudies/jehovah.htm (cited June, 2009) provides a good beginning point. In this book, "Jehovah" will be used as an understandable reference to God the Father.

2   It is true, of course, that the Holy Spirit also existed *before* the physical creation. By "physical creation," I am referring to the visible world which has a finite existence (1 John 2:15-17).

3   In Genesis 2:7, the word "breath" is from the Hebrew word *neshamah*, which can also be translated "wind," "inspiration," "soul," or "spirit" [Strong's #5397]. The word "soul" is from *nephesh* [Strong's #5315] which can be translated "creature," "spirit," "ghost," "mind," "appetite," and others. In other words, this verse seems to make an intentional connection: God's "breath" (Spirit) is what brings man's "soul" (life) into existence—in essence, makes man a "breather" of life. All Strong's number references are taken from James Strong's *Exhaustive Concordance* (STEP Files, Parson's Technology, Inc., 1998, electronic edition). This numerical indexing is used also by Thayer's Lexicon and other prominent references.

4   See also Ezekiel 37:1-14 for another (spiritual) application of this concept. "The new life of the redeemed Israel...is God's life because it is the product of God's creative Spirit" (C. K. Barrett, *The Holy Spirit and the Gospel Tradition* [Shreveport: Lambert Publications, 1966], 20.)

5   The "word of God" in this passage is most certainly the divine activity of the Holy Spirit—the "Him" in the verse to follow (Hebrews 4:13). This reference is *not* the literal Bible, for a book is not "living and active," nor does it have the ability to "judge" anything. More will be said on this passage later, but it is already clear that our souls are not overseen by mere words on a page, but by a "living" and life-giving Spirit.

6   Our "reconciliation" necessarily implies that we once enjoyed a favorable relationship with Him, but that this relationship has been interrupted by something—namely, our sin. The implication is the same as that in Matthew 5:23-24: one cannot be "reconciled" to a stranger with whom he had no previous fellowship, but he can be reconciled to a "brother," with whom he both *had* and is expected to *maintain* a favorable relationship.

7   This biblical citation, by itself, may not be convincing; but coupled with 1 Corinthians 2:11-16, where it is cited (in verse 16), Paul identifies God's *Spirit* as intimately associated with God's *mind*. I cover this thought in more detail

182

shortly after this reference.

8   There is a difference between omnipresence and omniperson: the Spirit's *presence* can be everywhere, but He remains one Personage; Christ is *in* us, yet He Himself remains at the right hand of God (Franklin T. Puckett, "The Holy Spirit," *Searching the Scriptures* [vol. 23, no. 7: July 1982], 151-152).

9   R. C. Sproul, *The Mystery of the Holy Spirit* (Wheaton, IL: Tyndale House Publishers, 1990), 125.

10   Ibid., 71; bracketed words are mine.

11   "He [the Holy Spirit] is never called a 'Person' in Scripture; and we only create a difficulty when we use the language of Theology instead of the words of God" (E. W. Bullinger, *Word Studies on the Holy Spirit* [Grand Rapids: Kregel Publications, 1985], 39). Yet the Spirit has the *nature* and *characteristics* of a "Person"; we would be wrong to call Him "a God," but there is nothing corruptive in referring to Him as a "Person(age) of God." In our limited understanding of the spiritual world, we have no better way by which to refer to Him.

12   Leo H. Boles, *The Holy Spirit: His Personality, Nature, Works* (Nashville: Gospel Advocate Co., 1973), 19.

13   Grammatical gender is not exactly comparable to biological gender. God is referred to with masculine pronouns, but this does not mean that He is biologically or anatomically "male." On the other hand, we cannot ignore the obvious implications: God—the Father, Son, and Spirit—is most certainly associated with *headship* and *authority*, which are also characteristics He assigns to earthly men (cf. 1 Corinthians 11:3). It is also true that there are no female entities described in the spiritual realm except for the "bride" of Christ, His church (Ephesians 5:25-27; Revelation 21:9).

14   Boles, *The Holy Spirit*, 27.

15   Some wish to limit the teaching of the Holy Spirit to Jesus' disciples-turned-apostles. It is true that Jesus spoke these words (John 14:26) to those disciples; it is also true that He did not promise all Christians what He promised them. However, it is not true that these words have no bearing upon us, or that *only* the eleven disciples heard these words (implied in Acts 1:21-22). While the Spirit imparted *miraculous* knowledge to the early church in lieu of the written Bible (1 Corinthians 12:8), it is wrong to assume that He cannot lead us to knowledge through whatever other means He chooses. Just because we cannot explain *how* the Spirit works in our lives today does not mean that *He does not work* in our lives. (We will address this topic further in a later chapter.)

16   The Holy Spirit hovering [lit., brooding] over the waters (Genesis 1:2) seems to parallel ancient "world-egg" depictions of the creation of the world; yet that concept assumes that the germ of life is in the "egg" itself. "The biblical idea is different. That over which the Spirit broods is not potential life; it is chaos. The life is not in the chaos; it is in the Spirit" (Barrett, *The Holy Spirit and the Gospel Tradition*, 18).

17   We should have no problem understanding the Holy Spirit to be referred to as "the Spirit of Christ," for Christ has always been in the background of the revelatory work of the Holy Spirit. In fact, in Romans 8:9, the "Spirit of Christ"

and "Spirit of God" are used interchangeably.

18   The word "inspired" (as in 2 Timothy 3:16) literally means "God-breathed" (or "[by the] breath of God") [Strong's #2315]. Those who were moved by the Holy Spirit to speak the oracles of God were, for all intents and purposes, filled with the "breath" of God. Just as God breathed life into Adam ("and the man become a living being"; Genesis 2:7), so God breathed His Spirit into His prophets and apostles and their message became a "living and active" word (Hebrews 4:12). To refer to such men as "God-breathers" is not far from a literal understanding of this concept.

19   It is difficult to understand exactly what is meant by this phrase, "the seven Spirits." Since the original language of the New Testament (*Koine* Greek) did not differentiate between upper and lower case usage, the translators capitalize "Spirit" based upon the context, not the language itself. But the context here is inarguably authoritative: the revelation is *from* God the Father, God the Son, and—because He is also "God"—God the Spirit. The Spirit's designation as "the seven Spirits" (Revelation 1:4 and 4:5) is not contradictory, but actually offers a fuller description (or explanation) of the nature of the Spirit. Just as God is three Persons, so the Spirit may be described as "seven Spirits." This description is not to suggest that there are seven *separate* Spirits, but only *one* Spirit defined in a seven-fold manner, depicting completeness, perfection, and heavenly origin, just as the number "seven" is consistently used elsewhere in Revelation. Thus, the seven-fold Spirit is described as fully mature, complete, perfect in every way, and (appropriately) forever in the Presence of the Father. Furthermore, this corresponds to the letters to the seven churches (Revelation 2 – 3), in which the phrase "let him hear what the Spirit says to the churches" is used each time. Again, this is not seven *separate* Spirits speaking, but *one* Spirit with seven separate appeals to the Lord's churches.

20   Boles, *The Holy Spirit*, 16.

Chapter Two

21   Virtually the same thought is expressed in Philippians 2:1. The word "partakers" (*metochos*, "fellows," "sharers") is also used in regard to the Spirit in the same way as it is with Christ; compare, for example, Hebrews 3:14 with 6:4.

22   Richard Rogers, "A Study of the Holy Spirit of God," *Sunset Study Series* (Lubbock, TX: Sunset School of Preaching, 1968), 1.

23   In fact, in some so-called "Christian Gnostic" texts (such as the "Gospel of Philip"), the Holy Spirit was considered a "divine Mother," possibly because the Hebrew noun for "spirit" (*ruah*) is feminine. This teaching also appears in the spurious "Gospel of the Hebrews" and "The Gospel of Thomas." The virgin birth of Christ, then, "was the mysterious union between the heavenly Father and the Spirit who is both Mother and Virgin. He [the author of the "Gospel of Philip"] concludes that Christ was indeed born from a virgin—the Holy Spirit" (Stanley Burgess, *The Holy Spirit: Ancient Christian Traditions* [Peabody, MS: Hendrickson Publishers, 1984], 43. This point is included here not because it has any theological merit, but simply to show the lengths to which some have gone to

try to explain some very difficult concepts.

24   Sproul, *The Mystery of the Holy Spirit*, 74.

25   Ibid., 61.

26   Earthly man also has a triune nature: he has a physical body, an earthly conscience, and an eternal soul. Each man is "one" in that he is a unified composite of these three aspects (Ashley Johnson, *The Holy Spirit and the Human Mind* [Delight, AR: Gospel Light Publishing Co., 1985], 139). He is also "two," in that he is both physical and spiritual all at once. But he is "three" (or triune) in that he does not exist *as* a man unless he has all three aspects—body, soul, and spirit—functioning all at once. God's message of truth appeals to and is in the best interest of every aspect of man's being (cf. 1 Thessalonians 5:23).

27   This does not contradict what was said earlier concerning the Son now sending the Spirit rather than the Father. A shift in *emphasis* (concerning Who does what) does not exclude the Father from making decisions; nor should we think that because the Father sends the Spirit of His Son into the heart of the believer that the Son Himself has nothing to do with this decision. In other words, this one expression in Galatians 4:6 does not invalidate or call into question all the other passages in which Christ's authoritative role is conclusive (Matthew 28:18; Acts 2:33, et al). It simply gives us another facet of the working cooperation within the Godhead.

28   Quoted by Henry Swete in *The Holy Spirit in the Ancient Church* (Grand Rapids: Baker Book House, 1966), 234. "Trinity," as Basil used the term and as it is used in this book, only refers to the triune Godhead: the Father, Son, and Holy Spirit. It is a descriptive term, not a doctrinal one. Its first recorded usage is by Theophilus (late 2nd century) in an apologetic written to Autolycus, who referred to the Godhead as the Father, the Logos (Christ), and the "Wisdom of God" (Holy Spirit) (ibid., 47).

29   It is tempting, yet inappropriate, to call the Father, Son, and Holy Spirit three "Gods" (a.k.a. "tri-theism"). It is true that "God" is three Persons—God the Father, God the Son, and God the Spirit—but it is not true that there are three "Gods." This may seem to be a petty argument in semantics to some, but in fact by referring to the triune God as "three Gods" is misrepresentative. Scripture nowhere describes the Godhead as three Gods, but does indeed recognize the Father, Son, and Spirit as three distinct Deities who are collectively known as "God" or the "Godhead" (*theios*, "divine nature" or "Godhead," used only in Acts 17:29; Romans 1:20; and 2 Peter 1:4).

30   Likewise, the "one flesh" of a husband and his wife (Genesis 2:24; Ephesians 5:31) does not nullify the individual persons or personalities of the two who are united by marriage.

31   Quoted by Swete, *The Holy Spirit in the Ancient Church*, 325-326.

32   From his treatise, "On 'Not Three Gods'" as quoted by Stanley Burgess in *The Holy Spirit: Ancient Christian Traditions* (Peabody, MS: Hendrickson Publishers, 1984), 145.

33   A. J. Gordon, *The Ministry of the Spirit* (Minneapolis: Bethany House Publishers, 1985), 95.

Chapter Three

34   Consider also, with regard to resurrection and regeneration, the overnight budding of Aaron's almond rod that was placed in the tabernacle (Numbers 17:1-8) and how this parallels, in a sense, the resurrection of Christ.

35   This picture of the two offices—of ruler and high priest—is also a prophecy of the Christ. The "Branch" (Messiah) would unite the two offices into one, and He would build a future "temple" (church) that would be greater than anything man himself could build (see Zechariah 6:12-13). Thus, Christ is both King over the kingdom of God and High Priest over His church, and He will not be succeeded or superseded in either of these offices.

36   Let us *never* reduce the Spirit to a mere "energy" or "force," however. The Spirit is not an impersonal "energy field" or a mindless, indistinct "power grid" that supplies God's kingdom with mysterious, supernatural capability. It is a terrible misrepresentation to characterize Him in any way that calls His divine Personage or living personality into question.

37   The "olive tree" in this passage (Romans 11:17-18) is meant to illustrate Israel, but the "root" (or trunk) of this "tree" cannot be anything or anyone other than the Christ, given the related passages (cited). The "branches" represent both Jewish Christians (natural branches) and Gentile Christians (grafted branches).

38   William Brown, *The Tabernacle: Its Priests and Its Services* (Peabody, MS: Hendrickson Publishers, 1996), 72.

39   Henry Soltau, *The Tabernacle: Its Priesthood and Its Offerings* (Grand Rapids: Kregel Publications, 1994), 347.

40   Consider again Genesis 6:3 ("My Spirit shall not strive with man forever") and the principle(s) derived from this. God provides each man with an opportunity for fellowship with Him, but in the face of open, impenitent rebellion, He has no choice but to withdraw His Spirit in order to protect His Name and holiness. The true nature of this rebellion is blasphemy, which is punishable by death (cf. Leviticus 24:16). As I understand it, it is the anticipation of this (spiritual) death that is described in Hebrews 10:26-29, which speaks of a Christian who no longer enjoys fellowship with Christ *or* the Holy Spirit because of his stubborn impenitence.

41   This Messiah would serve a dual role: "Not only was he the military hero who would restore the Jewish State and establish the kingdom on earth, he was the king of peace under whose rule Paradise would return to earth" (D. S. Russell, *Between the Testaments* [Philadelphia: Fortress Press, 1988], 131). Russell's book provides an excellent overview of the post-exilic and intertestamental messianic and eschatological perspectives, for those who are interested in pursuing these subjects.

42   In the 39 uses of the word *mashiyach* [Strong's #4899] or "messiah" in the Old Testament (Hebrew text), it is almost invariably used to describe the known positions of either a priest ("the anointed priest") or king ("His anointed one"). Only in Daniel 9:25-26 is the word used in reference to a specific but as yet unknown ruler who would eventually be king *and* high priest over Israel ("Messiah the Prince"). Ezekiel 44 – 48, in describing (in an ideal but not literal

sense) the forthcoming temple of God (i.e., the church) also employs the "Prince" descriptor, but does not refer to Him literally as "Messiah"—though it is clear that they are one and the same.

43   Jesus' dual nature as both Messiah (Christ) and Deity (Son of God) is crucial to His role as the "One who takes away the sin of the world" (John 1:29; 3:16; 1 John 2:1-2). If Jesus was not the Messiah of prophecy, then He was unable to fulfill the requirements of our Redeemer; if He was not the Son of God, then He did not have the authority to serve as Redeemer. This is what makes Peter's confession (Matthew 16:18) so important: Peter identified Jesus as both Christ and Son of God (see also John 20:31).

44   This is illustrated in the sprinkling of blood during the ratification of the covenant between God and Israel: Moses took the blood of the covenant offerings and sprinkled the people with it (Exodus 24:1-8; Hebrews 9:18-22). This is further illustrated in the sprinkling of the blood of the atonement offerings during the Day of Atonement (Leviticus 16:6-15).

45   In Exodus 40:34-35 and 1 Kings 8:10-11, at the consecration of the tabernacle and Solomonic temple (respectively), the sanctuary was filled with "the glory of the LORD," which the Jewish rabbis later called *shekinah* ("[He] that dwells"). This "cloud" was to signify the presence of God in the sanctuary, but God's presence is always intimately associated with God's Spirit. This also foreshadows the Spirit's presence in the life of a believer, especially since the individual Christian is referred to as a "temple" in which the Spirit dwells (1 Corinthian 6:19).

46   Gordon, *The Ministry of the Spirit*, 48.

Chapter Four

47   Already this will become a point of controversy with some: is the baptism with the Spirit speaking of what is done to an individual, or to the entire church? If this baptism refers only to select individuals, then what are we to say of all those who are not so baptized? A major thesis of this book will be that the baptism with which Christ baptizes refers to His entire church, not to a comparatively few people in the first century. However, this book will also maintain that the *visible effects* of this baptism were limited to the early church, since it was not necessary or advantageous to continue duplicating what has already been historically and genuinely established, namely, that Christ's church is indeed immersed "in the Spirit" (cf. Ephesians 2:22).

48   "It was not the Holy Spirit Himself who 'fell on' people; but He caused His power and His gifts that were bestowed by Him to fall on them 'from on high.'" So it was with the expression, "poured out": the Spirit Himself was not literally poured out, but His gifts. So also with "received": the Spirit Himself was not literally internalized, but His gifts were (Bullinger, *Word Studies on the Holy Spirit*, 34).

49   The Greek word for "by" (*en*) can also be translated "in," depending upon the context. "Most translators have adopted the reading *by* to reveal means or agency. ...Conversely, other translators believe that the Greek preposition *en*

denotes sphere or place and thus translate it "in." They point out that in the New Testament, the Holy Spirit is never described as the baptizer. Rather, the Spirit is the sphere into which the baptismal candidate enters" (Simon J. Kistemaker, *New Testament Commentary: 1 Corinthians* [Grand Rapids: Baker Books, 1993], 429).

50   "We must conclude, therefore, that 1 Corinthians 12:13 uses the expression 'by one Spirit are we all baptized into one body' as a description of the regeneration of all believers that is symbolized by water baptism, and does not picture a 'second work of grace' or a 'second infilling with the Spirit' or a 'second blessing' subsequent to and distinct from regeneration" (Anthony Hoekema, *What About Tongue-Speaking?* [Grand Rapids: Eerdman's Publishing Co., 1966], 63).

51   The "Zealots" (Greek) or "Cananeans" (Aramaic) or "Sicarii" (Latin) was a Jewish sect which apparently began when two men, Judas and Zadduk, led an open rebellion against Rome in Galilee (AD 6). The actual roots of the Zealots, however, may extend as far back as the Maccabean Revolt (167 BC): "As the Pharisees are the heirs of the Hasidim [lit., pious ones], so the Zealots are the heirs of the Maccabees"—in spirit, if nothing else (Russell, *Between the Testaments*, 54). The party that sprang from this incident was a group of extreme nationalists who viewed Rome as an illegitimate (ungodly) power and an intrusive enemy of the Jewish State. The Zealots' ambitions were as political as they were deeply religious. They believed that they were called by God to engage in a holy war against the "powers of darkness" in order to usher in the age of the Messiah (ibid., 37-40).

52   It was an ancient Oriental custom to have a herald go before the king's visit to a city, to warn that city to be prepared for the king's presence. Failure to properly "receive" one's king in this way warranted the king's wrath and judgment. This is exactly what Jesus referred to in Luke 19:41-44: Jerusalem (as a representative of all of Israel) refused to prepare for or receive her King; therefore, she was smitten with a divine curse. This was carried out in AD 69-70 when Jerusalem was besieged and then leveled to the ground by the Romans.

53   The word "baptize" is a transliteration of *baptizo* [Strong's #907], which means to dip, immerse, submerge, or make fully wet (to whelm with water). There is no hint of anything less than full submersion in water for anyone in the New Testament who was baptized.

54   R. P. Roth, "Baptism (Sacramentarian View)," *The Zondervan Pictorial Encyclopedia of the Bible*, ed. Merrill C. Tenney (Grand Rapids: Zondervan Publishing House, 1976), vol. 1, 465.

55   The Messiah did not merely put an end to the Law, but He *fulfilled* it. It is true that *in* fulfilling the Law, He put an end to it, but it is a terrible misrepresentation of the Messiah's covenant to say that it merely superseded God's covenant with Israel. The former covenant foreshadowed God's covenant with all men; the blood of bulls and goats (as prescribed by the Law) only pointed forward to a perfect blood sacrifice that would provide absolute redemption (Hebrews 10:1-4).

56   There is only "one baptism" which God requires of men (Ephesians 4:5),

and this is that which is explained and illustrated throughout the entire gospel: immersion in water. God cannot require men to be baptized in His Spirit, since this is something that is beyond us. If this were the case, then it would only be a demonstration of God's power (which He has already clearly proved), and not a demonstration of our personal faith in Him. "Evidently he [Paul, in Ephesians 4:5] has reference to the fact that there is one baptism which is an essential part of the unity of faith. Although many baptisms were mentioned in the New Testament, yet there is only one that was required of everyone" (James D. Bales, *The Holy Spirit and the Christian* [Shreveport: Lambert Publications, 1966], 18).

57   T. W. Brents, *The Gospel Plan of Salvation* (Nashville: The Gospel Advocate Co., 1973), 588.

58   Apostolic authority was most certainly *confirmed* with signs (2 Corinthians 12:12). Also, not every Christian received the ability to perform signs, but only those to whom the Spirit determined should have such ability (1 Corinthians 12:7-11).

59   Peter's statement in Acts 11:15-16 ("...in the beginning") necessarily indicates that Cornelius' baptism with the Spirit was not common or typical, but that it had only happened once before (ibid., 580). Foy Wallace, Jr., claims that what happened with Cornelius was *not* a manifestation of Holy Spirit baptism, but only "recalled" it (*The Mission and the Medium of the Holy Spirit* [Fort Worth: Foy E. Wallace, Jr. Publications, 1967], 100-101). He believes that otherwise this would impart to Cornelius power that was promised exclusively to the apostles. "There can be no degrees in Holy Spirit baptism. Any two men baptized in the Holy Spirit would have equal measure of it" (ibid., 101). While stated as a fact, there is nothing to substantiate this.

60   "The conclusion is...that the Holy Spirit having endowed to the apostles and having through them revealed all God has to say in this dispensation, and having borne public and convincing testimony to the truth that God's philanthropy includes both Jew and Gentile—the whole world—on the same condition [Acts 15:7-9], the baptism of the Holy Spirit is no longer needed in the administration of the affairs of the kingdom" (Johnson, *The Holy Spirit and the Human Mind,* 47). If Johnson means that the *effects* of this baptism are no longer needed, then this makes sense; but it cannot be implied that modern Christians are no longer in need of the Spirit, or that the baptism with the Spirit has no effect on the contemporary church.

61   "The practical issue...is this: Are there two levels of Christians—one kind that has the baptism of the Holy Spirit and another kind that does not?" (Sproul, *The Mystery of the Holy Spirit,* 143). The answer is obvious: there are not two levels. All who are in Christ are baptized *as a body* in the Holy Spirit.

62   L. Thomas Holdcroft, *The Holy Spirit: A Pentecostal Interpretation* (Abbotsford, Canada: CeeTeC Publishing, 1999), 93.

63   Ibid., 132-134.

Chapter Five

64   Peter does not intend to limit one's obedience to God to *only* repentance

and baptism. Certainly one must also believe in the Lord (John 3:16), deny himself, take up his "cross," and follow the Lord (Matthew 16:24), and whatever else is required by God as demonstrations of faith. But it is also true that both baptism and repentance are essential in one's conversion to Christ (Acts 22:16; Galatians 3:27; 1 Peter 3:21; et al).

65   Bales, *The Holy Spirit and the Christian*, 21; emphasis his.

66   For more on this idea, see Acts 2:21, 39; 22:16; Romans 10:11-13, and 2 Thessalonians 2:13-14. Salvation has never been a one-sided action. What God does (via grace) is infinitely greater than what we do (via faith), yet *both* parties must necessarily contribute to one's salvation (Romans 1:16-17; Ephesians 2:8-9).

67   In Acts 1:4-8, Jesus promised that the apostles would receive "power" while they waited in Jerusalem. This promise is only made to the apostles (verse 2), not to everyone. (Compare also 2:1 with 1:26: the "they" refers antecedently to the apostles, not to the "hundred and twenty" who had gathered in the upper room in 1:15.) We must be careful, then, to understand that *power* was given to the apostles, but the *signs* were given generally to the church (2:16-21), and specifically to whomever the Spirit chose for this (cf. 1 Corinthians 12:11). In the case of Cornelius, the Holy Spirit performed a miracle upon Cornelius, but we have no record that Cornelius was able to perform miracles at his own discretion after this.

68   Not every Israelite was literally anointed. The priests were anointed with holy oil on behalf of the Israelites, since their service was directly related to the tabernacle (Leviticus 8:12,30); likewise, the Levites were anointed (with "purifying water") because they served the priests and represented the first-born males of every Israelite family; see Numbers 3:5-12, 8:5-19.

69   Gordon, *The Ministry of the Spirit*, 27.

70   For an extensive discussion on the subject of grace, please read my book, *The Gospel of Grace* (Louisville, KY: Religious Supply, Inc., 2008). Go to: www.booksbychad.com.

71   Think of the words "church," "apostle," "works," or "world," for example: these terms are used in the New Testament differently, depending upon the context. We cannot, then, use the word itself to determine context, but just the opposite: it is the context which gives us the accurate meaning of the word.

72   Rogers, "A Study of the Spirit of God," 25.

73   Moses E. Lard, "The Gift of the Holy Spirit" (*Lard's Quarterly*, vol. 1, no. 4: June, 1864), 348; bracketed words are mine.

Chapter Six

74   The discussion of whether demon possession still occurs today as it did in Jesus' day takes us well beyond our present study. There is no doubt that demonic *activity* (or influence) is still very much alive and well today, but— "miracle-working" televangelists and exorcists notwithstanding—we have no real proof of literal possession. We should note, too, that there is a difference between a demon *possessing* someone (as we see in the gospels) and someone being under

the *control* of a demonic element. It seems evident that God allowed demons a much greater scope of activity in Jesus' day than He has ever since. The reason for this lies in passages like John 1:4-11, where the heavenly "Light" (Jesus) was purposely amplified against the backdrop of the darkness and hopelessness of man's corrupted world.

75 Boles, *The Holy Spirit*, 205.

76 Ibid., 204; emphasis his.

77 Such "knowledge" does not have to refer to literal divine revelations, as though in addition to the written Word. On the other hand, we are not told about all the different methods in which God *does* give knowledge to those who seek Him. Instead of handcuffing God to the limitations placed upon *us*, Christians would do well to realize that God has manifold options, opportunities, and resources at His disposal—without the employment of visible miracles—many of which we may never be aware.

78 It is hardly necessary to separate the power of Christ from the power of the Holy Spirit, since both "powers" are at work in the life of the believer. It is true that Christ has been given "all authority in heaven and on earth" (Matthew 28:18), and that He has sent the Spirit to work among His church (Acts 2:33), but it is virtually impossible for us to know the difference between the power of Christ and the power of the Spirit. As we have pointed out earlier, "Spirit of God" and "Spirit of Christ" can be used seamlessly (as in Romans 8:9). It is sufficient to say that in whomever the power of Christ is working, the Spirit is also working.

79 "Indwelling" is likened to "falling," as when the Spirit "fell upon" certain people. Obviously, the Spirit of God is not literally collapsing Himself upon any individual when He "falls" upon someone; the language is figurative, but does describe a real action. He "indwells" a person, but not to literally fill a person's internal body, and not with His entire Being. Nonetheless, the *process* is real, the *action* is real, and the *Spirit's presence* is real (Johnson, *The Holy Spirit and the Human Mind*, 262).

80 Again, even in the cases of demon possession recorded in the gospels, no one ever "sees" the demons, even when they are exorcised; they never are manifested in a physical way; they do not appear to occupy a physical space within a person's body. It is true that they *inhabited* a person's body, but not in a corporeal context.

81 Johnson, *The Holy Spirit and the Human Mind*, 29.

82 Robertson Whiteside, *Commentary on Romans*, 6th ed. (Denton, TX: Inys Whiteside, 1969), 173; bracketed words mine.

83 James P. Needham, *The Holy Spirit: His Nature & His Work* (Louisville, KY: Religious Supply, Inc., 1997), 19.

84 Ibid., 40.

85 Ibid., 25.

86 John says that *many* books would be required just to detail all that Jesus did in three years' time (John 21:25). How, then, should we think that the Bible could detail what the Spirit of God does over the entire course of our Christian lives or for all of history—both in the visible and invisible realms?

Chapter Seven

87   The cursing of the fig tree was not a parable originally intended for Christians, but was a message for the Jewish people of Christ's day. Most Jews refused to "recognize the time of [their] visitation" by their Messiah (Luke 19:44), and thus brought upon themselves a curse. Just as the fruitless fig tree was cursed, so fruitless Israel (as a theocratic *nation* that had failed to keep its covenant with God) would be destroyed. Jesus' prophecies concerning the ruin of Jerusalem and (thus) the special relationship that God had had with Israel (see Matthew 3:8-10; 21:43, Luke 19:41-44; 21:20-24; et al) were fulfilled in AD 70 when the Romans leveled the city to the ground and forever ended the Levitical priesthood and its intercessory sacrificial system.

88   Some believe that these "branches" represent different denominations of churches. However, there is no logical way that Jesus meant *churches* from a statement He made about *individual people* (see Romans 11:17-22, where the "branch" metaphor is used again, and where it is just as impossible for that instance to mean "denominations"). A vine can produce only one kind of branch, which can then produce only one kind of fruit; just as we do not expect multiple varieties of fruit from the same tree, so we should not expect multiple "faiths" or religions from the same "true vine."

89   "Excruciating" [lit., "from the cross (of crucifixion)"] is a most appropriate word here, for indeed discipleship is described as a cross-bearing experience (Matthew 10:38; 16:24; Galatians 2:20, et al).

90   Some Christians teach that such statements cannot possibly refer to hell, but are simply strong expressions of the undesirable state of being separated from God. There is no argument that such separation is undesirable—and what an understatement!—but I find it impossible to reduce Jesus' words here to mere expressions. Jesus does refer to a spiritual experience (i.e., one that takes place in a spiritual context), and thus the "fire" does not have to be literal flames and heat. At the same time, being separated from God will be as painful to the soul as it would be for one's body to be literally cast into a lake of fire without succumbing to death. All semantic appeals aside, the state of the lost soul is nothing less than hellish.

91   In Jeremiah 2:13, God calls Himself "the fountain of living waters" which the Jews had rejected for "broken cisterns that can hold no water." That which is the result of human effort simply cannot provide what only God is capable of providing, which is just as true today as it was in Jeremiah's day.

92   Quoted in Swete, *The Holy Spirit in the Ancient Church*, 263.

93   The fact that photosynthesis always creates waste product (oxygen) necessarily indicates that it is not a 100% efficient system. Of course, God makes good use of this "waste," but that takes us beyond our present illustration. The complex, spiritual transformation that occurs within the life of a disciple of the Lord, however, *can* be an entirely efficient process, as long as one's faith remains intently focused upon Christ. The only "waste" in this system is what we create when we fail to use that energy which God provides to its full potential.

94   We should not assume that a believer cannot bear any fruit *until* he

reaches maturity, for this is not true. Even a newborn Christian is immediately able to begin showing the "fruit" of his conversion to the Lord. However, it is also true that he is still child-like in his thinking (the implications of Hebrews 5:12-13 and 6:1-2), and is thus limited by this. Yet as he grows in grace and knowledge (cf. 2 Peter 3:18), he will become increasingly like his Master, and the fruit of this relationship will flourish proportionately.

95   This memorial, having been instituted by Christ Himself, is kept alive every week by those who believe in His death, burial, and resurrection—and His future return (1 Corinthians 11:23-26). In a spiritual sense, the memorial exists in an ever-present state, since it began on the night of Christ's death and continues in full effect "until He comes." It does not begin and end over and over, but lives on in the hearts of believers and in the heart of Christ perpetually (consider Matthew 29:29, for example, as not referring to a single instance, but a continuous spiritual communion Christ enjoys with those who worship Him). In a more practical sense, the memorial is re-created every first day of the week by groups of believers all over the world, and thus has no fixed location or earthly point of reference. This is a truly ideal memorial which—like the Christian himself—is suspended between heaven and earth, not being fully of one or the other.

Chapter Eight

96   Boles, *The Holy Spirit*, 198. "God's word" here cannot be limited to "the Bible," however, for we have records of people being converted to God without a written, completed Bible; however, *no one* comes to God without Him having first divinely *revealed* what is required of a person in order to do this. Thus, whether this information was revealed through the fulfillment of Old Testament prophecy (Acts 2:16-39; 17:2-3; et al), apostolic authority (Acts 11:13-14; Galatians 1:8, et al), or the written New Testament (1 Corinthians 14:37), the revelation *from* God is inseparable from one's conversion *to* God.

97   "Religious teachers have gone to two extremes—one is that the Holy Spirit has nothing [personally] to do in conversion and sanctification; the other is that the Holy Spirit does everything in conversion and sanctification. Be it remembered that the Holy Spirit is prominent and dominant in both; however, there is a happy medium between these two extremes" (Boles, *The Holy Spirit*, 235; bracketed word is mine).

98   Specifically, the seven radiation frequencies of the electromagnetic spectrum (from longest to shortest waves) are: radio waves, microwaves, infrared light, visible light, ultraviolet light, X-rays, and gamma rays.

99   This is the essence of what Albert Einstein proved in his Theory of Special Relativity. All physical mass can be expressed as potential energy, or energy in a fixed (but not permanent) state. Mass can be destroyed (i.e., reduced to the fundamental components of energy), but energy itself cannot be destroyed, according to the First Law of Thermodynamics.

100 Bales, *The Holy Spirit and the Christian*, 103.

101 This is *not* to suggest "total annihilation," a doctrine which assumes the literal destruction of the unregenerate soul. The Bible simply does not teach

this. Instead, the Bible teaches that those who refuse to "know God" or "obey the gospel of the Lord Jesus Christ" will be eternally separated from the Lord (Matthew 25:46; 2 Thessalonians 1:6-10, et al). This is the "death" I am referring to here: being cast into oblivion, forever separated from any fellowship with God, but continuing to exist nonetheless.

102 Boles, *The Holy Spirit*, 126.

103 F. B. Huey, Jr., "Seal," *Zondervan Pictorial Encyclopedia*, vol. 4, 319-324.

104 This is expressed symbolically in Revelation 7:1-8, where the "144,000" are "sealed" or identified with God as belonging to Him versus those who belong to the "beast" (chapter 13) and are thus marked for destruction. The scene is visionary, and is not to be taken literally. However, these symbols do point to literal truths: God knows His people (cf. 2 Timothy 2:19) and He specially identifies them with His own Spirit.

105 Henry Soltau, *The Tabernacle: Its Priesthood and the Offerings*, 384.

106 A. T. Robertson, *Word Pictures in the New Testament*, vol. IV (Grand Rapids: Baker Book House; orig. copyright 1931 by Sunday School Board of the Southern Baptist Convention), 519.

107 From *prosago*, "to bring to, to introduce"; (hence) "introduction, approach" (ibid., 355); in Romans 5:2, "that friendly relation with God whereby we are acceptable to him and have assurance that he is favorably disposed towards us" (Joseph Thayer, *Greek-English Lexicon of the New Testament* [Grand Rapids: Baker Book House, 1977], 544).

108 This is a further work of the Spirit, as expressed in John 14:26, although the context there is different than it is for us. In that passage, the Spirit is promised to the apostles for a specific purpose: to provide knowledge supernaturally so that they could carry out their work *as* apostles. We do not need this knowledge today, for whatever we need is already recorded for us in the gospel. However, *in principle* the Spirit still serves as our Helper or Comforter, since He seeks to convey the true intentions of our hearts to God for our best interest. Incidentally, the word for "Helper" is exactly the same Greek word translated "Advocate" in reference to Christ in 1 John 2:1-2. Thus, Christ is our Advocate and so is the Holy Spirit—each Divine Person carrying out separate but perfectly coordinated work in the life of the believer.

109 See Romans 8:12-13. The Spirit does not Himself "[put] to death the deeds of the body," for that is our responsibility. But He does, in full agreement with His revealed Word, prick our conscience and thus inspire us to do something about those areas of our lives that are in conflict with His gospel.

110 Olan Hicks, "'Restoration' Ideals Contrasting with Calvinism," <u>News and Notes</u>, Sept 2008.

111 Bales, *The Holy Spirit and the Christian*, 110.

112 Kenneth Wuest, *Wuest's Word Studies from the Greek New Testament*, vol 1 (Grand Rapids: Eerdman's Publishing Co., 1992), 221.

113 Bales, *The Holy Spirit and the Christian*, 64.

114 Brents, *The Gospel Plan of Salvation*, 642.

115   C. K. Barrett, *The Epistle to the Romans* (New York: Harper & Row, 1957), 168.

Chapter Nine

116   By implication, Paul's usage of Christ's "body" or "church" would necessarily include both those who are alive as well as those who have died in Christ (as mentioned in 1 Thessalonians 4:13). But our discussion involves only the physical church which exists in the earthly context, whose supra-human needs are fulfilled by the Holy Spirit.

117   I realize that this is a broad, sweeping statement, and that some *aspects* of what individual congregations do to fulfill this mission will be left up to human judgment, but the overall *principle* is valid. Christ's church as a whole is not governed by individual believers or congregations, but Christ Himself, and He has made His mission clear to us. We are to "make disciples" (Matthew 28:19)—then teach and encourage those who have become disciples—and whoever is not with Him in this is against Him (Matthew 12:30).

118   It is not as though the Father has divested Himself of all authority, but has legally transferred all of His authority to Christ (Matthew 28:18). The Father still retains His sovereign authority, as Paul points out in 1 Corinthians 15:27-28. This transfer of power is foreshadowed in Daniel 7:9-10,13-14, and is reviewed in Revelation 5:1-9.

119   "The work of the Holy Spirit was that of organizing, garnishing, and completing. When Jesus left earth, all the raw materials for the spiritual creation that God planned were in place. But nothing was organized. The church had not been [visibly—MY WORD] established, nothing had been written down, everything was ready to be completed, and that is exactly what the Holy Spirit was appointed to accomplish" (Alan Hitchen, "The Work of the Father, Son, and Holy Spirit," from a transcript of a series on "The Holy Spirit" presented in Kirkland, WA, October, 2004).

120   Boles, *The Holy Spirit*, 244; emphasis his.

121   The King James Version adds to 1 John 5:7-8: "For there are three that bear record in heaven, the Father, the Word, and the Holy Ghost: and these three are one. And there are three that bear witness in earth...." These words are not in any of the better, older manuscripts upon which the New Testament is based, and should be considered as questionable (see, for example, Simon J. Kistemaker, "James and I-III John," *The New Testament Commentary* [Grand Rapids: Baker Books, 1999], 353-354). The translation I am using is the New American Standard Bible (NASB), which relegates these extra words to a margin note.

122   The Anatolic School of Gnostics (late first century) maintained that Jesus "died when the Spirit that came down upon Him at the Jordan departed from Him" (quoted in Swete, *The Holy Spirit in the Ancient Church*, 58). While I cannot agree with this entirely, it does bring to mind a difficult question: What happened to the Holy Spirit's presence when Jesus died on the cross? It cannot be that the Spirit died with Him, for the incarnate Son of God was the only one of the Godhead that died, and God's Spirit cannot die. On the other hand, is it

specifically the departure of the Holy Spirit that Jesus referred to when He said, "My God, My God, why have You forsaken Me?" (Matthew 27:46)? I am not certain that this is *the* answer, but I offer this as a point for the serious Bible student to consider.

123   By implication, this man was either a Jew by birth who lived among the Diaspora—the scattering of Jews beyond Palestine—or (more likely) a proselyte to the Jewish religion. His status as a eunuch is what is remarkable here, especially in light of Isaiah 56:3-5; before this, no eunuch could enter into the holy assembly (Deuteronomy 23:1), which meant that the Ethiopian eunuch could enter Jerusalem, but was forbidden to enter the inner courtyard of the temple. It should be noted that "the term [eunuch] is also used of government officials of that day and perhaps should not be taken literally, for it does not mean that these men were deprived of their male functions" (Simon J. Kistemaker, *New Testament Commentary: Exposition of the Acts of the Apostles* [Grand Rapids: Baker Book House, 1990], 312; see also Lenski, *The Interpretation of the Acts of the Apostles* [Peabody, MS: Hendrickson Publishers, 1998], 338-339). However, it seems logical in this case that the man's status as a literal eunuch is being emphasized to indicate how the gospel had overcome all human limitations.

124   This is not meant to imply that the Spirit did (or does) exactly for others what He did with Philip and the Ethiopian. It simply means that the Spirit is involved in bringing together the two parties—the messenger and the one who needs to hear the message—through whatever means He deemed appropriate. Certainly this continues today through non-miraculous means, as when the Spirit brings people together through circumstances, allowing their paths to intersect, yet without any audible instruction or visibly miraculous intervention.

125   Lard, "The Gift of the Holy Spirit," 347; bracketed words mine.

126   We should note here: appealing to God's Word as the final standard is *not* a private "expectation." (The atheist appeals to his *own* authority, or the authority of mere *men*, which is inherently inferior to God's.) If someone says, for example, "I had a vision from God, wherein He revealed to me a new gospel," I would challenge that *not* because of my private expectations concerning miracles or revelations, but because of the divine authority of the gospel of Christ (cf. Galatians 1:8). That person may reply, "You are rejecting my revelation just because it doesn't fit your expectations!" No, but I reject it on the basis that it violates God's "once for all" revealed Word; it has nothing to do with *my* authority. There is a huge chasm between these two thoughts. Furthermore, this understanding will bear directly on our discussion of miracles in the next chapter.

127   "Christian denomination" is a contradictory phrase; likewise, multiple "faiths" (i.e., doctrinal teachings defining one's fellowship with God) are not found in the New Testament. Christ's unified church is neither to be "denominated" by men nor has it been divided by Christ (1 Corinthians 1:13). This is a comment on the denominational *system* (structure, hierarchy, government, etc.) and not a categorical reference to every person who is a member of a denomination.

128   There is no denying that we are united by the blood of Christ, for we are collectively a blood-bought people (Revelation 5:9). However, we do not

have Christ's blood coursing through our veins, but we *do* have the Spirit of God indwelling us. Even though this indwelling is *spiritual* in nature, it is nonetheless real and effective.

129   Someone poses the question, however: "What about those people who exhibit these 'fruits' but who are involved in religions whose teachings contradict the Bible?" This apparent conundrum is explained when we understand that one's manifestation of the "fruit of the Spirit" must be *consistent* and *habitual*. In other words, one may exhibit occasional kindness, patience, and self-control, but in order to exhibit godly *love*, for example, he must live according to God's *commandments* (John 14:15; 1 John 2:4-6; 5:1-3). One cannot manifest "fruit of the Spirit" that knowingly lives in opposition to the Spirit-revealed Word of God. Furthermore, one who is led by the Spirit will pursue this "fruit" as a matter of lifestyle, and not incidentally.

Chapter Ten
130   I say "still" as an implied reference to ancient times when miracles, signs, and wonders were an accepted part of how God (or "the gods," depending upon one's beliefs) interacted with people and the natural world. Some of this can be attributed to nature worship and superstition, such as how the ancient Egyptians deified the Nile River, the sun, animals, insects, and even death itself. But there are also credible instances of God's actual working of miracles among men, such as what He wrought through Moses during the exodus of Israel from Egypt. More specifically, it alludes to the era of the early church, the work of the apostles, and the supra-human abilities given to certain Christians at that time.

131   These Greek word definitions and studies are from Robertson's *Word Pictures in the New Testament*, Strong's *Concordance*, and Thayer's *Greek-English Lexicon of the New Testament*, cited *in loco*.

132   C. S. Lewis, *Miracles* (New York: HarperOne, 1996), 72.

133   "Glossolalia [i.e., miraculous tongue-speaking—MY WORDS] is closer to improvisational jazz than it is to language. One tongues-speaker made this comparison for me. The speaker uses syllables the way a musician uses notes. Glossolalia sounds have no fixed semantic meaning. Tongues-speakers cannot communicate specific ideas or facts, but they can use tongues as a vehicle to *express* themselves in the way music expresses emotional experience. This explains why some individuals claim to understand the message contained in a speaker's glossolalia 'prophecy.' They react to his tone of voice, to his breathing and to gestures rather than to the semantics of language" (William Samarin, "Glossolalia," *Psychology Today* [Aug 1972: 49], as quoted in James D. Bales, *Pentecostalism in the Church* [Shreveport: Lambert Book House, 1972], 11). On the other end of the spectrum, Holdcroft supports "angel tongues": "But even if a particular tongue is extraterrestrial, it still may communicate" (*The Holy Spirit: A Pentecostal Interpretation*, 107). Communicate *what*, exactly, he does not say; regardless, no angel in Scripture ever spoke to man in an "extraterrestrial" language.

134   See Nehemiah 9:9-38 and Psalm 78 for excellent synopses on this very

point.

135   Perhaps it would be good to quote C. S. Lewis here: "God does not shake miracles into Nature at random as if from a pepper-caster. They come on great occasions: they are found at the great ganglions of history—not of political or social history, but of that spiritual history which cannot be fully known by men. If your own life does not happen to be near one of those great ganglions, how should you expect to see one?" (*Miracles*, 273).

136   This can be understood both literally and figuratively. Jesus rebuked a storm, for example, as though it were a demon (Mark 4:35-41); likewise, He rebuked a fever in the same way (Luke 4:39). He spoke to inanimate things— wind, waves, a corpse, a tree, etc.—as though they were living entities. This is not to say that these things were literally demonic, but that the scope and exercise of His power extends beyond the human vision.

137   Lard, "The Gift of the Holy Spirit," 339.

138   Obviously, not everyone agrees with this point: "Cessation [of miracles— MY WORDS]…is a theological interpretation of pneumatology [the doctrine of the Spirit—MY WORDS], and in the opinion of Pentecostals, a non-biblical view of the person and work of the Holy Spirit" (Holdcroft, *The Holy Spirit: A Pentecostal Interpretation*, 139). Nonetheless, I believe that the arguments put forward in this chapter sufficiently argue otherwise.

139   The people of Chorazin, Bethsaida, and Capernaum saw many miracles, yet they did not believe or repent because of them (Matthew 11:21-24). This undercuts the argument that miracles are "necessary" today to persuade men. The fact is, if men can crucify the Son of God who for three years proved Himself to *be* the Son of God, then they can certainly refuse to believe in the Son's gospel message, which is filled with the accounts of miracles He performed.

140   This still does not prevent God from *performing* miracles today if He so chooses, or if there is a purpose which we do not know about. The point being made here regards the necessity of miracles in substantiating the gospel record *and* the purpose of miracles in general based upon what has been revealed in the Word, as well as what has been observed. Based upon the Word, there is no reason to expect miracles to continue; based upon modern observation, no proof has yet validated a single, irrefutable, visible miracle.

141   Holdcroft—an avid charismatic—writes: "In the church age the authority of written Scripture must stand above all other revelations, including prophecy. A [modern] prophetic utterance can neither contradict nor add to the Word of God. Unlike Old Testament prophecies, no prophecy today can bring any new revelation of abiding authoritative significance. …Most Pentecostal leaders discourage written transcriptions of prophetic messages in case such writings should become competitive with the Bible. …Primarily, the gift of prophecy is intended to sharpen, illumine, and energize the already revealed truths of Scripture" (*The Holy Spirit: A Pentecostal Interpretation*, 173). On the one hand, Holdcroft supports modern-day Spirit-given prophecy; on the other hand, such prophecies are "discouraged" from being written down in case the Spirit accidentally contradicts Himself.

142   This is how it is *supposed* to be, when the original divine intent is carried out. However, the Hebrews writer chastised those who were supposed to be mature Christians but still had need of "milk" and not "meat" (5:11-14). In other words, they had not matured as God had intended, but had actually reverted back to an immature state. But Paul's comments in 1 Corinthians 13 speak idealistically, and thus are not nullified by poor examples to the contrary.

143   "At the time of the Reformation some of the best minds of Europe searched the Scriptures diligently to rediscover the New Testament patterns of doctrine and life. Not one of the Reformers, however, found that tongue-speaking belonged to the normal gifts God had permanently bestowed on the church" (Hoekema, *What About Tongue-Speaking?,* 19).

144   Rogers, "A Study of the Spirit of God," 39ff.

145   The "eleven apostles," to which Matthias was added, are mentioned in Acts 1:26. In the next verse (2:1), the pronoun "they" has no other logical antecedent than those twelve men. Furthermore, the comments of those who heard the tongue-speaking refers to these same men (2:7), as did Peter himself (2:14). Still further, it was only the apostles who were performing signs and wonders, not the entire company of believers (2:43). The text simply will not support this "power"—which was promised only to the apostles—to be given to the "hundred and twenty" men and women who met in the upper room (1:13-15).

146   This gives the "hundred and forty-four thousand" (Revelation 7:4, 14:3) meaningful context. This number is twelve squared times ten cubed, or a powerful yet symbolic representation of the physical church upon the earth. Likewise, the "twenty four elders" who surround the throne of God serve to represent all such believers in the very presence of God Himself—two witnesses (cf. 2 Corinthians 13:1) for every group of "twelve" (in essence, for every church). These numerical expressions are not coincidental, but further underscore the consistency and continuity of how God identifies His people to Himself.

147   This is a necessary inference: Saul performed no miracles before this (Acts 9:26-28). Also, there is no reason to assume a different procedure for Saul than for the Samaritans: as the Samaritans were baptized in water, so was Saul (9:18, 22:16); as the Samaritans required the laying on of the apostles' hands, so did Saul. Ananias laid *his* hands upon Saul so that he could "be filled with the Holy Spirit"—not to perform miracles, but to be sanctified as an obedient disciple (2:38, 5:32). Ananias was not an apostle; what he performed upon Saul was not the work of an apostle. It is presumptive to impose apostolic authority upon Ananias at the mere mention of laying on of hands and the Holy Spirit. Instead, Peter could have—indeed, *must* have—laid *his* hands upon Saul when he [Saul] spent 15 days with him on his visit to Jerusalem early in his apostolic career (Galatians 1:15-18).

148   As to the authenticity of Paul's apostleship, there is no doubt; but *when* he was literally ordained *as* an apostle is difficult to know exactly. Some assume it happened immediately upon his "road to Damascus" experience; others, upon his having been summoned by Barnabas (Acts 11:22-26); still others, when he was set apart by the Spirit for his missionary journey (13:2-3). None of these

explanations is satisfactory; they all raise questions of some sort. It seems clear, however, that Paul was not chosen in the same way that Matthias was. It is also clear *why* his selection process would be different: he was bereft of the three year ministry with the Lord that the other apostles enjoyed; he was not part of "the twelve" that preached to Israel; and his apostleship was unique in scope and objective (see 1 Corinthians 15:6-10). However, *at least* by the time of his first missionary journey, Paul was serving *as* an apostle in a sense and authority that far exceeded that of his companion Barnabas.

149   There is absolutely no indication that Cornelius ever had the ability to confer the power to perform miracles upon someone else. In fact, there is no record of Cornelius involved in any miraculous activity outside of that which we read in Acts 10:44-48.

150   Johnson, *The Holy Spirit and the Human Mind*, 167.

151   "The Faith-Healing practice leads to the production of 'professionals' standing between the soul and God. There is grave danger in a soul permitting an unauthorized intermediary to take up a position between it and the gracious activities of God toward it" (Benjamin B. Warfield, *Counterfeit Miracles* [London: Banner of Truth Trust, 1972], 195).

152   Bales, *Pentecostalism in the Church*, 24

153   Robert E. Gromacki, *The Modern Tongues Movement* (Philadelphia: Presbyterian and Reformed Publishing Co., 1967), 124.

Chapter Eleven

154   Such is the opinion of noted scholar F. F. Bruce, *The Book of the Acts* (Grand Rapids: Eerdmans Publishing Co., 1964), 144; Caiaphas held the office of high priest until AD 36.

155   Stephen—really, the Spirit—involved the temple in his defense because of the accusation made against him, namely, that he was conspiring to destroy it (Acts 6:14). This was the same accusation made against Jesus (Matthew 26:59-61), which completely distorted what He had actually said (John 2:18-21). Thus, the Jews revered (i.e., idolized) their temple yet showed great contempt for God's Son.

156   This point of the Jews having *always* resisted the Holy Spirit (see also Psalm 106:33, Isaiah 63:10, Zechariah 7:12, et al) clearly indicates that the Spirit had been communicating with them long before the gospel of Christ had been preached.

157   On this allusion to being "uncircumcised in heart and ears" (Acts 7:51), see also Deuteronomy 10:16, 30:6, Jeremiah 9:25-26, and Romans 2:25-29. The "true circumcision" is that which is performed by Christ upon the human heart at the time of one's baptism (Colossians 2:11-12, Philippians 3:2-3).

158   By "Scripture," Paul refers to what we call the Old Testament scriptures. I am not ignoring this when I link "Scripture" to the "gospel of salvation." But it is true that the gospel of Christ has existed since eternity (Ephesians 3:11), and that the New Testament is incomplete apart from the Old Testament. The *covenants* of both are different, but the *message* is the same: God saves *all* men

by grace through faith, a process which is ultimately made possible through the redeeming work of His Son, Jesus Christ.

159　We could add Revelation 22:18-19 *in principle*, although the immediate context of that passage deals with the revelation given to John (which he recorded as a "book") and not the entire Bible.

160　Bales, *The Holy Spirit and the Christian*, 127, 140.

161　Dave Miller, *Piloting the Strait* (Pulaski, TN: Sain Publications, 1996), 385.

162　Because our relationship with the Spirit is *real* and *personal*, we are able to cause Him grief. This could not be the case if by "the Spirit" Paul simply meant "the Bible." We cannot bring grief to a written word; our sins do not cause the Bible sorrow; we cannot disappoint a mere book.

163　Bales, *The Holy Spirit and the Christian*, 75.

164　Boles, *The Holy Spirit*, 168.

Chapter Twelve

165　I say this with a grateful nod to four different but related (and highly recommended) works: *Inside Out* by Dr. Larry Crabb; *The Sacred Romance* by Brent Curtis and John Eldredge; *Point Man* by Steve Ferrar; and *The Screwtape Letters* by C. S. Lewis (see bibliography for publisher information).

166　For example, see http://www.bible-history.com/tabernacle/TAB4The_Shekinah_Glory.htm (accessed May, 2009). There is a considerable amount of modern-day Jewish commentary on *shekinah*. It is not my intention here to expound upon the Jewish interpretation of "the glory of the LORD," but only to say what is relevant for our present study.

167　At least one scholar wants this passage to read, "be filled *through* [or *by*] the Spirit," not "with." "It was not the Person 'with' whom they were to be filled, but by or through whom they were to be filled" (Bullinger, *Word Studies on the Holy Spirit*, 30). The Spirit, then, is the "filler" here (ibid., 31). This grates against the context, however. Paul is comparing being filled with wine against being filled with the Spirit; just as it would be awkward to consider wine to be the "filler" of drunkenness, so it would be improper to assume the Spirit as the "filler" of the music of the heart. A much more natural conclusion is: because of the Spirit's presence *in* the believer's heart, that person responds with songs of praise and encouragement.

168　Having Christ "living" within us (Galatians 2:20) seems to be synonymous with being filled with the Spirit, since we cannot have the one without the other. Christ works in the life of the believer *through* the Spirit of God, so that there is no need to make a distinction between the activities of each Divine Personage *in this context*. It would be wrong, however, to suggest that Christ works independent of the Spirit, or that the Spirit is able to redeem the human soul. Only Christ has died for us; only His body and blood serve to redeem man from his condemnation (cf. Hebrews 9:13-14, 10:5-10). The Spirit of God has not died for us, but He *is* directly involved in consecrating the soul for service to God and prepares the soul for its presentation before God, as we have discussed in earlier chapters.

Chapter Thirteen

169   Proponents of the "Bible only" position take issue with the "Bible only" descriptor, saying that it is not accurate (Needham, *The Holy Spirit: His Nature & His Work*, 58-59). Since they *do* claim that the Spirit is at work, therefore to say "Bible only" omits the Spirit altogether. However, this chapter—as well as what has already been stated in this book—proves that this is an indefensible, if not self-refuting, position. "Bible only" means God uses *nothing but the Bible* to lead, train, inspire, and sanctify the Christian, which is exactly what this position maintains. The Holy Spirit is involved only passively or indirectly, as the One who has provided the Bible, but not as an active, dynamic agent of transformation of the human heart. "Bible only" is not only an accurate description of this position, but (as will be shown) would be improper to have it stated otherwise.

170   Arthur W. Atkinson, "The Holy Spirit" series, *The Gospel Guardian* (vol. 11, no. 27: Nov 1959), 425.

171   Franklin Camp, *The Work of the Holy Spirit in Redemption* (Bowling Green, KY: Guardian of Truth Foundation, 1972), 200.

172   Ibid., 253.

173   Jimmy Tuten, Jr., "Modern Pentecostalism," *The Gospel Guardian*, special edition (vol. 20, no. 15 – 17: Aug 1968), 253.

174   Wallace, *The Mission and the Medium*, 12.

175   I will be capitalizing "Word" when it refers to the divinely-revealed gospel, to distinguish it from all other "words" (just as Scripture is often capitalized for the same reason). When quoting the literal Bible text, however, I will use whatever case (upper or lower) that the translators themselves have chosen to use—not necessarily because I agree with their decisions on this, but to maintain the integrity of the translation itself.

176   Johnson, *The Holy Spirit and the Human Mind*, 124.

177   "The Spirit and the word worked together harmoniously. There is no proof that in conversion they ever worked apart. The word without the Spirit would be dead and the Spirit without the word would be without the effective instrument" (ibid., 29).

178   I am referring here, of course, to the Ten Commandments, which the Lord wrote with His own "hand" (see Exodus 24:12, 31:18, and 34:1). These commandments [lit., "ten words"] certainly define the holy nature of God as it was to be practiced among His covenant-bound people, but it would be absurd to think that, just because God had given Israel written instructions as to how to live, God's presence among them was no longer needed.

179   Needham, *The Holy Spirit: His Nature & His Work*, 23.

180   The word "blessing" here (Ephesians 1:3) is *eulogia*, from which we get "eulogy" [Strong's #2129]. It is a benediction, or (by extension) a blessing conferred upon someone. Such blessings are not visible miracles, but they are *miraculous* in nature, inasmuch as they pertain to the spiritual, supernatural world of God. At the same time, they are *real*, and are really applied to us. To deny God's divine activity in the life of the believer is to render these "spiritual blessings" as nothing more than hollow words and empty promises.

181 Just because we have no evidence of His miracles today does *not* mean that God is incapable of performing them. If God wants to perform a miracle, certainly our reservations or protests are not going to stop Him. God does what He does; we should not assume that He must comply with our beliefs or expectations before He acts. At the same time, I have already made sufficient arguments concerning modern miracles in an earlier chapter, and it is not my intention to re-address all of those arguments in the present one.

182 Atkinson, "The Holy Spirit" series (vol. 11, no. 48: Apr 1960), 755; bracketed words are mine.

183 Russell, *Between the Testaments*, 41-48.

184 Camp, *The Work of the Holy Spirit in Redemption*, 16.

185 "The phrase 'through the Word' does not mean the *Word only*. The preposition *through* expresses medium—it is the Spirit working through the Word. There is a wide difference between the word only and the phrase *only through the word*" (Wallace, *The Mission and the Medium*, 14; emphasis his). Claiming that the Spirit works "through the word" as though this were an expected, perfectly natural means of God interacting with man—but *not a miracle*—is convenient, but not explanatory. Wallace wants to say that the Word is the only acceptable medium by which the Spirit can do anything; but the Word itself never says this. No one denies that the Spirit works through His Word; but this "working" requires *something more* than what mere words are able to accomplish. Reading the Bible is one thing; having the Spirit work upon one's heart *because* of what he has read is quite another.

186 Camp, *The Work of the Holy Spirit in Redemption,* 15.

187 As stated, for example, by C. D. Plum in "The Work of the Holy Spirit in the Conversion of Sinners," *Gospel Guardian*, special edition (vol. 20, nos. 15 – 17: Aug 1968), 227.

188 Brents, *The Gospel Plan of Salvation*, 642; emphasis his.

189 Camp, *The Work of the Spirit in Redemption*, 20.

190 "...What could the Spirit of Truth abiding directly in one's heart accomplish that the Spirit working through the Word [Bible] could not? If by the Spirit-revealed Scriptures we are made 'perfect, thoroughly furnished unto all good works' (2 Timothy 3:16-17), what is left for the direct agency of the Spirit?" (Keith Sharp, "The Indwelling of the Holy Spirit" [*The Preceptor*, vol. 28, no. 4: 1979], 16). "Now, just as surely as the word is all-sufficient, we don't need anything separate and apart from it and in addition to it. We cannot say that the word is all-sufficient if we need something separate and apart from and in addition to it. ...[Otherwise] the word is not all-sufficient" (Needham, *The Holy Spirit: His Nature & His Work*, 69).

191 It is not necessary to limit God to the working of a visible miracle in order to answer a single prayer. God has already proved His gospel with miracles; He does not need to "prove" prayer in the same way. One's faith in what the gospel says ought to provide all the confidence that person needs that God can and will answer prayers sufficiently and appropriately. However, the fact that God promises to answer our prayers means that He will do *something* for us—not in the form of visible miracles, but unseen, divine activity all the same.

Selected Bibliography

Atkinson, Jr., Arthur W. "The Holy Spirit" (series). The Gospel Guardian, vol. 11, nos. 6, 9, 14, 18, 22, 27, 31, 35, 43, 48: 1959-1960; vol. 12, no. 2: 1960.

Bales, James D. *Pentecostalism in the Church.* Shreveport: Lambert Book House, 1972.

_____. *The Holy Spirit and the Christian.* Shreveport: Lambert Publications, 1966.

Barrett, Charles Kingsley. *The Epistle to the Romans.* New York: Harper & Row, 1957.

_____. *The Holy Spirit and the Gospel Tradition.* Shreveport: Lambert Publications, 1966.

Boles, H. Leo. *The Holy Spirit: His Personality, Nature, Works* Nashville: Gospel Advocate Co., 1973.

Brents, T. W. *The Gospel Plan of Salvation.* Nashville: Gospel Advocate Co., 1973.

Brown, William. *The Tabernacle: Its Priests and Its Services.* Peabody, MS: Hendrickson Publishers, 1996.

Bullinger, E. W. *Word Studies on the Holy Spirit.* Grand Rapids: Kregel Publications, 1985.Originally titled, *The Giver and His Gifts* (London: Eyre & Spottiswoode, 1905).

Bunch, Larry A. "The Holy Spirit." The Preceptor, vol. 26, no. 1: 1976.

Burgess, Stanley M. *The Holy Spirit: Ancient Christian Traditions.* Peabody, MS: Hendrickson Publishers, 1984.

Camp, Franklin. *The Work of the Holy Spirit in Redemption.* Bowling Green, KY: Guardian of Truth Foundation, 1972.

Comfort, Philip W. *The Origin of the Bible.* Wheaton, IL: Tyndale House Publishers, 1992.

Crabb, Dr. Larry. *Inside Out.* Colorado Springs: NavPress, 1988.

Curtis, Brent and John Eldredge. *The Sacred Romance: Drawing Closer to the Heart of God.* Nashville: Thomas Nelson Publishers,1997.

Farrar, Steve. *Point Man.* Sisters, OR: Multnomah Books, 1990.

Gordon, A. J. *The Ministry of the Spirit.* Minneapolis: Bethany House Publishers, 1985.

Gromacki, Robert E. *The Modern Tongues Movement.* Philadelphia: Presbyterian and Reformed Publishing Co., 1967.

Hoekema, Anthony A. *What About Tongue-Speaking?* Grand Rapids: Eerdman's Publishing Co., 1966.

Holdcroft, L. Thomas. *The Holy Spirit: A Pentecostal Interpretation* (rev. ed.). Abbotsford, Canada: CeeTeC Publishing, 1999.

Johnson, Ashley. *The Holy Spirit and the Human Mind.* Delight, AR: Gospel Light Publishing Co., 1985 (orig., 1903).

Kistemaker, Simon J. *New Testament Commentary: Exposition of the Acts of the Apostles.* Grand Rapids: Baker Book House, 1990.

_____. *New Testament Commentary: 1 Corinthians.* Grand Rapids: Baker Book House, 1993.

Lard, Moses E. *Commentary on Romans.* Delight, AR: Gospel Light Publishing Co. [no date].

_____. "The Gift of the Holy Spirit." Lard's Quarterly, vol. 1, no. 4: June 1864.

Lenski, R. C. H. *The Interpretation of the Acts of the Apostles.* Peabody, MS: Hendrickson Publishers, 1998.

Lewis, C. S. *Miracles.* New York: HarperOne, 1996.

_____. *The Screwtape Letters.* New York: Macmillan Publishing Co., 1982.

Luther, Martin. *Three Treatises.* Philadelphia: Fortress Press, 1994.

Manchester, M. F. "The Promise of the Spirit." Vanguard, vol. 8, no. 7: July 1982.

Miller, Dave. *Piloting the Strait.* Pulaski, TN: Sain Publications, 1996.

Needham, James P. *The Holy Spirit: His Nature & His Work.* Louisville, KY: Religious Supply, Inc., 1997.

Plum, C. D., Robert C. Welch, et al. Gospel Guardian (special edition), vol. 20, nos. 15 – 17: Aug 1968.

Puckett, Franklin T. "The Holy Spirit"; "The Gift of the Holy Spirit." *Searching the Scriptures*, vol. 23, no. 7: July 1982; vol. 23, no. 8: Aug 1982.

Robertson, A. T. *Word Pictures in the New Testament* (five volumes). Grand Rapids: Baker Book House; © 1930 by Sunday School Board of the Southern Baptist Convention.

Rogers, Richard. "A Study of the Holy Spirit of God," *Sunset Study Series.* Lubbock, TX: Sunset School of Preaching, 1968.

Russell, D. S. *Between the Testaments.* Philadelphia: Fortress Press, 1996.

Sharp, Keith. "The Indwelling of the Holy Spirit." The Preceptor, vol. 28, no. 4: 1979.

Soultau, Henry. *The Tabernacle: Its Priesthood and the Offerings.* Grand Rapids: Kregel Publications, 1994.

Sproul, R. C. *The Mystery of the Holy Spirit.* Wheaton, IL: Tyndale House Publishers, 1990.

Stanley, Charles F. *Living in the Power of the Holy Spirit.* Nashville: Nelson Books, 2005.

Swete, Henry Barclay. *The Holy Spirit in the Ancient Church.* Grand
Rapids: Baker Book House, 1966.

Sychtysz, Chad. *The Gospel of Grace.* Louisville, KY: Religious
Supply, Inc., 2008.

Tenney, Merrill C., ed. *The Zondervan Pictorial Encyclopedia of the
Bible.* Grand Rapids:Zondervan Publishing House, 1976.

Thayer, Joseph. *Greek-English Lexicon of the New Testament.* Grand
Rapids: Baker Book House, 1977.

Tuten, Jr., Jimmy. "The Gift of the Spirit." The Preceptor, vol. 30,
no. 1: 1980.

Wallace, Jr., Foy E. *The Mission and the Medium of the Holy Spirit.*
Fort Worth: Foy E. Wallace, Jr. Publications, 1967.

Warfield, Benjamin B. *Counterfeit Miracles.* London: Banner of Truth
Trust, 1972.

Whiteside, Robertson L. *Commentary on Romans* (6th ed.). Denton,
TX: Inys Whiteside, 1969.

Wuest, Kenneth. *Wuest's Word Studies from the Greek New Testament.*
Grand Rapids: Eerdman's Publishing Co., 1992.

More Bible workbooks that you can order from Spiritbuilding.com or your favorite Christian bookstore.

BIBLE STUDIES

Inside Out (Carl McMurray)
Studying spiritual growth in bite sized pieces
Night and Day (Andrew Roberts)
Comparing N.T. Christianity and Islam
We're Different Because..., w/Manual (Carl McMurray)
A workbook on authority and recent church history
From Beneath the Altar (Carl McMurray)
A workbook commentary on the book of Revelation
1 & 2 Timothy and Titus (Matthew Allen)
A workbook commentary on these letters from Paul
The Parables, Taking a Deeper Look (Kipp Campbell)
A relevant examination of our Lord's teaching stories
The Minor Prophets, Vol. 1 & 2, w/PowerPack (Matthew Allen)
Old lessons that speak directly to us today
Esteemed of God, the Book of Daniel, w/Manual (Carl McMurray)
Covering the man as well as the time between the testaments
Faith in Action: Studies in James (Mike Wilson)
Bible class workbook and commentary on James
The Lion is the Lamb (Andrew Roberts)
Study of the King of Kings, His glorious kingdom, & His promised return
Church Discipline, w/Manual (Royce DeBerry)
A quarter's study on an important task for the church
Communing with the Lord (Matthew Allen)
A study of the Lord's Supper and issues surrounding it
Seeking the Sacred (Chad Sychtysz)
How to know God the way that HE wants us to know Him
1 Corinthians & 2 Corinthians study workbooks (Chad Sychtysz)
Detailed studies to take the student through these important letters
Living a Spirit Filled Life, w/PowerPack (Matthew Allen)
An overview study of Galatians & Ephesians with practical applications
From Fear to Faith (Matthew Allen)
A study to build a greater assurance of personal salvation
Behind the Preacher's Door (Warren Berkley, editor)
A call to personal purity for preachers & all Christians
The AD 70 Doctrine (Morris Bowers)
A study of this false and growing doctrine of men
The Last Mile of the Way (Kipp Campbell)
An examination of the last week of Christ's life on earth

TEENS/YOUNG ADULTS

Transitions, w/PowerPack (Ken Weliever)
A relevant life study for this changing age group
Snapshots: Defining Moments in a Girl's Life (Nicole Sardinas)
How to make godly decisions when it really matters
The Path of Peace (Cassondra Givans)
Relevant and important topics of study for teens
The Purity Pursuit (Andrew Roberts)
Helping teens achieve purity in all aspects of life
The Gospel and You (Andrew Roberts)
Thirteen weeks of daily lessons for Jr High and High School ages
Paul's Letter to the Romans (Matthew Allen)
Putting righteousness by faith on an understandable level
God's Plan for Dating and Marriage (Dennis Tucker)
A look at some pitfalls to avoid during dating & a study of marriage.
Eye to Eye with Women of the Bible (Joanne Beckley)
A workbook for teen girls

WOMEN

Reveal In Me... (Jeanne Sullivan)
A ladies study on finding and developing one's own talents
I Will NOT Be Lukewarm, w/PowerPack (Dana Burk)
A ladies study on defeating mediocrity
Will You Wipe My Tears? (Joyce Jamerson)
Resources to teach us how to help others through sorrow
Bridges or Barriers, w/Manual (Cindy DeBerry/Angie Kmitta)
Study encouraging harmony with younger/older sisters-in-Christ
Learning to Sing at Midnight (Joanne Beckley)
A study book about spiritual growth benefiting women of all ages
Forgotten Womanhood (Joanne Beckley)
Workbook which covers purity of purpose in serving God
Re-charging Your Prayer Life (Lonnie Cruse)
Workbook for any woman wanting a richer prayer life
Heading for Harvest (Joyce Jamerson)
A study to help ladies digest the fruit of the Spirit
Does This Armor Make Me Look Fat? (Lonnie Cruse)
A study of Ephesians 6:10-18 for women

PERSONAL GROWTH
Compass Points (Carl McMurray)
22 foundation lessons for home studies or new Christians
Marriage Through the Ages, w/Manual (Royce & Cindy DeBerry)
A quarter's study of God's design for this part of our life
Parenting Through the Ages, w/Manual (Royce & Cindy DeBerry)
Bible principles tested and explained by successful parents
What Should I Do?, w/Manual (Dennis Tucker)
A study that seeks Bible answers to life's important questions
When Opportunity Knocks, w/Manual (Matthew Allen)
Lessons on how to meet the JW/Mormon who knock on your door

SPECIAL INTERESTS
In the Eye of the Hurricane - AUTISM (Juli Liske)
A family's journey from the shock of an autistic diagnosis to victory
I Cried Out, You Answered Me - DEPRESSION (Sheree McMillen)
What happens when faith and depression live in the same home
Her Little Soldier - DIABETES (Craig Dehut)
The journey of a young man suffering from Type 1 Juvenile Diabetes
For However Brief a Time (Warren Berkley)
A son's human interest tales of his father in a time now gone by
Family Bible Study Series (Ken Weliever) *A series of 16 quarters of Bible class curriculum ideas*

JUST FOR KIDS
Greta's Purpose (Rebecca Helvey)
A children's book about a Great Dane who struggles with fitting in
Rudy's Path (Rebecca Helvey)
A story of a chocolate colored dog who finds belief, a family, and a name
Gus and Phil Stories Audio CDs (Ivan Benson)
Stories of true friendship and Christian values
Spiritbuilding Bible Challenge on CD (Mark Hudson, Alayne Hunt)
An entertaining CD-ROM series of Bible questions & answers
Bucky Beaver (Julie Robbins)
Children's book which teaches biblical lessons of obedience & diligence

*All PowerPacks include PowerPoint presentations +
Teacher's Manual

Breinigsville, PA USA
15 June 2010
239879BV00002B/3/P